Investigations in Sociohistorical Linguistic

In the last 500 years or so, the English langu ___gone
remarkable geographical expansion, bringing it into contact with other
languages in new locations. This also caused different regional dialects
of the language to come into contact with each other in colonial
situations. This book is made up of a number of fascinating tales of
historical-sociolinguistic detection. These are stories of origins – of
a particular variety of English or linguistic feature – which together
tell a compelling general story. In each case, Trudgill presents an
intriguing puzzle, locates and examines the evidence, detects clues
that unravel the mystery, and finally proposes a solution. The solutions
are all original, often surprising, sometimes highly controversial.
Providing a unique insight into how language contact shapes varieties
of English, this entertaining yet rigorous account will be welcomed by
students and researchers in linguistics, sociolinguistics and historical
linguistics.

Peter Trudgill is Professor of Sociolinguistics at the University
of Agder, Kristiansand, Norway.

Investigations in Sociohistorical Linguistics

Stories of Colonisation and Contact

Peter Trudgill
University of Agder

CAMBRIDGE
UNIVERSITY PRESS

CAMBRIDGE UNIVERSITY PRESS
Cambridge, New York, Melbourne, Madrid, Cape Town, Singapore,
São Paulo, Delhi, Dubai, Tokyo, Mexico City

Cambridge University Press
The Edinburgh Building, Cambridge CB2 8RU, UK

Published in the United States of America by
Cambridge University Press, New York

www.cambridge.org
Information on this title: www.cambridge.org/9780521132930

© Peter Trudgill 2010

This publication is in copyright. Subject to statutory exception
and to the provisions of relevant collective licensing agreements,
no reproduction of any part may take place without the written
permission of Cambridge University Press.

First published 2010

Printed in the United Kingdom at the University Press, Cambridge

A catalogue record for this publication is available from the British Library

Library of Congress Cataloguing in Publication data
Trudgill, Peter.
  Investigations in sociohistorical linguistics : stories of colonisation and
  contact / Peter Trudgill.
    p. cm.
  Includes bibliographical references and index.
  ISBN 978-0-521-11529-2 (hardback) – ISBN 978-0-521-13293-0 (pbk.)
  1. Sociolinguistics. 2. Historical linguistics. 3. Language and
  languages–Variation. 4. Linguistic change. 5. Languages in
  contact. I. Title.
  P40.T7475 2010
  306.44–dc22
  2010026386

ISBN 978-0-521-11529-2 Hardback
ISBN 978-0-521-13293-0 Paperback

Cambridge University Press has no responsibility for the persistence or
accuracy of URLs for external or third-party internet websites referred to in
this publication, and does not guarantee that any content on such websites is,
or will remain, accurate or appropriate.

Contents

Maps

Tables

Acknowledgements

I owe a very special debt of gratitude on the publication of this book to the co-authors who were involved in the work of preparing and writing the original versions of some of the papers which now appear here as chapters. They are Elizabeth Gordon, Gillian Lewis, Daniel Long, Margaret Maclagan, Terttu Nevalainen, Daniel Schreier, Jeffrey P. Williams and Ilse Wischer. I am grateful to you all for so cheerfully and graciously giving me permission to publish your work under my own name.

I am also very grateful to very many other people who helped and advised me on the original versions of the chapters that appear here, and/or on the work that has gone into this new book. I apologise sincerely to anybody who I have inadvertently omitted, but the list of names I have tried to keep complete reads as follows: Bas Aarts, Anders Ahlqvist, David Allerton, Laurie Bauer, Allan Bell, Leiv Egil Breivik, David Britain, Juan Manuel Hernández Campoy, Jack Chambers, Sandra Clarke, Jan Terje Faarlund (and other members of staff at the Toten Center for Advanced Studies), Małgorzata Fabiszak, Paul Fletcher, Remus Gergel, Elizabeth Gordon, Mark Greengrass, Patrick Griffiths, Walter Haas, Jack Hawkins, Jennifer Hay, Dick Hudson, Ernst Håkon Jahr, Toni O'Brien Johnson, Jeffrey Kallen, Anders Källgård, Ian Kirby, William Labov, Stephen Laker, Karen Lavarello-Schreier, Gillian Lewis, Angelika Lutz, Sharon Millar, Jim Milroy, Mike Olson, Dennis Preston, Daniel Schreier, Peter Schrijver, Janet Smith, Andrea Sudbury, Sali Tagliamonte, Hildegard Tristram, David Willis, Walt Wolfram and Laura Wright. Thank you all very much!

As for financial and institutional support, different aspects of the research reported here were funded in part by grants from: the

Marsden Fund of the Royal Society of New Zealand; the New Zealand Foundation for Research, Science and Technology; the University of Canterbury, Christchurch, New Zealand; and the British Council. The original versions of Chapters 2–8 were written while I was working in Switzerland, first as Professor of English Linguistics at the Université de Lausanne, and then as Professor of English Linguistics at the Université de Fribourg/Universität Freiburg Schweiz. I also benefited greatly during that period from research time spent at Canterbury University, Christchurch, New Zealand. The present book, including Chapter 1 in its entirety and the – often substantially – revised new versions of the other chapters, has taken form while I have been, gratefully, affiliated to the Research Centre for Linguistic Typology at La Trobe University, Melbourne, Australia; the University of East Anglia in my home city of Norwich, England; and the new University of Agder in Kristiansand, Norway. I have also been able to work on the book at the Christos Research Centre, Lesbos; and while enjoying visiting professorships at the Ohio State University, Albert-Ludwigs-Universität Freiburg, the University of Hamburg and Memorial University Newfoundland. I am also very grateful to Andrew Winnard of Cambridge University Press, whose idea this was.

My most grateful thanks, however, are reserved for two people. My mother, Hettie Trudgill, has over the decades been a fount of wisdom on very many things, but crucially for this book on the subject of East Anglian dialect forms, and she has always helped and encouraged me. And my wife and companion of thirty years, Jean Hannah, has increased my enjoyment in the writing of this book immeasurably by just being there; and has helped enormously with the research, the writing of the original papers, their presentation at conferences and meetings, the structure of the book itself, and the selection of papers. If any errors of judgement or deficiencies of organisation do remain, they are there simply because I did not heed Jean's advice quite as much as I should have done.

SOURCES

Eight of the ten sections in this book are (sometimes very considerable) revisions, reworkings, and/or expansions of previously published papers, or parts of previously published papers, as follows:

Chapter 2: Peter Trudgill, 1996, Language contact and inherent variability: the absence of hypercorrection in East Anglian present-tense verb forms. In J. Klemola, M. Kytö and M. Rissanen (eds.), *Speech past and present: studies in English dialectology in memory of Ossi Ihalainen*, 412–25. Frankfurt: Peter Lang; and Peter Trudgill, 1998, Third-person singular zero: African American vernacular English, East Anglian dialects and Spanish persecution in the Low Countries. *Folia Linguistica Historica* 18.1–2, 139–48.

Chapter 3: Peter Trudgill, Daniel Schreier, Daniel Long and Jeffrey P. Williams, 2003, On the reversibility of mergers: /w/, /v/ and evidence from Lesser-Known Englishes. *Folia Linguistica Historica* 24, 23–46.

Chapter 4: Peter Trudgill and Daniel Long, 2004, The last Yankee in the Pacific: eastern New England phonology in the Bonin Islands. *American Speech* 79.4, 356–67.

Chapter 5: Peter Trudgill, Terttu Nevalainen and Ilse Wischer, 2002, Dynamic *have* in North American and British Isles English. *English Language and Linguistics* 6: 1–15.

Chapter 6: Peter Trudgill, 1999, A window on the past: "colonial lag" and New Zealand evidence for the phonology of 19th-century English. *American Speech* 74.3: 1–11.

Chapter 7: Peter Trudgill and Elizabeth Gordon, 2004, Predicting the past: dialect archaeology and Australian English rhoticity. *English World-Wide* 27.3: 235–46.

Chapter 8: Peter Trudgill, Margaret Maclagan and Gillian Lewis, 2003, Linguistic archaeology: the Scottish input to New Zealand English phonology. *Journal of English Linguistics* 31: 103–24.

Epilogue: Peter Trudgill, 2001, On locating the boundary between language contact and dialect contact: Low German and continental Scandinavian. In E. H. Jahr (ed.), *Språkkontakt:*

innverknaden frå nedertysk på andre nordeuropeiske språk (= Skrift nr. 2 fra prosjektet "Språkhistoriske prinsipper for lånord i nordiske språk"). Copenhagen: Nordisk Ministerråd, 71–86; Peter Trudgill, 2008, Colonial dialect contact in the history of European languages: on the irrelevance of identity to new-dialect formation. *Language in Society* 37.2: 241–54; Peter Trudgill, 2008, On the role of children, and the mechanical view: a rejoinder. *Language in Society* 37.2: 277–80.

Prologue: Colonisation and contact

My friend, colleague and former doctoral student Professor David Britain once told me that, of the papers I had written, the ones he enjoyed reading most were those where it seemed as if I was telling a story – particularly, he said, where they were detective stories. I had never thought of myself as writing detective stories before, but I did come to realise that David had offered an insight about my work that I had never been clever enough to arrive at myself. Some of my writing has indeed consisted of articles which begin with a historical-sociolinguistic puzzle, and then attempt to come up with a solution on the basis of the available evidence. And they are, I now see, written in such a way that the reader is left waiting to find out what the solution to the mystery is until the very end of the story. Even if there is no punchline as such, there may well be a final punch-paragraph.

This book, then, is made up of a number of such historical-sociolinguistic tales of detection which I hope, individually, will tell a coherent story; and which will also, I hope, combine to produce an overall, more general story which is also coherent. This general story has to do, I suppose, with the belief that great explanatory power in finding the solution to linguistic mysteries is to be derived from the study of vowels, consonants and grammatical constructions in combination with the study of macro- and micro-level social factors and historical events. Happily, there are many linguistics scholars who have greater goals than this – linguists who seem to be most highly motivated by the very laudable desire to learn more about the very big picture: a quest for a greater understanding of the vitally important question of why human language is like it is, in terms, perhaps, of the nature of the human language faculty. For me, this question has always seemed to be far too hard, and I am happy to leave it to others. I have contented myself with doubtless less important questions, but those which I feel might be more within my capabilities. These questions, as asked in this book, are all of a particular type: I ask not so much why language is like it is, but more why is this *particular* language or dialect like it is? How did it get to be like that? Why does it have these linguistic characteristics and not others?

The chapters in this book all deal with varieties of the English language as it is spoken around the world: the British Isles, North America, the Caribbean, the Southern Hemisphere, the Pacific Ocean. I am concerned with issues such as why American English is like it is; how New Zealand English got to be that way; what factors led to the English of the Bonin Islands being as it is; why the English of my native East Anglia is not exactly like any other kind of English; and so on. There is always a historical explanation for such things, of course, but I have generally supposed that answers to this sort of question will also be as much sociolinguistic as purely linguistic-internal.

In all the papers in this volume, contact turns out to be a key problem for, and/or a key solution to, the riddles I have been trying to solve. This sometimes involves language contact, sometimes dialect contact, and often both. The English language has, in the last 500 years or so, experienced a remarkable history of geographical expansion which led it to undergo contact with other languages, indigenous and non-indigenous, in new locations. It also led to different regional dialects of the language coming into contact with each other in colonial situations, in a way that had never happened before. For example, new dialects of English developed on the east coast of North America as a result, in part, of contact between different regional dialects of English English. These new dialects then took part in further dialect contact processes with the westward journey of the language across the continent, as the colony itself began colonising. West coast varieties of American English must result from mixtures of mixed dialects which were themselves the result of dialect mixture of mixed dialects. One type of puzzle which I attempt to deal with in this book, therefore, is the unravelling of the different, complex strands involved in the mechanisms of contact and mixture which gave rise to the varieties under examination.

The book starts, however, with an examination of the very first process of colonisation in which English was involved, a process that began more than fifteen hundred years ago – with the original coming into being of the English language itself; and with the role that the study of contact has to play in producing explanations for why, even in the early centuries of its existence, the English language was like it was.

I What really happened to Old English?

We begin these studies at the beginning, with an investigation into Old English. This study deals with the first five hundred years or so of the history of the language in which the present book is written; and it exemplifies the concerns with immigration and colonisation, and with language and dialect contact, which run throughout all the chapters of this work.

We start this chapter with the observation that it is generally agreed that Old English, as it first developed on the island of Britain, was typologically very different from the Middle English that it later became. Old English was of the morphological type known as *fusional* and *inflecting*; Lass (1992: 94) says: "Old English is a highly synthetic inflecting language." It had three grammatical genders; three numbers; five cases; inflectional case-marking on nouns, adjectives, demonstratives and pronouns; strong versus weak nominal declensions; inflectional person-marking on verbs; and large numbers of irregular 'strong' verbs, which also made a distinction between the root vowels of singular and plural preterite forms, as in the verb *findan* 'to find':

	singular	plural
1st	*fand*	*fundon*
2nd	*funde*	*fundon*
3rd	*fand*	*fundon*

There were also large numbers of conjugations and declensions; and it had relatively free word order.

Middle English, on the other hand, was much less fusional, showing a clear move towards a much more *isolating* type of morphology: "the Middle English evolution consists primarily in a shift towards a more analytic structure" (Lass 1992: 94). Middle English had no grammatical gender;[1] two numbers rather than three; three cases rather than five; and many fewer inflections, conjugations and declensions. There was also a reduction in case-marking and in subjunctive verb forms; and the distinction between the root vowels of the singular and plural preterite forms of strong verbs also disappeared, as did the strong/weak nominal declensions. Middle English also showed a much greater trend towards fixed SVO word order.

As just one numerical indication of the degree of the typological change, Hawkins (2004: 76–7) computes the amount of morphological complexity to be found in different Germanic languages in terms of the number of distinctive inflections found for third-person nominals (determiners, nouns, adjectives, pronouns). Hawkins looks at three genders (masculine, feminine, neuter), two numbers (singular and plural) and three cases (nominative, accusative, dative), so the maximum number of distinct forms mathematically possible in his calculations would be eighteen. Old English had in fact an elevenitem system, while by Middle English this had reduced to seven, although this arithmetical difference conceals to a very considerable extent the degree to which there was a "reduction in morphological expressiveness: both in the number of categories per word, and the number coded at all" (Lass 1992: 95).

LaPolla (2005: 481) gives an extended example of this kind of development in English. He lists Old English examples from the words corresponding to Modern English *stone*, *gift* and *hunter*. These items came in many different forms:

	singular			plural		
nom.	*stan*	*giefu*	*hunta*	*stanas*	*giefa*	*huntan*
acc.	*stan*	*giefe*	*huntan*	*stanas*	*giefa*	*huntan*
gen.	*stanes*	*giefe*	*huntan*	*stana*	*giefa*	*huntena*
dat.	*stane*	*giefe*	*huntan*	*stanum*	*giefum*	*huntum*

---

[1] Kastovsky (1999) indicates that the loss of grammatical gender was a long and complex process that was not fully complete until the 1300s.

The adjective corresponding to *good* had the following weak forms:

	masc.	fem.	neut.	pl.
nom.	goda	gode	gode	godan
acc.	godan	godan	gode	godan
gen.	godan	godan	godan	godena
dat.	godan	godan	godan	godum

The modern system consists of two forms each for the nouns and one form for the adjective. And LaPolla does not even mention (because it was not necessary for the point he was making) that the above declension for *good* only represents the 'weak' forms of the adjective. There is also a set of 'strong' forms which are used in conjunction with definite forms of the noun phrase:

	singular			plural		
	masc.	fem.	neut.	masc.	fem.	neut.
nom.	god	god	god	gode	goda	god
acc.	godne	gode	god	gode	goda	god
gen.	godes	godre	godes	godra	godra	godra
dat.	godum	godre	godum	godum	godum	godum
inst.	gode	godre	gode	godum	godum	godum

The nature of the overall trend of the linguistic changes which took place between Old English and Middle English is, then, clear. What is not clear – and this is the mystery which this chapter confronts – is: why did these changes take place? Linguistic change as between Old English and Middle English is in itself not a mystery, since change is a feature of all human languages; but the question is: why did the changes that occurred in English during this period take this particular form?

SIMPLIFICATION

In attempting to answer this question, we can note that one way of describing the typological transformation that English underwent between Old English and Middle English is to say, with Milroy (1992: 177), that what happened represented "a trend towards simplification in Middle English": the changes outlined above can all indeed be referred to by the typological cover-term that Milroy uses – *simplification*.

In Trudgill (1996a), and following Mühlhäusler's pioneering work (1977) as well as important earlier work such as that of Ferguson (1959, 1971), I suggest that there are three crucial, linked, components to the simplification process. These are:

(1) the *regularisation* of irregularities. In regularisation, obviously, irregularity diminishes, so that, for example, irregular verbs and irregular plurals become regular, as in the development in English of *helped* rather than *holp* as the preterite of *help*; and the replacement of *kine* by *cows* as the plural of *cow*.

(2) an increase in lexical and morphological *transparency*: for example, forms such as *thrice* and *seldom* are less transparent than *three times* and *not often*, and any (partial or complete) replacement of the former by the latter would represent simplification.

(The above two components are often linked. Obviously, forms such as *cows* are also more transparent, analytic and iconic than forms like *kine*.)

(3) the loss of *redundancy*. All languages contain redundancy, which seems to be necessary for successful communication, especially in less than perfect, i.e. normal, circumstances. But the fact that redundancy can be lost suggests that some languages must have more redundancy than others. Redundancy, and therefore the loss of redundancy, takes two major forms. The first occurs in the form of *repetition of information*, or syntagmatic redundancy

(Trudgill 1978), as for example in grammatical agreement, where there is more than one signal that, say, a noun phrase is feminine. Here reduction in redundancy will take the form of a reduction in the number of repetitions, as in the loss of agreement, such as happened in Middle English. The second type of redundancy loss involves the *loss of morphological categories*. Sometimes loss of the morphological expression of grammatical categories is compensated for by the use of more analytical structures, as in usage in Modern English of prepositions instead of the dative case of Old English:

godan huntan → *to the good hunter*

Analytical structures are also obviously more transparent than synthetic ones.

Sometimes, however, no compensation occurs. A good example of this latter type is the loss of grammatical gender. Grammatical gender disappeared in Middle English, as we have just noted, without, apparently, this loss having had any structural consequences.

DIALECT CONTACT

Different explanations have been advanced for this dramatic typological difference between Old English and Middle English, with Middle English, as we have noted, demonstrating considerable simplification. Many of these explanations have focussed on *contact*.

In the Prologue to this work, I said that this book would be concerned with both language contact and dialect contact. Let us therefore consider, first, the possibility that dialect contact might have been involved in this case, because the earliest example of colonial dialect mixture involving English surely concerned the actual development of English itself. It is well known, and we have evidence of various non-linguistic sorts, that southern and eastern England, and southeast Scotland, were initially settled by Germanic-language speakers coming from all along the North Sea littoral, from Jutland in the north to the mouth of the Rhine: these were Jutes, Angles, Saxons, Frisians, all speaking different dialects. But is it possible that contact between these different Germanic dialects led to dialect mixture, and therefore perhaps eventually to simplification?

Nielsen (1998: 78, 79) certainly argues that Old English was in origin a mixed dialect resulting from contact; and he supplies linguistic evidence. He suggests that Old English was the result of a mixture of West Germanic dialects from continental Europe; and argues that it is because of dialect mixture that Old English initially had a greater degree of variability than the other Germanic languages of the time where no colonial dialect mixture had been involved. He gives examples as follows:

(1) Old English had a surprising number of different, alternating forms corresponding to the Modern English word *first*. And this variability, Nielsen indicates, could be linked to origins in different dialects from the European mainland: *ærest, forma, formesta* and *fyrst*. He also points out that it is interesting that these forms resemble, respectively, Old High German *eristo*, Old Frisian *forma*, Gothic *frumists* and Old Norse *fyrstr*. There is, however, no claim of a direct link to these languages, even though we do suppose (see above) that Frisians at least were directly involved in the settlement (Morgan 2001: 62).

(2) Similarly, Old English had two different paradigms for the present tense of the verb *to be*, one apparently resembling Old Norse and Gothic, and the other Old Saxon and Old High German (see more on this below):

	Gothic	O.Norse	O.English I	O.English II	O.Saxon	OHG
1sg.	*im*	*em*	***eom***	***beom***	*bium*	*bim*
2sg.	*is*	*est*	***eart***	***bist***	*bist*	*bist*

(3) Old English was also variable in terms of the form of the interrogative pronoun meaning 'which of two'. The form *hwæðer*

relates to Gothic *hvaðar* and West Norse *hvaðarr*, while the alternative form *hweder* corresponds to Old Saxon *hweðar* and Old High German *hwedar*.

So the implication of Nielsen's suggestion is that even if we did not know from other non-linguistic evidence that southern and eastern Britain were initially settled from many different locations on the continent, there would have been some linguistic evidence that would have led us in the direction of that conclusion. And in any case there is evidence (Morgan 2001) that many of the bands of raiders and settlers were of mixed ethnic origins. In addition, we know that in modern colonisation episodes whose consequences we have been able to observe more closely, such as the anglophone settlement of New Zealand, dialect mixture is a more or less inevitable result of dialect contact (Trudgill 2008).

A good case can be made, then, for dialect contact and dialect mixture in early Anglo-Saxon Britain. But can we ascribe the simplification that we outlined above to this contact? On reflection, this actually seems unlikely. The cases of dialect-contact-induced simplification described, for example, in Trudgill (1986) are generally of the type in which regularisation occurs, and unmarked forms are selected or developed. But they do not extend to wholesale loss of morphology such as occurred in the transition from Old English to Middle English. That is, a case could be made for suggesting that the reduction of, say, Old English declension types in Middle English was due to dialect contact; but it would be very hard to do the same thing for the loss of, say, grammatical gender.

LANGUAGE CONTACT

It therefore seems, although we cannot rule out dialect contact altogether, that it would be more fruitful to continue this investigation by looking at the involvement of language contact. And indeed many authors have plumped for just this solution. James Milroy, for example, says of the simplification which occurred that "it seems clear that such a sweeping change is at least to some extent associated with *language contact*" (1992: 203).

His case is a strong one, because simplification is very well known to be associated with language contact, and his thesis would therefore seem to be relatively uncontroversial. And the fact that he regards the change as 'sweeping' again makes the case for language contact being involved, as opposed to dialect contact.

There is very considerable agreement in the sociolinguistics literature that language contact does indeed lead to simplification: pidgins and creoles are widely and uncontroversially agreed to owe their relative structural simplicity to language contact; and agreement about the role of contact in producing simplification in languages other than pidgins and creoles is also widespread in sociolinguistics.

What is not uncontroversial, however, is the precise nature of the particular contact involved in this transition between Old English and Middle English. The puzzle we have to address is, if simplification in English did occur as a result of contact between Old English and some other language, then which language (or languages) was it? There is certainly more than one language to choose from: as is well known, in the first several centuries of its existence Old English experienced major contact in Britain with three other languages.

First, there was contact with the language of the indigenous population of Britain at the time of the West Germanic invasions of the island – the Brittonic Celtic language which was the ancestor of Cornish, Modern Welsh and, probably, Breton. This contact began in the fourth century and became widespread in the fifth century with the first permanent settlements of the Angles, Saxons, Jutes and Frisians from the continent and their colonisation of eastern England and southeastern Scotland, spreading out over the course of the next centuries until they occupied most of what is now England.

Secondly, as a consequence of the Viking invasions of Britain, there was contact between the West Germanic language Old English and the North Germanic language of the Scandinavian (mainly Danish and Norwegian) invaders and settlers, which we can refer to as Old Norse. The Viking settlements took place mainly during the ninth and tenth centuries, and led to many areas of eastern and, especially, northern England containing a heavily Scandinavian or Scandinavianised population, as famously witnessed by hundreds of Norse place names. The numbers of Scandinavians who actually arrived and settled in Britain is, however, unknown and the subject of much controversy (Härke 2002; Holman 2007).

Finally, from the eleventh century onward, there was contact with the Romance language of the Norman conquerors, Norman French, beginning after 1066. The number of French speakers who actually settled in England is again not known, but it is agreed that they can never have formed a very large proportion of the population (Härke 2002; and see below).

NORMAN FRENCH

To consider the probability of the involvement of these candidates in the production of simplification in reverse chronological order, it is totally clear that contact with French did indeed have a very considerable impact on English. As is mentioned in all histories of the English language, this was especially true of English lexis, with 40 per cent often being cited as the proportion of French-based lexis in the modern language.

More important for the present discussion, it is also true that Bailey and Maroldt (1977) have argued that Middle English was a creole that developed as a result of contact and interaction between English and French. And of course creoles are characterised, as we have already noted, by contact-induced simplification. However, the case for accepting French as the language responsible turns out to be a weak one. Bailey and Maroldt's theory, and indeed their usage of the term *creole*, have not been widely accepted; and Görlach's (1986) careful rejection of their claims is particularly powerful.

The chronology and demography of the contact of Old English with French also argue against this language being the key to the simplification that occurred. The number of native Norman French speakers in Britain was never very high – Carpenter (2004) gives a figure of 8,000 for the year 1086; and in any case evidence of the beginnings of simplification in English comes from well before the Conquest: Strang (1970), for example, cites numerous examples of morphological regularisation as having occurred in the period 770–970.

OLD NORSE

The argument in favour for Old Norse is much stronger, and has been argued for more often and by many more writers, starting with Bradley (1904). In particular, the chronological and demographic case for Old Norse is much more powerful than that for French. Contact began in the appropriate period, with settlements dating from the ninth century, as we have noted. And the Scandinavian element in the population was much higher, although, as we have also noted, not known with any certainty. The Old Norse-speaking population, moreover, was geographically concentrated in the north of England, where the grammatical simplifications which occurred in Old English are generally said to have begun, before spreading southwards.

In fact, in historical linguistics, something almost like a consensus about the importance of the role of Old Norse seems to have been achieved. For example, Poussa has it that contact with Old Scandinavian was responsible for "the fundamental changes which took place between standard literary Old English and Chancery Standard English, such as the loss of grammatical gender and the extreme simplification of inflexions" (Poussa 1982: 84). Kroch *et al.* (2000) make precisely the same point; and so does McWhorter (2007: 90ff), who argues particularly powerfully for the role of Old Norse in producing morphological simplification on the basis of a detailed examination of the extent and nature of "the striking losses which English suffered in the centuries during and in the wake of the

Scandinavian invasions" (2007: 103). Further extensive and detailed discussions of the nature, extent and consequences of Old Norse–Old English contact are found in Townend (2002) and Thomason and Kaufman (1988: 275–304).

A more detailed and widely touted view is that Old Norse and Old English were closely related Germanic languages, and that at the time of the Viking settlements in northern and eastern England there was still enough similarity, especially lexical similarity, between the two languages that communication was possible. However, the similarity did not extend to morphology, and therefore "inflexions were largely non-functional in Anglo–Norse communication" and "Anglo–Norse contact was indeed an important factor in the atrophy and loss of inflexions" in English (Townend 2002: 201). In fact, the degree of mutual intelligibility that existed between Old English and Old Norse remains controversial.

CELTIC

However, there is an alternative thesis to the importance of Old English–Old Norse contact. This is that it was contact between Old English and the Celtic Brittonic language of the original inhabitants of Britain which was the determining factor in producing simplification (Tristram 2002).

That there was contact between the ancestors of modern English and Welsh is of course indisputable. However, to argue the case in favour of the role of Celtic, it has been necessary for writers who favour this hypothesis to counter two factors which have been widely considered to militate against it: first, that there was relatively little contact between the two languages because Celtic speakers either fled from the Germanic invaders as they arrived and/or were rapidly exterminated or absorbed by the incomers; and, secondly, that the chronology does not work, in that the simplification which occurred in Old English did not happen until many centuries after the Celtic Brittonic language had died out in England and the Old English-speaking areas of Scotland.

The first factor has now been argued against by writers who find evidence that the Celtic language that can conveniently be called Late British survived for much longer than has often been supposed. It is generally accepted that Late British did survive in places even after the arrival of Norman French: in the form of Cumbrian, which is said to have been spoken in the Lake District of north-western England and in the adjacent Strathclyde area of Scotland as late as the twelfth century (see Jackson 1953); and of course it also survived in Wales, Devon and Cornwall. However, Schrijver (2006) has argued that Late British survived, if not quite that long, then at least up till the tenth century in much more of Highland Britain than that. This Highland area can be distinguished from Lowland Britain[2] along a line which may, if only uncertainly, be drawn in England from south to north, from Dorchester via Bath, Gloucester, Wroxeter, Leicester, Lincoln, and York to Corbridge and Carlisle.[3] In other words the boundary passes through the (traditional) counties of Dorset, Somerset, Gloucestershire, Worcestershire, Shropshire, Staffordshire, Leicestershire, Nottinghamshire, Lincolnshire, Yorkshire, Durham and Northumberland, leaving the whole of the English counties of Herefordshire, Cheshire, Derbyshire, Lancashire, Westmoreland and Cumberland on the Highland side, in addition to the whole of Wales, and most of Scotland (see Map 1).

This is not a view held only by linguists: in a superb overview, Laker (2008: 21) indicates that "there is much agreement from scholars working in neighbouring disciplines that there was significant survival of the Romano-British population in the fifth and sixth centuries, especially in northern and western Britain"; and "there are few archaeologists these days who believe that the native Romano-British population of Britain was wiped out or driven out of Britain, cp. Henson (2006: 79): 'Incredibly, some scholars still talk of the possibility of genocide or population displacement'."

---

[2] For the original presentation of this distinction, see Fox (1932).
[3] Peter Schrijver, personal communication (2008).

Map 1 Late British survival in Highland Britain

More detail about the nature of the Celtic survival is given by Tristram (2004), who suggests that "in some areas of the Midlands and Northern zone, speakers of the post-conquest Anglian and Mercian dialects ruled the native population of the Britons as their slaves. These continued to speak Brittonic, their native language, for perhaps as many as six or seven generations, before they shifted to Old English." Gelling (1993: 55) allows for more than four hundred years for the shift from Brittonic to Old English to have been completed and suggests that the process was only complete around AD 900.

Interestingly, Schrijver (2002) argues that by the time of the Anglo-Saxon invasions, the Lowland zone was in fact not monolingual Late British-speaking but that a British form of Vulgar Latin, a language which, had it survived, would have ended up being very like Old French – he links them together as "Northwestern Romance" – was also extremely widely used by Celts, especially the upper-classes, as a native language or second-language lingua franca. His argument is based on a detailed linguistic analysis which shows that Brittonic experienced considerable linguistic influence, notably phonological, from British Latin, suggesting that Latin was spoken in one way or another by a large proportion of the Lowland population.

Schrijver (2009) further argues that it was large-scale language shift from British Latin to Late British on the part of refugees fleeing from the Lowland into the Highland zone that led to the simplification that is well known to have occurred in Brittonic at this period (Jackson 1953).

As far as the second factor – the chronology – is concerned, Tristram (2004) has argued for the relevance of the persistence of a written-language/spoken-language *diglossia* in Anglo-Saxon England. The suggestion is that simplification occurred in Old English very much earlier than has hitherto been thought, at a time when contact with Celtic would provide a very reasonable explanation. The fact is, however, that these fundamental changes occurred in the spoken language but did not make their way into the written language – which of course provides the only data that we now have. The written evidence that has survived came from the pens of a small upper-class elite who preserved a knowledge of how Old English was supposed to be written, long after the original morphological complexity had disappeared from everyday speech, very much in the way that knowledge of how Latin was supposed to be written survived in areas where massive linguistic changes had produced a situation where the population as a whole were now speaking, say, a precursor to Old French. (As Clackson and Horrocks say, nonstandard spoken Latin of the later Empire "is hidden behind the façade of the uniform written idiom which we find in most texts" (2007: 262).) According to Tristram (2004: 113), "the theocratic elite of late Anglo-Saxon England deliberately enforced the standardization of Old English as a means of political control".

Evidence of simplification then appears in the written record only after the social breakdown brought about by the Norman Conquest had led to the disappearance of this diglossia, producing the first evidence available to us of changes which had occurred several centuries earlier:

> Unfortunately, we know nothing about spoken Old English to the extent that it differed from the language as it was committed to writing, which was an instrument of power enforcement in the hands of a very few monastics belonging to the elite. In Old English literature we seldom hear about non-aristocratic people; they were given no voice. The spoken language only became visible (literally) after the Norman Conquest, after William the Conqueror effectively replaced the Anglo-Saxon aristocracy by Norman-French-speaking barons, clerics and their followers. Spoken Old English therefore only started to be admitted to the realm of writing at the beginning of the twelfth century.
>
> (Tristram 2006: 203)

EVIDENCE FROM SOCIOLINGUISTIC TYPOLOGY

The choice, then, would seem to lie between Old Norse and British Celtic (in the form of Late British). Distinguished and erudite linguists, accepting the case for the role of language contact in the simplification which occurred in Old English, have nevertheless argued about what really happened, some stressing the role of Old Norse, others the role of Late British. This, then, is our puzzle. Does it make more sense to argue that the simplification which Middle English demonstrates relative to Old English is the result of contact between the Germanic language of the Anglo-Saxon invaders and Celtic Late British? Or is it more reasonable to suppose that it was contact with the Old Norse of the Vikings which was the major factor?

In the rest of this chapter, I attempt to solve this puzzle by approaching it from a different angle, namely from the perspective of sociolinguistic typology (see Trudgill 2009). Sociolinguistic typology examines the hypothesis that the distribution of linguistic structures and features over languages is sociolinguistically not entirely random. The suggestion is that there may be a tendency for different types of social environment and social structure to give rise to, or at least be accompanied by, different types of linguistic structure (Trudgill, in preparation).

Now we saw above that there is widespread acceptance in the sociolinguistics and related literatures that language contact produces simplification. However, what was not mentioned above was that the view from sociolinguistics is by no means shared by linguists who have other research interests. It is very striking, in fact, that there is a very widespread acceptance in the linguistic-typological literature of the completely *opposite* point of view. For example, Johanna Nichols writes that "contact among languages fosters complexity, or, put differently, diversity among neighbouring languages fosters complexity in each of the languages" (1992: 192).

This remarkable conflict between these two opposing positions has remained widely unnoticed, though it has been noted by historical linguists, who have, however, not attempted to adjudicate in the conflict or tried to come up with a solution. They have generally contented themselves with observations such as that of Thomason

(2001: 65), who writes wryly that "all the examples that support the claim that interference leads to simplification are of course counter-examples to the opposite claim".

This is an acknowledgement that we are here confronting yet another puzzle: who is right? Is it the sociolinguists and creolists, experts on language contact, who are correct when they assert that contact between languages leads to simplification? Or is it the typologists, who after all know more about languages than most of us, who are right when they say that contact produces complexification?

In fact, I suggest that it is very important, in our attempt to solve this second puzzle, to acknowledge that both schools of linguists are actually correct. Language contact does lead to simplification, but it also leads to complexification: the two different types of outcome do indeed both occur in contact situations. Crucially, however, the resolution of this mystery is to be located in sociolinguistic insights which suggest that the two different types of outcome result from *two different types of contact* (see Trudgill 2009). Here I follow Thomason and Kaufman (1988), who have convincingly shown that a distinction needs to be drawn between different contact scenarios.

Anttila, for example, allies himself with the creolists when, in a recognition that language contact situations obviously lead to language learning, he says that "language-learning situations, in general, are responsible for various simplifications" (1989: 189). However, an examination of both the typological and sociolinguistic literature shows that it is very much a matter of *who does the learning, and under what circumstances*. In Trudgill (1983: 106) I argued that "it is legitimate to suggest that some languages actually are easier for adults to learn, in an absolute sense, than others" and that these 'easier' languages are more analytical languages "which have experienced more contact". The clue to our conundrum lies in the phrase "easier for adults to learn". The point is that whenever adults and post-adolescents learn a new language, *pidginisation* can be said to occur (Trudgill 2003); and pidginisation includes as a crucial component the process of simplification.[4] This in turn – although other factors such as motivation may be involved – is due to the difficulty human adults face in learning new languages perfectly.

This inability is due to the differential language-learning capabilities of adult and adolescent humans, on the one hand, and small children, on the other. According to Lenneberg (1967), adults are speakers who have passed the *critical threshold* for language acquisition. Lenneberg's term, whether or not one actually accepts 'threshold' as the most appropriate metaphor for what is most likely actually simply a gradual tailing off, refers to the well-known fact, obvious to anyone who has been alive and present in normal human societies for a couple of decades or so, that while small children learn languages perfectly, adults do not. Dahl (2004: 101) writes of "children's ability to learn large amounts of low-level facts about language". He also claims (2004: 294) that "human children indeed seem to have an advantage compared to ... adult members of their own species". Tristram (2004: 200) agrees that "the proficiency of child and adult L2 acquisition differs considerably. Adult L2 learners are far less successful in their replication of target languages than children are: the younger the children, the better their proficiency." And, as Trask (1999: 63) has it, "young children learn perfectly any language to which they are adequately exposed ... [while] few adults can perform the same feat". Trask then goes on to say (1999: 64) that "strong support for Lenneberg's hypothesis comes from the obser- vation of feral children who ... have been denied normal access to language in early life" and who fail to learn language after being first exposed to human contact as teenagers. There is also excellent experimental evidence for this point of view from second-language acquisition studies (Johnson and Newport 1989), as well as very per- suasive evidence from studies in the deaf community, with age of

---

[4] Pidginisation is a common process which only very rarely, and in very unusual circumstances, leads to the development of a pidgin language (see Trudgill 1996a, 2000).

exposure to Sign Language being closely related to success in its acquisition (Hyltenstam 1992). As Pinker says, "acquisition of a normal language is guaranteed for children up to the age of six, is steadily compromised from then until shortly after puberty, and is rare thereafter" (Pinker 1994: 298).

The view from sociolinguistics (e.g. Labov 1972) is that children acquire new dialects and languages more or less perfectly up to the age of about eight, and that there is no or very little chance of them learning a language variety perfectly after the age of about fourteen. What happens between eight and fourteen will depend very much on the circumstances and on the individual. Although it must be the case that sociological and sociopsychological factors are also partly responsible for the relatively poor language-learning abilities of adults in natural acquisition situations, developmental factors play an obvious and vital role.

The importance of the role of the age of the learner in producing simplification is supported by Kusters (2003: 21), who, in making the point that inflectional/fusional morphology is implicated in complexity, crucially specifies that it is "outsider complexity" he is referring to. Here an 'outsider' is "a *second language learner*, who is not acquainted with the speech community of which s/he is learning the language, and who wants to use the language to transmit meaningful messages" (2003: 6 [my italics]). And of course it is the fact that we are dealing with post-threshold *adult* second-language outsider-learners here that is the crucial one: Dahl (2004: 294) uses the term "L2-difficult".

Indeed, the relevance of contact to the study of developments in Old English is made clear by Kusters (2003), who cites Clahsen and Muysken (1996) and Meisel (1997) as demonstrating that L2 learners have serious problems specifically with inflection, and that inflection is one area where "adults have clearly more learning difficulties than L1 learners" (Kusters 2003: 48). Eubank (1996) also argues that the capacity to learn inflection in language is innate, but that for adults and adolescents this capacity is no longer accessible.

Now the picture becomes clearer. Simplification in language contact does not result from non-native language learning as such, but from post-critical-threshold non-native language learning. Labov (2007: 382) states that contact phenomena he has studied "share the common marker of adult language learning: the loss of linguistic configurations that are reliably transmitted only by the child language learner". Simplification will occur in sociolinguistic contact situations only to the extent that *adult* second-language learning occurs – and not only occurs, but dominates.

I have argued (1983) that we have become so familiar with this type of simplification in linguistic change – in Germanic, Romance, Semitic – that we may have been tempted to regard it as normal, as a diachronic universal. However, it is probable that

> widespread adult-only language contact is a mainly post-neolithic and indeed a mainly modern phenomenon associated with the last two thousand years, and if the development of large, fluid communities is also a post-neolithic and indeed mainly modern phenomenon, then according to this thesis the dominant standard modern languages in the world today are likely to be seriously atypical of how languages have been for nearly all of human history.
>
> (Trudgill 2009: 109)

Nichols (2007: 176) agrees that contact "may well have been rare in prehistory though it is responsible for much reduction in morphology in Europe over the last two millennia".

If we define linguistic complexity as being related to[5] the difficulty of acquisition of a language, or a subsystem of a language, for adolescent and adult learners (Trudgill 2009), then it is clear why simplification, at its most extreme in the development of pidgins, takes the form it does. Post-threshold learners have difficulty in coping with irregularity and opacity; redundancy adds to the burden for learner-speakers. Highly irregular and non-transparent features are

---

[5] But it is not necessarily identical with this – see Dahl's (2004: 39) discussion of complexity versus cost and difficulty.

harder to learn and remember: arbitrariness in grammar produces material which has to be learnt without any generalisations being possible. And high redundancy means that there is more to learn (see Bakker 2003).

Indeed it does seem reasonable to characterise complexity in this way. As Andersson says:

> The terms simple and complex rather refer to structural aspects of the language: a simple language has fewer rules, paradigms and grammatical forms than a complex one. Furthermore, a simple language (in this structural sense) is easier to learn (in terms of time and effort) than a complex language.
>
> (Andersson 2005: 40)

Speech communities which have frequent contacts with other societies involving adult dialect or language acquisition are therefore relatively more likely to produce languages and dialects which demonstrate simplification, the most extreme though least usual cases typologically being pidgins and creoles. Changes such as a move from synthetic to analytic structure, reduction in morphological categories, and grammatical agreement and other repetitions, increase in regularity and increase in transparency make for greater ease of adult learnability. As Wray and Grace say, "a language that is customarily learned and used by adult non-native speakers will come under pressure to become more learnable by the adult mind, as contrasted with the child mind" (2006: 557).

This now, in turn, helps us to appreciate under which circumstances contact will lead to the reverse process, complexification, as pointed to by Nichols and other typologists. As we noted above, a study of the relevant literature shows that there actually is considerable evidence that language contact can indeed lead to an *increase* in linguistic complexity. This clearly occurs as a result of the addition of features transferred from one language to another: for example, Dahl (2004: 127) refers to "contact-induced change" in terms of the spread of grammatical elements from one language to another. One well-known European example is the acquisition of (postposed) definite articles by Bulgarian as a result of its participation in the Balkan *Sprachbünd*. This is then *additive* borrowing, in which new features derived from neighbouring languages do not replace existing features but are acquired in addition to them.

But our overview of the role of adult language learning indicates that we can expect to see additive complexity developing only in stable, long-term, co-territorial contact situations which involve childhood – and therefore proficient – bilingualism. It is this kind of situation which gives rise to the phenomenon of the *Sprachbünd* or *linguistic area*. "Strong linguistic areas are typically characterised by large numbers of small linguistic communities *on good social terms*. Their members are in frequent contact and often become multilingual" (Mithun 1999: 314 [my italics]). And the length of time that may be involved in this kind of co-territorial contact and bilingualism, sometimes stretching back thousands of years, is illustrated in what Mithun has to say in connection with her work on Californian languages:

> California is home to tremendous genetic diversity. The most ambitious reductive hypotheses have grouped the languages into seven possible genetic units ... Yet we see striking parallelisms in abstract grammatical structure which cross-cut genetic lines. The languages are characterized by pervasive, often elaborate sets of means/manner prefixes and locative/directional suffixes, structures that are relatively rare outside of the area. The situation is strongly suggestive of transfer through language contact. Relatively little is known for certain of the prehistory of the California groups before their contact with Europeans, but it is clear that there was an extensive period of intense social contact, multilingualism, and intermarriage in this area.
>
> (Mithun 2007: 146)

It is clearly also this type of (very) long-term contact that Heine and Kuteva are mainly interested in when they write that "contact-induced language change is a complex process that not infrequently extends over centuries, or even millennia" (2005: 5).

A sociolinguistic-typological consequence of *this* type of language contact is therefore that languages which have experienced relatively high degrees of contact are more likely to demonstrate relatively higher degrees of this type of additive complexity than languages which have not.

To sum up this section, then, we can say that sociolinguistic-typological considerations lead us to suppose that typically, and on average, and allowing for the fact that this is a very simplistic version of what actually happens in human societies, and that all of the categories I am employing represent continua which permit of many degrees of more-or-less, the following is the case:

- high-contact, long-term contact situations involving childhood language contact are likely to lead to complexification through the addition of features from other languages;
- high-contact, short-term post-critical threshold contact situations are more likely to lead to simplification.

Because of the differential language-acquisition abilities of young children as opposed to adults and adolescents, simplification occurs at its most dramatic in short-term language-contact situations involving language learning by adults. Complexification, on the other hand, develops in long-term co-territorial contact situations involving childhood bilingualism – as often occurs in the case of *Sprachbünd*-type outcomes.

OLD NORSE VERSUS LATE BRITISH

If accepted, this distinction between the two types of contact immediately seems relevant to the solution to our puzzle. Contact between Old English and Old Norse speakers in England, after the Viking raids and depredations, soon turned in the north of England into one of long-term co-territorial co-habitation and intermarriage. Townend sees the significance of "Anglo-Scandinavian integration and the continued practice of mixed marriage" (2002: 204). And Laing and Laing (1979: 185) speak of "the cultural fusion of Angle and Dane in the north".

Moreover, not only did large numbers of words make their way from Old Norse into English but, as a very persuasive piece of actual linguistic evidence for the intensity of the long-term contact, the English third-person plural pronominal forms *they, them, their, theirs* also have their origins in Old Norse, as is well known. The borrowing of pronouns from one language to another is a rare type of development which one sees, not ever in short-term adult contact situations, but only in long-term co-territorial contact of the type which typifies the growth linguistic areas/*Sprachbünde*, as discussed above. As Law (2009) says, the conventional wisdom in linguistics is that "pronouns are unlikely to be borrowed". Rankings of borrowability by different authors "consistently place them among the least likely to be borrowed" (Law 2009: 215). It is true that pronoun borrowing is not located at the very bottom of Thomason and Kaufman's (1988: 74–8) borrowing scale, but this form of borrowing does occur, according to them, only in contexts of intense contact. Campbell (1997) and Thomason and Everett (2005) list a number of cases where the borrowing of pronominal forms from one language to another has occurred – and all of these cases without exception involve long-term contact and proficient bilingualism. For example, among American languages, Miskito (Nicaragua) has borrowed certain pronouns from Northern Sumu, and Alsea (Oregon) borrowed Salishan pronominal suffixes; Campbell also cites cases of pronoun borrowing from Austronesian and Papuan languages. The crucial point for our discussion is that, according to Nichols and Peterson (1996: 242), the "borrowing of pronouns points to *unusually close contact*" [my italics].

The fact that the contact was "unusually close" and sufficiently intimate and long term that pronouns could be borrowed would therefore now seem to render much less tenable the popular thesis that it was contact with Old Norse which led to simplification in Late Old English. Old Norse and Old English "were roughly adstratal in Viking Age England" (Townend 2002: 204). Contact between Old Norse and Old English was of the sociolinguistic type that makes not for simplification but for complexification.

In fact, of course, we see no evidence of complexification as such: this is no surprise since the complexification typical of this kind of situation involves, as Nichols says, the borrowing of additional morphological categories. But Old English and Old Norse were sufficiently closely related that there were no significant differences in the inventory of morphological categories between the two languages, so none could be borrowed. As Dixon says, with languages in a close family-tree relationship "there is little opportunity for grammatical forms to be borrowed" (1997: 22).

The intensity and co-territoriality of the Old Norse – Old English contact in turn makes it more likely that the simplification that occurred in Old English was due to contact with speakers of Celtic Late British.

COMPLEXIFICATION IN OLD ENGLISH

There is, it is true, evidence that initially the contact between Late British and Old English speakers may have been of the complexification type also. A number of writers, including Ahlqvist (2010), Filppula (2003), Laker (2008), Lutz (2009) and Vennemann (2000), have discussed the possibility that Old English might have acquired morphological categories from Late British.

One example is the distinction between the two paradigms of *be* that was mentioned at the beginning of this chapter. Lutz points out that there is the possibility of Late British influence here in that not only are there two present-tense declensions for the verb *to be* in Old English: *ic eom, þu eart, he/heo/hit is*, pl. *we/ge/hie sint* [*sindon, sindun*] vs. *ic beo, þu bist, he/heo/hit bið*, pl. *beoð*, but that this is actually a functional distinction. The importance of this for our current story is most persuasively made by the distinguished Celtic linguistic scholar Anders Ahlqvist (2010), who describes what he calls "a curious parallelism": the functional distinction lay in the fact that the Old English *eom* declension was used only for the actual present, while the other declension with forms beginning with *b-* was employed only for the expression of the future or habitual. According to Ahlqvist, this system is not only peculiar to Old English among the Germanic languages; the distinction is also precisely the one which is found in Welsh. And not only that – there is also the remarkable phonological similarity between the forms of Old Welsh and Old English: the "true present" in both has forms without *b-*, while the habitual/future has forms with *b-*. More particularly, the Welsh form corresponding to the Old English third-person singular habitual *b-* form *bið* is *bydd*, which goes back to earlier **bið*. Ahlqvist stresses that this resemblance – or indeed identity – is even more remarkable because the short vowel of Old English *bið* is difficult to account for in that it is not a regular development from earlier Germanic, while the Welsh form actually is a regular development.

Laker (2002) agrees that this is an extraordinary parallel, but states that the present-tense verb paradigms of the verb *be* in other West Germanic languages also have two different stems. This could suggest that there were also two functionally distinct paradigms of *be* earlier in continental West Germanic. Compare the first-, second- and third-person Old Saxon present-tense singular forms *bium, bist, is*, for example, with the more regular North Germanic Old Norse *em, ert, er*. Thus, Laker says, there is the possibility that the two West Germanic paradigms might have been preserved in Old English, but not in other West Germanic varieties, as a result of Brittonic influence, rather than being acquired from Brittonic. Alternatively, I would suggest that the presence of the two paradigms may well result from initial West Germanic dialect mixture as suggested by Nielsen (1998); but then the functional sorting out of the two different paradigms occurred as a result of the *reallocation* process that often accompanies new-dialect formation (Trudgill 1986, 2004), with the precise nature of the reallocation in this case being due to the grammatical/semantic influence of Late British.

It is also possible that the two functionally distinct paradigms of *be* in earlier continental West Germanic were indeed the result of contact with Celtic, but that the Celtic/West Germanic contact which gave rise to this phenomenon actually occurred in continental Europe before the migrations of the Anglo-Saxons to Britain, rather than in Britain itself. After all, Schrijver (1999) has argued for a similar development as far as Celtic phonological influence on West Germanic is concerned.

A second example of possible borrowing and complexification concerns the grammaticalisation of the progressive aspect (Filppula 2003; Lutz 2009; Mittendorf and Poppe 2000; White 2002): the progressive is generally considered not to be a typical feature of the Germanic languages, and therefore to be a good candidate for an example in English of influence from Brittonic, where it was and is an established feature. Laker (2002) does caution that there are also examples of the present participle being used to indicate progressive aspect in Old High German, and in Old Frisian Law codices, but concedes that "for the present we can agree that some British influence may be detectable in the Old English texts" (2008: 19) as far as this feature is concerned. Nickel (1966) argues that it is an example of a change which was spontaneously generated in Old English itself.

Ahlqvist, however, gives a reasoned and highly persuasive account – and one informed by a profound knowledge of Celtic linguistics and of the relative chronologies involved – that the argument that the English progressive results from influence from a Celtic source is a sound one. I cannot do his detailed argument justice here, but one stage of it involves Middle Welsh verb forms which are clearly the result of univerbation involving compound forms of *bot* 'to be'. The verb *gwybot* 'to know' has forms including the following:

	present	habitual present/future
1sg.	*gwnn*	*gwy**byd**af*
2sg.	*gwydost*	*gwy**byd**y*
3sg.	*gwyr*	*gwy**byd***
1pl.	*gwdom*	*gwy**byd**wn*
2pl.	*gwydawch*	*gwy**byd**wch*

	present	**habitual present/future**
3pl.	*gwydant*	*gwy**b**ydant*
imper.	*gwys*	*gwy**b**ydir*

	imperfect	**habitual past**
1sg.	*gwydwn*	
2sg.	*gwydut*	*gwy**b**ydut*
3sg.	*gwydyei*	*gwy**b**ydei*
1pl.	*gwydem*	*gwy**b**ydem*
2pl.	*gwydewch*	*gwy**b**ydwch*
3pl.	*gwydynt*	*gwy**b**ydant*
imper.	*gwydit*	*gwy**b**ydit*

(Evans 1964: 147–8)

The marker -**b**- in the right-hand column, derived from the -**b**-root of the verb *to be*, shows that this is a composite paradigm, consisting of inherited, older, clearly synthetic forms in the left-hand column and newer, univerbated, formerly periphrastic forms in the habitual. Given this evidence for the frequent occurrence of periphrastic locutions with *bot* plus other verbs early enough for them to have ended up as univerbated verbal forms in Middle Welsh, "it seems possible to assume that their very presence – obviously fairly abundantly so – in the language made it possible for them to become functionally differentiated from non-periphrastic ones, thereby giving rise to the grammatical category progressive" (Ahlqvist 2010: 60). Periphrastic verbs forms are well known to have occurred in Middle Welsh. But the point here is that Ahlqvist has shown that we can deduce from the Middle Welsh compound habitual forms – originating from morphologisation of forms of *be* – that the periphrastic verb forms must have been common and frequent enough even in Primitive Welsh and Old Welsh (AD 600–1150, Evans 1964: xvi) to give rise in the case of a few verbs to univerbation. This frequency contrasts with evidence from Early English verbal morphology, which does not contain signs of having verbal forms that can be derived by morphologisation from earlier periphrastic ones. This in turn means that the "environment from which progressive forms might have arisen" was "much more restricted" in English than in Welsh, which "strengthens the argument that the progressive forms of English are the result of influence from a Celtic source" (Ahlqvist 2010: 60).

Laker (2002) also cites as other candidates for Celtic influence features which have been proposed by a number of different scholars: periphrastic *do* (van der Auwera and Genee 2002; White 2002); the "Northern Subject Rule", whereby present-tense verbs have -*s*, except when they are directly preceded by a pronoun subject (Klemola 2000); the loss of the external possessor construction, as in German *die Mutter wäscht dem Kind die Haare* 'the mother washes the child's hair' (Vennemann 2002); the negative comparative particle *bigger* **nor** *him* (Laker 2008); and *it*-cleft constructions (Tristram 2000: 22).

Schrijver (1999, 2002, 2009) also argues, again on the basis of a detailed linguistic analysis, that Old English *phonology* was heavily influenced by contact with British Vulgar Latin and/or Celtic – the point being that there was a transitivity here (see Vennemann 2000) such that if the influence on Old English was from the Celtic of eastern Britain, this had itself already been influenced by British Latin (see above).

The sociolinguistic typological approach adopted here, however, suggests that if there was in fact contact of the type that would lead to Late British features being introduced into Old English, it is likely that this contact occurred at a time when Old English speakers were relatively few in number, and the relationship between the two ethnic groups had settled down to be one that developed for a while on a basis of relative equality. This contact would have taken place in the earlier decades of Anglo-Saxon settlement in the Lowland zone, quite likely after the fleeing of the British Latin-speaking upper-classes to the Highland zone.

SIMPLIFICATION IN OLD ENGLISH

Crucially, however, in those Highland areas where, later on, Late British survived the West Germanic invasion in the long term, and indeed for many centuries, its speakers were in a very different type of contact situation with Old English speakers: Late British was in a substratal, not adstratal relationship with Old English (Tristram 2004, 2006), and there was perhaps something like a caste system.

The Britons were often slaves, a point made by Lutz (2009) among others: Lutz devotes extensive discussion to the important work on Anglo-Saxon slavery by Pelteret (1995). And according to Whitelock (1952: 111), "the unfree class consisted of persons of different origins. Some were the descendants of the British population, as the word for 'Briton' to mean simply 'slave' testifies. The menial tasks described in some Anglo-Saxon riddles are performed by 'Britons'." And a number of writers (see Woolf 2007) have actually described the situation as being one of "apartheid": Thomas *et al.* (2008) write that the genetic evidence suggests that "an apartheid-like social structure remains the most plausible model to explain the high degree of northwest continental European male-line ancestry in England", and that "people of indigenous ethnicity were at an economic and legal disadvantage compared with those having Anglo-Saxon ethnicity – leading to differential reproductive success – and that the two groups were, to an extent, reproductively isolated". So the two linguistic groups were hardly "on good terms", in Mithun's phrase. "From the textual evidence we have, the social barriers between the free and land-holding elite of Anglo-Saxon society and their dependents were perhaps fairly stable until the advent of the Normans" (Tristram 2004: 202).

Residential patterns will also have been important: as Coates (2007: 190) says, separate villages where "homogeneous slave communities might be retained" could "lead to 'slave coloured' varieties of English". There is considerable evidence for this residential separation from place names. Ekwall (1960) lists about fifty different places in England containing the Old English element *walh, wealh*

'Briton, serf', including Walbrook, Walburn, Walcot, Walden, Walford, Wallington, Walmer, Walshford, Walton and Walworth. There are as many as twenty Waltons with this origin. And these towns and villages are to be found as far apart as the southwest (Dorset, Wiltshire, Worcestershire, Herefordshire, Oxfordshire, Berkshire), the southeast (Kent, Middlesex, Sussex, Surrey, Hertfordshire), East Anglia (Essex, Suffolk, Norfolk), the Midlands (Leicestershire, Derbyshire, Lincolnshire, Shropshire, Staffordshire, Warwickshire, Northamptonshire) and the north (Durham, Lancashire, Yorkshire).

Linguistically, then, as Tristram (2004: 202) has it, "if we assume that the native Britons in the South West, the Midlands and the North slowly shifted to Old English in the course of two to four centuries (fifth to ninth), the type of linguistic contact and of language acquisition would have had to be that of the adult learner type". She suggests that for Britons acquiring Old English, especially perhaps in the Highland zone, the first step was that of unstructured adult acquisition of the Old English target dialects as L2:

> Perhaps, initially, there may have been only a small stable group of adult bilinguals who mediated between the speakers of Late British and the Old English dialects. Social segregation ... may have generally kept the two population groups apart. As long as the social barrier lasted, this scenario will have meant for adult bilinguals a native-like acquisition of the lexicon but transfer on the level of phonology and morphosyntax because of their unconscious, imperfect replication of the target language.
>
> (Tristram 2004: 202)

I do not, however, share Tristram's view that the simplification which occurred took place through actual transfer from Late British as a result of the fact that it was by that time a non-inflecting language as far as the nominal system was concerned. I regard simplification, as being a feature of adult L2 acquisition which occurs regardless of the nature of the L1. Features which are "L2 difficult" are not rendered any easier simply because similar complexities are present in one's mother tongue. For example, learning and remembering the more-or-less arbitrary gender assignment of nouns in, say, German, is surely no easier for Russian speakers than for English speakers.

Laker (2002, 2009) also argues for phonological transference from Brittonic to Old English at this stage: for example, he proposes Brittonic substratum influence for the change of /kw/- and /hw/- to /xw/- in northern English dialects of Old English, giving e.g. *quick* as *"wick"* (from earlier *"hwick"*) in some modern northern Traditional Dialects. He argues that since Old Welsh had neither /kw/-, nor /hw/-, Brittonic speakers shifting to Old English replaced both of them with the closest approximation in their own speech, namely /xw/-; and it is most likely that this occurred at this stage as a typical instance of shift-induced substratum interference (Thomason 2001).

In any case, the pidginised form of Old English that Tristram hypothesises would have been increasingly passed on to subsequent generations: "children would have learned the imperfectly acquired L2 from their parents as their L1 and subsequently passed on their linguistic knowledge of the modified target language to their own children" (Tristram 2004: 202), and the simplified version of the language eventually became the dominant variety. The scenario would have resembled the one in which the colonial Dutch of South Africa, while maintaining a continuous tradition of transmission from one generation of native speakers to another, underwent considerable simplification even in the version spoken by native speakers, as witnessed by modern Afrikaans, as a result of widespread language contact and non-native acquisition.

Demography would have been very important for these developments: "The current discourse [of historians and archaeologists] advocates the theory of an elite take-over of the c. two-million Romano-British population by Anglo-Saxon 'fringe barbarians'" (Härke 2002: 167). "This means that the great mass of the Brittonic or British Latin speaking menial population of the island of Britain suffered an Anglo-Saxon take-over from the top" (Tristram 2004: 14).

The Anglo-Saxon elite then continued to consist of a small number of aristocrats: William the Conqueror replaced no more than 4,000 Anglo-Saxon nobles by Norman barons within his first twenty years. Below the Anglo-Saxon aristocracy, there was the class of the freemen, but the majority of the population were unfree people or slaves (Whitelock 1952).

In the Highland zone, then, it was the pidginised form of Old English which came to dominate, and it is therefore not surprising that it is in the north of England that we first see the greatest degree of linguistic simplification. As noted earlier, this northern locus has more usually been cited as evidence in favour of the influence of Old Norse; but White (2002, 2003) has argued that the inflectional attrition which occurred as a consequence of the pidginisation resulting from Late British–Old English contact may later have been *reinforced* by contact with Old Norse. Kroch *et al.* (2000) also argue convincingly for the loss of verb-second order in English as being the result of a rather complex series of linguistic events due initially to contact between Old English and Old Norse.

This double dose of language contact would explain why the north of England was by far the most innovating region in the late Old English/early Middle English period. White also argues that the English southeast was the most conservative area because it experienced very little language contact after the earliest period, while East Anglia and the southwest were intermediate in terms of degree of change because they experienced only one contact phase each, with Old Norse and Late British respectively.

The simplification, however, did not appear in written texts until much later. Tristram assumes that the diglossia that arose between the Late British-derived Old English and the elite Old English spoken by the comparatively small number of people forming the aristocracy was very significant: "only the language of the elite, the high variety of Old English narrowly monitored and standardised, seems to have been codified in writing, and it was this version of the language which remained remarkably constant over many centuries" (Tristram 2004: 202).

The solution to our puzzle thus seems to be that it was contact between a minority of Old English and a majority of socially inferior Late British speakers, in northern England, that set the process of simplification going as the Britons shifted to (their form of) English, and Late British was eventually lost.[6] Further contact with Old Norse in the north may then also have been involved, so, as is often the case, the answer to our conundrum of Celtic vs. Old Norse would appear to be that the advocates of the two positions are both likely to be correct, even if one of the positions is even more correct than the other.

The language contact that occurred in England between Brittonic, Latin, Old English and Old Norse over many centuries was an extended, fluid and complex process. The different stages of language contact that may have been involved were, chronologically over several centuries:

(1)   interference and additive complexification in early Old English (with transfer of some Brittonic phonological and grammatical features) as a result of (eventually) intimate contact with an adstratum of lower-class Brittonic and/or British Latin speakers in the Lowland zone, with eventual shift from Brittonic to Old English;

(2)   simplification of Brittonic in the Highland zone as a result of adult language contact with a superstratum of upper-class refugee British Latin speakers, with eventual shift from Latin to Brittonic;

(3)   simplification of later Old English as a result of adult language contact, mainly in the Highland zone, with a substratum of at least partly enslaved Late British speakers, with eventual shift to Old English. This is the crucial stage for the problem being addressed here. The substratum role also accounts for

---

[6] Except in Wales and Cornwall.

the paucity of lexical borrowings from Late British into Old English (Ahlqvist 2010), bearing in mind, however, that Breeze (e.g. 2002) has argued that there were more such loans than is traditionally considered to be the case;

(4)   intimate contact between Old English and an adstratum of Old Norse speakers, mainly in the north, with lexical and indeed pronoun borrowing, but no evidence of complexification because of close structural similarities between the languages.

2 East Anglian English and the Spanish Inquisition

The geographical focus of this chapter is on one of the areas where the contact between Germanic and Brittonic (Brythonic) which we have just been discussing first occurred – namely the area of eastern England now known as East Anglia. Chronologically, however, the investigation starts where the previous one left off, in the Middle English period, and then takes us in terms of its principal focus up to the sixteenth and seventeenth centuries.

We start, however, by working backwards from the 1960s and 1970s, when East Anglian dialects of English had their brief moment of international academic glory. The big sociolinguistic issue of the day in the English-speaking world was the historical origins of African American Vernacular English (AAVE), or American "Nonstandard Negro English", as it was then called. To simplify rather considerably, there were two major groups of American academic linguists in competition on this issue. One group, the Creolists, argued that, to the extent that AAVE was linguistically different from White varieties of English, this was due to the fact that AAVE had its origins in an earlier creole similar to Gullah and to the other English-based Atlantic creoles (Bailey 1965): AAVE was a decreolised creole or "post-creole" which still retained some creole features. The other group, who we can call the Dialectologists, argued that, without denying that Black and White varieties of American English differed, it was not necessary to postulate a creole history. They argued instead that differences were due to differential loss and retention of original features of British Isles English, together with subsequent independent developments (see the presentations in Dillard 1970; Burling 1973).

This chapter is dedicated to Jim Milroy, without whom I would not have ventured to write it.

A number of features of AAVE were advanced as evidence for and against these hypotheses. One of these was the absence from verb forms in this variety of third-person singular present-tense -*s* (see Fasold 1972).

The Creolists pointed out that loss of -*s* represented a typical case of regularisation or simplification of the sort which often happens in language contact situations, as we saw in Chapter 1, and that the Caribbean and other Atlantic English-based creoles also demonstrated this feature. If White American speech had -*s* and vernacular Black varieties had zero, then this was not surprising in view of the large-scale processes of language shift, pidginisation and creolisation that the speech of the ancestors of modern black Americans had been subject to as a result of their enforced transplantation from West Africa to slavery in the Americas (see Dillard 1970).

The Dialectologists' view (see Kurath 1928) was that third-person singular present-tense zero was a feature of certain British Isles dialects, and the obvious explanation was that Black varieties had acquired and retained this original British Isles feature, while White dialects for the most part had not retained it.

The British Isles dialects in question were those of the English region of East Anglia, where forms such as the following are the norm (see Trudgill 1974, 1990):

> He like it, do he?
> That go ever so fast.
> She buy some every day.

The creole or non-creole history of AAVE continues to be discussed in the sociolinguistic literature today, though these more recent discussions tend to be based on more sophisticated data and argumentation from historical linguistics and variation theory (Poplack 2000). The antiquity, status and grammatical function of third-person singular zero in AAVE has also been called into question, as has the role of *s*-marking on persons other than the third-person singular

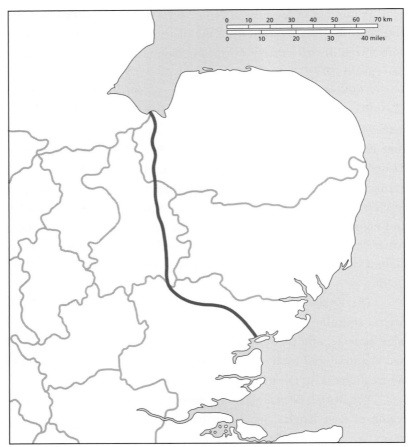

Map 2 East Anglian third-person singular zero

(see Schneider 1983; Poplack and Tagliamonte 1989; Winford 1992; McElhinny 1993; Montgomery *et al.* 1993; Poplack 2000).

However, there was one obvious question which nobody in the 1960s and 1970s ever thought to ask, and which has never been asked since: why is it that the dialects of *East Anglia* lack present-tense *-s*? That is the puzzle that this chapter now addresses.

EAST ANGLIAN DIALECTS

Third-person singular present-tense zero is currently a well-known feature of the traditional dialects of an area which includes the counties of Norfolk, Suffolk and Essex (see Map 2, from Trudgill 2001). The publications of the *Survey of English Dialects* show zero-marking for this verb form in northern Essex, all of Suffolk and all of Norfolk except the Fens. According to David Britain (p.c.), who is an expert on the sociolinguistics of the area (see Britain 1991), the non-Fenland Norfolk town of Downham Market has zero while the Cambridgeshire Fenland town of Wisbech has -*s*. Emneth, which is a suburb of Wisbech but is administratively in Norfolk, also has -*s*.

Local dialect literature confirms that third-person zero is a typical feature of the Traditional Dialects. For example, Charles Benham's *Essex ballads*, originally published in Colchester in 1895, contain verses such as:

> I loike to watch har in the Parson's pew
> A Sundays, me a-settin' in the choir;
> She *look* jest wholly be'tiful, she *do*.
> That fairly *seem* to set my heart a-fire.
> That *seem* ridic'lous nons'nse this, I doubt,
> A-tellin' on yer how she *make* me feel,
> But who's to help it when she *walk* about
> More like a angel than a gal a deal.

> *(Miss Julia: the Parson's Daughter)*

Similarly, the Norfolk dialect poet John Kett in more recent writings uses forms such as:

> That *seem* as though, whenever I sow seeds
> They fare t'come up slow, or not a'tall.
> An' them there hollahocks agin that wall
> In't haalf as big as them untidy weeds.
> But I'll say one thing, bor, an' that in't tew –
> Now Winter's come, an' that ole North wind *blow*,
> My garden's buried und'ra foot o' snow ...
> That *look* like all the others now, that *dew*!

> *(My Garden)*

We find examples in many other sources, including the correspondence of Horatio Lord Nelson, who was born and grew up in north Norfolk, such as "Captain Lambert have been very fortunate" and "the *'Lady Parker'* have done a great deal of mischief around the island".

ENGLISH PRESENT-TENSE VERB SYSTEMS

The East Anglian verb system of course contrasts with the modern Standard English system, which is often held to be typologically unusual among the world's languages: of its present-tense verb forms, only the third-person singular shows morphological marking. This is very odd, as typologists are of the opinion that this is precisely the verb form which is *least* likely to receive special marking, and that Standard English is unusual in this respect. Battistella, for instance, says that "the third singular is the least marked person number category" (1990: 112).

It is therefore not at all surprising that many dialects of English do not share this characteristic of Standard English. Many dialects of British Isles English, for example, have a system in which present-tense -*s* occurs with all persons. In north of England dialects where it occurs, it is likely that this represents a survival of the original Middle English system. (There is, however, the further complication that many north of England varieties, like Scottish and northern Ireland varieties, have a subject agreement rule often called the Northern Subject Rule, as we saw in the previous chapter, such that third-person present-tense plural verb forms take -*s* unless they are governed by the pronoun *they*. This constraint has also been found in some American varieties (e.g. Wolfram and Christian 1976) and elsewhere (Poplack and Tagliamonte 1989), and has been argued by Bailey *et al.* (1989) to have been present at earlier periods at least in parts of the south of England.) The generalised -*s* system, however, is also very prevalent in large areas of southwestern England and south Wales (see Hughes and Trudgill 1995), where it must represent a more recent regularisation.

Conversely, there are many other varieties of English which have achieved regularisation by having no person-marking at all for any person in the present tense. Certain forms of English have, like East Anglian dialects, regularised this unexpected and irregular system by having zero-marking for all persons. These varieties are rather considerable in number, but it is of great interest that all of them except East Anglian English are spoken outside the British Isles. We have already mentioned AAVE and the creole Gullah in the United States. The other relevant varieties are mostly English-based pidgins, creoles, post-creoles and creoloids.

This latter term, *creoloid*, refers to varieties like Afrikaans, which, when compared with some source variety like Dutch, resemble a post-creole in that they show some features of simplification as a result of the influence of imperfect learning by non-native-speaker adults, but which have maintained a continuous native-speaker tradition, unlike pidgin-derived creoles and post-creoles. It could be argued, then, on the basis of Chapter 1, that Middle English was a creoloid relative to Old English.

Many of the English-based creoles are found in the Caribbean and West Africa, while other varieties which have third-person zero include the South Pacific pidgin and creole varieties Tok Pisin, Bislama and Solomon Island Pidgin; the language spoken on Pitcairn and its sister language on Norfolk Island; and the English of Saint Helena, which is perhaps best described as a creoloid (see Chapter 3). In Pitcairnese, for example, we find utterances such as the following (Ross and Moverley 1964: 127):

> If any want one melon, first up *get* it.
> [If anyone wants a watermelon, the first up there gets it.]
> It *make* I think its lost ball.
> [It makes me think it's a lost ball = a ship not going to stop.]

Zero-marking is also found in some institutionalised second-language varieties, such as the "New Englishes" of Singapore, Malaya and elsewhere.

What all these non-British Isles varieties have in common, of course, is that they are varieties with a history of considerable language contact. Pidgins and creoles are our prime examples of contact languages; and creoloids and second-language Englishes are also obviously the result of the acquisition of English by non-native speakers in a contact situation. And as we saw in Chapter 1, adult language contact is well known to lead to simplification, so loss of *-s* in these varieties is not at all surprising.

East Anglian English would therefore appear to be the odd one out here: it is the only British Isles, as opposed to overseas, variety which demonstrates third-person singular zero. This fact – that East Anglian dialects, alone of all British varieties, coincide with the overseas contact varieties on this point – therefore leads us to ask the following question: *is it possible that third-person singular zero is a contact feature in East Anglian English also?*

THE CHRONOLOGY OF EAST ANGLIAN VERB FORMS

Any explanation for the absence of third-person singular *-s* from East Anglia must necessarily look at the history of the development of *-s* in modern English itself.

Middle English present-tense verb forms had a regional distribution as follows, illustrated from the verb *to thank* (see Fisiak 1968):

	South	Midlands	North
1sg.	*thanke*	*thanke*	*thanke*
2sg.	*thankest*	*thankes(t)*	*thankes*
3sg.	*thanketh*	*thanketh/es*	*thankes*
pl.	*thanketh*	*thanken*	*thankes*

The Midland plural form *-en* was borrowed from the subjunctive, and provided a singular/plural distinction not available in the other dialects. During the Middle English period, this form gradually spread to the other dialects, and the *-n* was increasingly lost. With eventual loss of final /ə/, only the second- and third-person singular forms retained inflectional endings. With the subsequent loss of the singular second-person *thou* forms in favour of plural *you* forms, the third-person singular forms were left as the only ones distinct from the base.

As can be seen, and as is well known, the third-person singular ending in the south was *-(e)th*, in the north *-(e)s*. The origin of the northern *-es* form is somewhat controversial. Hogg (1993: 306) writes:

> In Northumbrian only, final /θ/ in [the third-person singular and in the plural present indicative] is often spelled as <s> ... The morphological restriction on these forms indicates that the shift could take place only under favourable morphological conditions, but its spread to the plural shows that the stimulus cannot solely have been an analogy with Scandinavian.

Whatever its origins, the originally northern form gradually spread south. According to Brook (1958), "the forms in *-es* spread from the north to the East Midlands and the North-West Midlands in Middle English, and by the fifteenth century spread to London English". (A number of third-person zero forms also occurred from the 1400s onward (Holmqvist 1922), but these were very infrequent indeed: Kytö (1993) reports seven (= 1.5 per cent) examples out of a total of 461 third-person singular present-tense verb forms in the Helsinki corpus for 1500–70.)

Baugh and Cable (1993) claim that the spread of *-es* forms to the south is "difficult to account for, since it is not easy to see how the Northern dialect, where they were normal, could have exerted so important an influence on the language of London and the South". Nevertheless, spread they did. The general consensus is that this spreading process was gradual and effected colloquial speech first, and that there was a long period in the London area when both forms were available to differing extents. It is often pointed out that Shakespeare, for instance, was able to use both *-th* and *-s* forms depending on the needs of style and metre. In *Hamlet*, for example, we find:

> … and sweet religion make**s**
> A rhapsody of words: heaven's face do**th** glow.

According to Baugh and Cable, *-s* forms predominated in the London area by 1600. The geographical diffusion of this form did not, of course, end in London, and forms in *-th* are known not to have been replaced by *-s* in Traditional Dialects in the far southwest of England (Devon and Cornwall) until the early years of the twentieth century (see Wakelin 1972).

As far as East Anglia is concerned, what evidence we have from the Middle English of the area shows that, from the eleventh to the fifteenth centuries, it shared the fully inflected present-tense verb systems of other Middle English dialects (though for the analyst, distinguishing unmarked subjunctive from indicative forms in texts can be a problem (Wright 2001)). Given that Norwich is about as far from the north of England as London is, the regional location of East Anglia would lead us to expect that southwards geographical diffusion would have led to the replacement of southern *-th* by the originally northern *-s* form in Norwich at about the same time as in London, namely during the 1500s in colloquial speech and during the 1600s in more formal prose (see Baugh and Cable 1993).

Important evidence on this comes from the Paston letters, which are a highly important source of information about the vernacular English of the period. They form a collection of letters and papers from correspondence written by members of the Paston family between 1422 and 1509 (Davis *et al.* 2004–5); and crucially for our investigation the family were Norfolk gentry – the village of Paston lies about fifteen miles northeast of Norwich. Importantly, these letters show third-person singular *-th* throughout.

On the other hand, if we try to focus on the question of at what point after 1509 the current East Anglian dialect zero form came into being, it is certainly clear that third-person singular zero has been a feature typical of East Anglian English since at least 1700. This is apparent from the work of the Norfolk clergyman the Rev. R. Forby, who was probably born in 1732 and died in 1825. In his posthumously published *The vocabulary of East Anglia*, Forby (1830) describes the East Anglian dialect "as it existed in the last twenty years of the eighteenth century", i.e. from 1780–1800. He writes of East Anglian speakers that "we so stubbornly maintain that the first and third persons are of the very same forms 'I love, he love'" (1830: 142). And we can in fact assert with confidence that zero was typical of Norfolk English even well before 1780: zero forms occur in the correspondence of a later member of the Paston family, Lady Katherine Paston [c. 1578–1629], who was writing during the period 1603–27 (Hughey 1941; Hogg and Denison 2006: 295).

We therefore have a clear indication that, if we want to consider a contact-based explanation for why modern East Anglian dialects have third-person singular present-tense zero, we must consider sociolinguistic factors that date from the hundred years between, say, 1510 and 1610; if we want to solve the puzzle, we have to ask the crucial question: *what exactly happened in the sixteenth century?*

Before we ask this question, however, we must note that there are presumably two possible historical-linguistic scenarios: (a) either East Anglian English arrived at the modern zero-marking system via an intermediate *s*-marking system, in between the *-th* of the early Paston letters and the zero of Katherine Paston and the Rev. Forby, as it were; or (b) there was no intermediate stage, and East Anglian dialects lack *-s* because they never acquired it in the first place:

(a) *-eth* → *-es* → -Ø
(b) *-eth* → -Ø

What, then, are the relevant sixteenth-century sociolinguistic factors, and which is the correct scenario, (a) or (b)?

SPANISH PERSECUTION IN THE LOW COUNTRIES

I now present historical sociolinguistic evidence from the sixteenth century which suggests, first, that third-person singular present-tense zero in East Anglian dialects is indeed a contact feature; and, second, that it is the second scenario which is the correct one.

As far as contact is concerned, histories of the English language, having dealt with the influence of Norman French and Old Norse on English, as we did in Chapter 1, rarely thereafter comment on language contact or multilingualism in England at all, with the possible exception of a brief mention of the shift from Cornish to English in Cornwall, which was completed in the eighteenth century. A consideration of the earlier history of English, however, suggests that language contact of different types has frequently occurred not just in Ireland, Scotland and Wales, but also in England. Consider the linguistic history of East Anglia itself.

After the gradual replacement between the fifth and seventh centuries of the ancestor of modern Welsh – and what Latin there was, again as discussed in Chapter 1 – by the Anglo-Saxon spoken by the invading Angles and Frisians, East Anglia must have remained fairly monolingual for a century or so until the arrival of the Danes in the ninth century. For the next few hundred years, however, multilingualism must have been a frequent feature. After the Norman Conquest, for instance, Norwich itself in the twelfth century must have had, in addition to the original speakers of English and Danish, speakers of the newly arrived Norman French, as well as the Breton and Flemish spoken by many of the Normans' followers. Large numbers of Jews also arrived with the Normans, and they may have been speakers of Ladino (Judaeo-Spanish). Later, during the fourteenth century, there were also numerous Flemish-speaking weavers who arrived in the city.

It is very unlikely, however, that these particular instances of language contact had any kind of effect on the present-tense verb system of East Anglian English. Historical events which do appear to be relevant are the following. From 1348 onwards, the different provinces of the Low Countries, for the most part modern Belgium and the Netherlands, came gradually under the control of the Dukes of Burgundy. Mary, the daughter of Charles the Bold, Duke of Burgundy, married Emperor Maximilian of Austria. Their son Philip married Joanna, the daughter of Ferdinand of Aragon and Isabella of Castile, and thus control of the Low Countries ultimately passed to their son, who as Charles V was Holy Roman Emperor, as well as being King Charles I of Spain. When he abdicated in 1556, the imperial office went to his brother, Emperor Ferdinand I. The crown of Spain, however, together with control over the Low Countries and other colonies such as Naples and Milan, went to his son, King Philip II.

Although Charles had been educated in the Low Countries, his son Philip had been brought up in Spain. Philip was also a devout Catholic, and most of his domestic, colonial and foreign policies were focussed on stamping out Protestantism. It was therefore inevitable that there would be friction in the Low Countries where, in the northern provinces (now the Netherlands), Calvinism had taken deep root.

Under the control of Philip's sister, Margaret of Parma, the stationing of Spanish troops in the Low Countries, the prosecution of "heretics" and the Spanish Inquisition led to an insurrection in the colony against Spanish domination even in the mainly Catholic south (modern Belgium), where loss of autonomy was resented. In 1567, Philip sent the Duke of Alva with an army of 20,000 Spaniards to the areas which are now Belgium and the Netherlands to quell this anti-Spanish, anti-Catholic revolt. Many prominent people were executed, estates were confiscated and opposition was ruthlessly suppressed. In particular, penal edicts against "heresy" led to considerable persecution, including torture, of Protestants.

Not surprisingly, thousands of inhabitants of the Low Countries, at that time probably the wealthiest and most civilised part of Europe, fled abroad. Equally unsurprisingly, very large numbers indeed of these fled across the North Sea to independent,

Protestant England. And a very large number of those who fled to England arrived in the largest city of eastern England, Norwich.

Dutch, Flemish and Walloon refugees escaping to England from this Spanish persecution also settled in Sandwich (Kent), London and Colchester, but the group of refugees that found its way to Norwich was the biggest by far. They were probably attracted at least in part by an already established group of invited weavers. In 1565, the mayor and aldermen of Norwich had invited thirty "Dutchmen" and their families – no household was to exceed ten persons – to Norwich in an attempt to modernise the local textile industry, which was of great economic importance to the region, but which had been lagging behind in terms of technology, design and skills. In the event, twenty-four Flemish and ten Walloon master textile makers arrived and settled in Norwich (Rickwood 1984; Vane 1984). The refugees themselves, although predominantly also textile workers, included ministers, doctors, teachers, merchants and craftsmen. They were mostly from Flanders and Brabant, but there were also many Walloons from Armentieres, Namur and Valenciennes (note that at this period, the border with France was further south than it is today), and even some German speakers from Lorraine. The large size of the colony of foreigners, and the very high proportion of "Strangers", as they were called, in the city, did lead to a certain amount of friction, and there was at least one attempted revolt against them; but generally, the absorption of a very large number of refugees into the population, while it undoubtedly caused overcrowding, seems to have been relatively trouble free. The economic benefits of the reinvigorated textile trade were plain for all to see.

The impact of the refugees must have been enormous. The population of Norwich in 1579 was 16,236. Of that number, approximately 6,000 were Dutch- and French-speaking refugees. With about 37 per cent of the population being native speakers of a language other than English, then, Norwich at the turn of the sixteenth century was the scene of very considerable language contact indeed.

Some of the Flemish community returned to the Low Countries during the 1600s, ironically as a result of religious persecution, but during the seventeenth century the foreign community was further strengthened by the arrival of some French Huguenots after the revocation of the edict of Nantes in 1685. Subsequently, the Dutch and French languages survived in Norwich for a considerable time. According to Moens (1888), "in the first half of the seventeenth century, as much Dutch and French was spoken in Norwich as English". The first books ever to be printed in Norwich were in Dutch, and orders for the conduct of the Strangers were written in French in 1659. According to Ketton-Cremer (1957), church services in Dutch and French were maintained in the churches that had been given over to the immigrant communities "for many decades", and the congregations seem to have remained vigorous until 1700 or so. Then, "slowly but inevitably the Strangers became merged into the surrounding population and the community lost its separate identity" (Ketton-Cremer 1957). French and Dutch continued to survive, but by 1742 the congregations attending church services held in these languages were small, and the churches decayed. The last French-language service in Norwich was in 1832, and the last in Dutch in the 1890s, but by then the languages were only used for liturgical purposes. Now only French and Dutch surnames survive, and most of those in anglicised form.

I conclude that the Dutch and French languages, having arrived in the period 1565–70, finally fell out of use as native languages in Norwich during the 1700s. Norwich was a genuinely trilingual city for perhaps as much as two hundred years.

CONTACT AND CHANGE

The direct linguistic influence of this influx on Norwich English seems to have been minimal as far as French is concerned: I have been able to find a single dialectal lexical item, *lucam* 'attic window', from French *lucarne* 'skylight'.

Dutch, however, has made a rather clear lexical contribution. This, of course, has to be distinguished from the contribution of Dutch to English generally, which, though nothing like that of French, is of some importance and reasonably well established. Dutch-origin words in general English tend to fall into a limited number of semantic fields. It is not surprising, given the maritime trading connections between the Low Countries and Britain, that numerous nautical words have been borrowed:

> *bluff, boom, buoy, cruise, deck, dock, drill, freebooter, iceberg, keelhaul, leak, morass, pump, skipper, sloop, smack, smelt, smuggle, yacht*

Other words borrowed from Dutch are probably or possibly trade related:

> *to bluff, brandy, bundle*

There are a few, later words to do with art:

> *etch, easel, landscape, sketch*

and others of no particular provenance:

> *cackle, frolic, grab, offal, roster, skate, slurp*

The degree of actual Dutch influence on the Norwich dialect is somewhat difficult to determine for the rather obvious reason that Dutch and English are closely related languages, both descended from West Germanic, and resemblances between Dutch and forms of English are therefore most usually due not to the influence of Dutch on English, or vice versa, but to their common origin.

Nevertheless, when we find English words that resemble Dutch and that are found *only or mainly* in East Anglia, then it is worth considering whether or not they derive from close contact across the North Sea, or from the Flemish speakers who arrived with the Norman Conquest, or from the Flemish weavers who arrived in the fourteenth century, or – as is relevant to this chapter – from the massive numbers of Dutch-speaking Strangers who arrived in the sixteenth century. Indeed, Pettersson (1994) shows that there are many more words of Dutch and/or Low German origin in English dialects than in Standard English, as revealed by her study of the *Survey of English Dialects* (SED) materials. In particular, she reports that the areas with the largest number of such words are Lincolnshire, Norfolk and Essex. She suggests that this is natural since the Dutch came across the North Sea and primarily settled in the areas in which they first landed.

Crucially for our purposes, the likelihood of Dutch lexical influence stemming from the presence of the Strangers in Norwich is indicated by the way in which the candidate dialect words all fall into semantic fields which are different from those associated with Dutch words borrowed into English generally. They comprise no nautical words, for instance, but rather include domestic vocabulary and words concerned with the urban landscape. For example, in Norwich and other Norfolk towns, open urban areas are not called *squares*, as they would be elsewhere, but *plains*, from Dutch *plein* – Norwich has among others *Bank Plain*, *St Andrews Plain* and *Palace Plain*, and in Sheringham, on the coast, there is *Lifeboat Plain*.

Other Norfolk dialect words may well be of Dutch origin: *dwile* 'floorcloth' comes rather obviously from Dutch *dweil*, which has the same meaning; *crowd* 'to push, as of a wheelbarrow or bicycle' may very likely have come from Dutch *kruien* 'to push a wheelbarrow'; *deek* 'dyke, ditch' is probably from Dutch *dijk*; *fye out* 'clean up' may well be connected to Dutch *vegen* 'to sweep'; *push* 'boil, pimple' is quite possibly derived from Dutch *puist* 'pimple'; and *foisty* 'mouldy, musty' is basically the same word as *fusty*, and may derive from Dutch *fust* 'cask', which is equivalent to French *fût*, Old French *fust* – so this may just represent a further example of French lexical influence in Norwich. Another possible candidate is *dwainy* 'weak, sickly', which is perhaps from Old English *dwinan* 'to waste away', Middle English *dwine*, which survives in Modern English only in the form *dwindle*; on the other hand, the Norfolk word may come from early Modern Dutch *dwijnen* 'to vanish'. And *hake* 'hook over a cooking fire, pothook' may be from Dutch *haak*.

Given that there is some direct, lexical evidence of language contact in Norfolk, even if this is not overwhelming, I now therefore turn to a search for evidence of the indirect effects of language contact, of a type which could help to confirm the role of the Strangers in the development of third-person singular zero. We must begin by reiterating the point made above about adult language contact being well known to lead to linguistic simplification. My suggestion, specifically, is that East Anglian third-person singular present-tense zero is in origin a contact feature which developed as a result of the presence of large numbers of non-native speakers in Norwich who, in using English as a lingua franca among themselves and with the native population, failed to master – as non-native speakers of all types often do – the non-natural person-marking system of English verbs.

This simplification of the English verb system occurred in the speech of the Strangers in the same way and for the same reason that it occurred in the other varieties of English such as AAVE which also have third-person singular zero. It will be recalled from Chapter 1 that contact-induced simplification consists, among other processes, of the regularisation of irregularities, and loss of redundancy. Clearly, the modern East Anglian present-tense verb system contains no redundancy and is entirely regular. (It would not have been relevant that the Flemish and Walloon dialects spoken by the incomers themselves had third-person singular marking on verbs – as I argued in Chapter 1, that would not have helped. Irregularity and redundancy cause acquisition difficulties for all adult language learners, regardless of the structures of their own languages. As we saw in Chapter 1, arbitrariness in grammar produces material which has to be learnt without any generalisations being possible; and high redundancy means that there is more to learn.)

What happened next was, I hypothesise, as follows. Once the simplification had become an established part of the Norwich dialect of English, it subsequently spread outwards from Norwich, as the dominant *central place* (Christaller 1950), in the well-known pattern of geographical diffusion of linguistic innovations (see Trudgill 1983: 57–87) until it covered the whole area of East Anglia. In fact, we can say that "East Anglia" as a linguistic area (Trudgill 2001) is precisely the region of England which is dominated by Norwich as its biggest and most important urban centre. Today the greater urban area of Norwich has a population of about 250,000 and is by no means one of the largest cities in England. In mediaeval times, however, and up until the seventeenth century, Norwich was the largest city in England apart from London, with the possible exception of Bristol and York. Green and Young (1964) give a population for Norwich in 1662 of 29,200 and say that "Norwich was then probably the largest provincial town in England". It was certainly therefore by a very long way the dominant urban area of East Anglia: Ipswich in the 1660s had a population of only about 7,500, Colchester had 10,000 and Cambridge 6,000. Even today the city nearest to Norwich which is bigger than it in terms of population is London, 120 miles away. We can therefore imagine that it would be normal for social and cultural developments taking place in sixteenth- and seventeenth-century Norwich, as the dominant central place, to diffuse geographically down the urban hierarchy and out into the rural areas of the whole of East Anglia, and that this would have included linguistic developments.

THE COINCIDENCE

But there remains a further and rather obvious problem: why would the simplified verb system as employed by the Strangers "become an established part of the Norwich dialect"? Why should this feature of foreigner English be adopted by the majority of native speakers of English in Norwich in this way?

Above I compared the present-tense verb system of East Anglian English to that of English-based pidgin and creole languages around the world. However, there can be no suggestion that East

Anglian English was or is, as a whole, in any way a creole or other form of contact variety like, say, Pitcairnese or even AAVE. Clearly it is not. The modern dialect of Norwich contains no features at all other than third-person singular zero which can be described as being the result of contact-induced simplification; nor indeed does it demonstrate any other phonological or grammatical (as opposed to lexical) features which appear to be the result of direct interference or borrowing from Dutch or French. Norwich English, like other forms of East Anglian English, bears no resemblance to a creoloid. Indeed, we would not expect Norwich English to resemble a creoloid like Afrikaans because the degree of language contact was not nearly so great nor as prolonged. At all times, in spite of the large numbers of foreigners in the city, native speakers outnumbered non-natives by at least two to one. Indeed the situation in general seems to have developed rather quickly into the kind of language-contact situation – long-term co-territorial contact involving child language acquisition – which we discussed in Chapter 1 as not being conducive to simplification.

So the problem is that we have to provide an explanation for why the language contact that undoubtedly took place resulted in the simplification of this one particular grammatical feature, third-person singular zero, and of no others. It is clear that, under normal circumstances, given that the Strangers were in a minority, albeit a large one, the zero form would never have been victorious.

I propose the following explanation – an explanation which focusses on the fact that the circumstances were not normal. By far the most important explanatory factor for the unfolding of this development lies in the chronology of the arrival of the Strangers in Norwich. The fact is that these immigrants arrived *exactly* at the time when the present-tense system of verbs in English was in a state of flux in Norwich. As a result of the southward spreading of the newer -s ending, there was considerable variability in Norwich at this time between -th and -s forms. In other words, at any other time in history, competition between minority non-native zero forms and majority native forms with third-person-marking would *not* have led to the replacement of native by non-native forms. In the late sixteenth century, however, competition was *not* between zero and a single native form. On the contrary, competition was between zero and -*th* and -*s*. It was, that is, a much more equal struggle, as it were, and one in which the non-native form had the advantage of linguistic naturalness and simplicity: I have already pointed to the typological oddity and highly marked nature of marking only third-person singular verb forms in the present tense – such an unusual system must be more susceptible to simplification than most. (As pointed out to me by Laura Wright, it is also possible that the zero form received further support from present-tense subjunctive forms, given the weakening of the grammatical and semantic distinction between subjunctive and indicative during this period.)

We can imagine a situation, then, where, as far as this feature was concerned, the non-natives were not outnumbered two to one. If the native population were varying between -*s* and -*th* endings, there must have been a crucial decade or so, to simplify enormously, when each of the three forms had approximately one-third of the population supporting it, so to speak, with the indigenous citizens divided fifty–fifty as to their usage of the older and newer forms:

	natives	
non-natives	**older**	**newer**
-∅	-*th*	-*s*
(100% = 33% of total)	(50% = 33% of total)	(50% = 33% of total)
[linguistically favoured		
by being unmarked]		

In this equal struggle, it was the regular, originally non-native form which eventually won the day.

We can conceive of the situation, as far as third-person singular present-tense verb forms were concerned, as being one of dialect contact, i.e. contact between the original Norwich English dialect with *-th*, the newer indigenous dialect with *-s*, and the form of English spoken by the Strangers with zero. And it often happens in dialect-contact situations that, *other things being equal* – and for this particular feature alone in Norwich they *were* equal – simple, regular forms tend to win out over more irregular, non-natural ones (see Trudgill 1986: Ch. 3).

It was also of very considerable importance that there were at this time not one but two foreign-language communities in Norwich. The fact is that English was not only used by the Strangers to communicate with the indigenous population; it was also used as a lingua franca for communication between French speakers and Dutch speakers. Whinnom's (1971) "tertiary hybridisation" three-language model of pidginisation, when applied to our Norwich scenario, suggests that the usage of non-native English as a means of communication between the two different groups of non-native speakers would have led to the crystallisation of a common "agreed" form of non-native usage, further reinforcing the non-native morphology, and focussing (see Le Page and Tabouret-Keller 1985) on the zero form.

I conclude that the explanation for the absence of third-person singular *-s* in East Anglian English is similar to, if somewhat more complex than, the explanation for its absence from other varieties, including AAVE. The explanation lies in language contact. My thesis is that Norwich English has had zero-marking ever since the more-or-less simultaneous arrival in the city of (a) third-person singular *-s* from the north of England and (b) the Strangers from the Low Countries.

HYPERCORRECTION

There is now one final problem we have to address on the subject of East Anglian zero.

Today in Norfolk and Suffolk, at least, this feature continues to be very characteristic of the modern dialects. In the city of Norwich, for example, working-class speakers use forms without *-s* most of the time. Percentage of usage correlates with social-class background and with formality of style, but zero predominates in informal colloquial speech (see Trudgill 1974). The same is true for other urban areas in the region such as Ipswich and Great Yarmouth. Trudgill (1974) shows the following extent of -s usage for Norwich:

| | % -s | |
speakers	informal	formal
lower working-class	3	13
middle working-class	19	36
upper working-class	25	62
lower middle-class	71	95
upper middle-class	100	100

An obvious explanation for this variability would appear to lie in contact between the original Traditional Dialect forms, which lacked -s, and the prestigious Standard English of the education system and the media, which of course does have -s. This explanation also appears to be favoured by the strong and obvious correlation of percentage of usage of standard forms with social class and formality of situation.

However, if contact between the local dialect and Standard English lies at the root of the variability we find in modern East Anglian English, we would then expect to find at least spasmodic, individual occurrences of hypercorrect forms on the part of East Anglian speakers, especially perhaps those with less education. We would imagine that, in attempting to speak in a more statusful or "correct" manner, some speakers would employ standard -s but, because of a faulty analysis of the Standard English system, they would also from time to time add -s to persons other than the third-person singular. There are many examples in the literature of similar forms of contact between standard and nonstandard varieties leading to instances of hypercorrection. For example, hypercorrect -s occurs in the speech of native speakers of forms of Caribbean English which lack third-person -s in their basilectal form (see Edwards 1979). Similar hypercorrect forms are reported in some varieties of AAVE (Schneider 1983).

However, it is an interesting and perplexing fact that in East Anglian English, hypercorrection does not occur for this feature. I have to recognise, of course, that it is always difficult to argue for the total absence of a phenomenon, and some sociolinguists will doubtless find my assertion difficult to accept. The absence does, however, seem to be genuinely total. There are, for example, no hypercorrect present-tense forms at all in the scores of hours of data from the Trudgill (1974) Norwich study; and in a lifetime of observation of speakers in the area, I have never heard a single example of -s being added to persons other than the third-person singular. When East Anglian speakers use more standard or formal styles, it is true that they do variably add -s to third-person singular forms, but they always get it right and never append it to other persons. Is it possible to explain why this is?

INHERENT VARIABILITY

Before I started considering this problem, it had always seemed to me to be probable that this current social and stylistic variability involving -∅ and -s in the English of Norwich and other parts of East Anglia was a relatively recent phenomenon, resulting from twentieth-century and perhaps nineteenth-century interaction between the local dialect, on the one hand, and the Standard English of the education system, on the other. The absence of hypercorrection seems, however, to detract from the probable validity of this scenario. I now hypothesise that this variability, totally free from hyperadaptation as it is, may be the direct and continuing result of the way in which -∅ forms were introduced into Norwich English in the first place. There is, once again, a historical explanation.

The originally non-native zero ending, as we have seen, appeared in the English of Norwich, the capital city and central place of East Anglia, simultaneously with the new -s form which had spread geographically from the north of England. The two new forms, however, must have been differentially influential in replacing the original -*th* in different sections of the community. A large number of the Strangers, although they brought wealth to the city, remained among the poorer sections of the population, as is often the case with immigrants and refugees (Rickwood 1984). It is probable, therefore, that their non-native English had a greater influence in the city on the developing English of the lower-classes, of which many of them became a part, than on that of the upper-classes, who would have been subject to greater influence from the fashionable new -*s* forms that were also taking over in London and elsewhere in the south. Alternation between zero and -*s* may therefore have been a permanent and continuing feature of Norwich English ever since the more-or-less simultaneous arrival in Norwich of the Strangers and present-tense -*s*.

In my work on dialect contact (Trudgill 1986), I have shown that, in a dialect-mixture situation, if new-dialect formation takes place it is usual for only one variant of a given feature from the mixture to survive. However, where, unusually, more than one variant survives, it is usual for the two or more surviving variants to be subject to *reallocation*.

A local phonological example of this is provided by the fact that the modern Norwich dialect has three variant pronunciations of the vowel of words from the lexical set of *broom, room*: /ʊ/, /ʉ:/ and /u:/. It is clear from rural dialect studies that each of these pronunciations is to be found in the immediate rural hinterland of Norwich, /ʊ/ to the south, /ʉ:/ to the north and east, and /u:/ to the west (see Trudgill 1986: 112–19). In the urban dialect, however, as a result of the involvement in the development of the dialect of rural in-migration, followed by dialect mixture and reallocation, /u:/ is now the middle-class variant, /ʊ/ the upper-working-class variant, and /ʉ:/ the lower-working-class variant.

If we conceive, as we did above, of language contact in sixteenth-century Norwich as leading to a situation of contact between three dialects, as far as third-person verb forms were concerned – the older indigenous dialect with -*th*, the newer indigenous dialect with -*s*, and the Strangers' more regular but lower-status dialect with -∅ – then we can see the current situation as resulting from a similar process of reallocation that took place four hundred years ago. In the case of East Anglian -*s* versus -∅, however, the reallocation of variants took place according to *both* style *and* social class. In the three-way competition between the different third-person singular present-tense forms, -*th* was lost forever, but both -*s* and -∅ survived because they were allocated different functions in the local dialect. The ability of native speakers of Norwich and East Anglian English generally to switch stylistically between zero and -*s* without hypercorrection may thus be the result of centuries of familiarity with a system that originated in language contact and dialect mixture, and which produced, as a result of reallocation of variants from different dialects – native -*s* and non-native zero – long-term and thus genuinely inherent variability.

3 On Anguilla and *The Pickwick Papers*

The principal chronological focus of the previous chapter was on historical-sociolinguistic events involving the English language in the 1500s and 1600s. This new investigation once again starts where the previous one left off, in the 1600s; but geographically the focus is now greatly expanded, reflecting the world-wide expansion of the English language itself which began in this period. In 1600, English was a rather small and unimportant language on the world stage, and had no very significant role as a foreign or second language anywhere. It was spoken natively in a very small area of the globe indeed: it was the native language only of the indigenous population in most of England and in the south and east of Scotland. It was, however, absent from much of Cornwall, and from Welsh-speaking parts of Shropshire and Herefordshire; most of Ireland was Irish-speaking; nearly all of Wales was still Welsh-speaking; the Highlands and Hebridean Islands of Scotland spoke Gaelic; Orkney and Shetland spoke Scandinavian Norn; the Isle of Man was Manx-speaking; and the Channel Islands were still Norman French-speaking.

However, during the course of the 1600s this situation changed dramatically. As a result of colonisation, English arrived as a native language in Ireland, in what is now the United States, and in Bermuda, Newfoundland, the Bahamas, and the Turks and Caicos Islands. It also spread during this time into many island and mainland areas of the Caribbean: Anguilla, Antigua and Barbuda, Barbados, the Cayman Islands, Jamaica, Montserrat, St Kitts and Nevis, the British Virgin Islands, the American Virgin Islands, and the mainland areas of Guyana and Belize. And, as is not so widely known, there were also other areas that received anglophone settlement: eastern coastal and island areas of Honduras, Nicaragua and

Colombia remain English-speaking to this day. The Dutch island colonies of Saba, St Maarten and St Eustatius have also been English-speaking since the early 1600s; and the mainly Papiamentu-speaking Dutch colony of Bonaire has a sizeable number of indigenous anglophones too.

During the eighteenth century English began its expansion into Wales and northwestern Scotland, and into mainland and maritime Canada. And in the nineteenth century, again as a result of colonisation, English expanded to Hawaii, and into the Southern Hemisphere – not only to Australia, New Zealand and South Africa, as is well known, but also to the South Atlantic Islands of St Helena, Tristan da Cunha and the Falklands, and in the Pacific to Pitcairn and Norfolk Island. There was also expansion from the Caribbean islands to eastern coastal areas of Costa Rica and Panama, and the repatriation of African Americans to Sierra Leone and Liberia, as well as an African-American settlement in the Dominican Republic. During this time also Caribbean islands which had hitherto been francophone started on a slow process of becoming anglophone to different degrees: Dominica, St Lucia, Trinidad and Tobago, Grenada, and St Vincent and the Grenadines. Other little-known anglophone colonies which still survive today were also established during the nineteenth century: in Americana, southern Brazil, by American Southerners fleeing the aftermath of the Civil War; on the Bonin Islands of Japan by New England and Hawaiian whalers and seamen; and on one of the Cook Islands in the South Pacific.

Of all the areas just mentioned, it is safe to say that only the English of the British Isles, mainland North America, Australasia, South Africa and, to a lesser extent, the creoles of the Caribbean and the South Pacific have attracted large amounts of attention from historical linguists. In this chapter, however, I direct attention to some of the other, lesser-known varieties of the language (see Schreier *et al.* 2010). In this investigation, I consult data from these varieties in an attempt to solve a puzzle for historical linguistics which concerns a rather small area of southern England.

The problem is as follows. Conventional linguistic wisdom has it that phonological mergers cannot be reversed: "it is generally agreed that mergers are irreversible: once a merger, always a merger" (Labov 1994: 311). The reason for this is clear: once two phonemes have converged, speakers have no way of knowing which one of the two original units belongs in which of the two original lexical sets, so restoration is impossible. As is well known, however, there are a number of reports in the historical linguistics literature of phonological mergers which actually have been reversed. One often-quoted example is that of the merger in English of items such as *mate*, from the FACE lexical set, which had Middle English /aː/, and *meat*, which had Middle English /ɛː/. This merger is well attested from earlier periods of the language, but has now been undone and superseded by the FLEECE merger (Wells 1982: 194) such that it is now *meat* and *meet* which are homophonous.

This "once a merger, always a merger" maxim has quite naturally led historical linguists to consider how to explain these reports of reversed mergers. In earlier work on this topic, historical linguists (e.g. Kökeritz 1953) typically employed explanations for this puzzling phenomenon which were based on dialect contact. They agreed that mergers could not be reversed as such, but their thesis was that while, say, *mate* and *meat* were indeed genuinely merged in some dialects, the merger was later undone as a result of contact between speakers of these dialects and speakers of other dialects where it had not occurred. That is, later generations of speakers were able to "repair" the merger accurately by consulting the distribution of vowels over lexical sets in the speech of speakers of the non-merging dialects. Wyld (1956: 210) writes that we have to assume that the *mate* and *meat* part of the English vowel system was "differentiated among different classes of speakers – whether in a Regional or a Class dialect I am unable at present to say – into two types", and that the unmerger was not a sound change as such but "merely the result of the abandonment of one type of pronunciation and the adoption of another" (Wyld 1956: 211).

More recently, an intriguing alternative explanation has been advanced by Labov: these mergers were never actually mergers at all but rather "near-mergers". That is, they may have been perceived – and therefore reported and spelt – as mergers because of a very close phonetic proximity between the two phonemes concerned, but they were in fact not actually identical. Labov (1994: 349–70) discusses this issue at considerable length. He cites several instances of speakers, remarkably, being able to produce a very small phonetic distinction without themselves being able to perceive it. How they do this, however, is, as Labov says, "not at all clear" (1994: 371). These small differences are big enough to be apparent to investigating linguists but are not observed by speakers themselves. Therefore, because a total merger has not actually taken place, the two phonemes may in some cases move phonetically further apart again at a later date, leading to reports of unmergers as in the case of *meat* and *mate*.

All the reversed and therefore – according to the Labovian thesis – near-mergers discussed in the literature so far have concerned vowels (see Labov 1994: 349–90). In this chapter I discuss a well-known but little-discussed phonological merger which involves English consonants. The merger is of special interest because, if it actually was a merger, it has clearly been totally reversed in the geographical area for which it was reported. Here I examine what is known about this merger, and attempt an examination of the viability of the "dialect contact" versus "near-merger" explanations as solutions to the puzzle of what actually happened.

THE MERGER OF /v/ AND /w/

The facts concerning this merger, as they are generally reported, are that in many of the local varieties spoken in the southeast of England in at least the 1700s and 1800s, prevocalic /v/ in items like *village* was replaced by /w/. The reports focus on word-initial /w/ in items such as *village, victuals, vegetables, vermin*. All the data that we have from England are consistent with the view that the change [v] → [w] took place only in syllable-initial position and that

[v] was still retained in words such as *love*. We can assume, therefore, that there was a single phoneme which had two allophones, [w] in syllable-initial and [v] in syllable-final position.

Below are some of the reports of this merger.

(1) Ellis (1889) describes the southeast of nineteenth-century England as being, at the Traditional Dialect level, the "land of wee" (as opposed to "vee").

(2) Wright (1905: 227) says that "initial and medial v has become w in mid-Buckinghamshire, Norfolk, Suffolk, Essex, Kent, east Sussex". Given the geographical location of Hertfordshire between Buckinghamshire and Essex, we can suppose that the merger was probably a feature of the dialect of that county also.

(3) Wakelin (1972: 95–6) writes that the *Survey of English Dialects* (SED) materials (from the 1950s and 1960s) show that "in parts of southern England, notably East Anglia and the south-east, initial and medial [v] may appear as [w], cf. V.7.19 *vinegar*, IV.9.4 *viper* (under *adder*), V.8.2 *victuals* (under *food*) ... The use of [w] for [v] was a well-known Cockney feature up to the last century." Here we note an indication that the original merger had by then died out in London.

(4) Wakelin (1984: 79) also states that "Old East Anglian and south-eastern dialect is noted for its pronunciation of initial /v/ as /w/ in, e.g., *vinegar*, *viper*; a very old feature, which was preserved in Cockney up to the last century."

(5) Further examination of the published SED materials shows other sporadic instances of this merger from the area mentioned by Wright. The spontaneous responses to Question VIII.3.2, for instance, show *very* with initial /w/ in Buckland and Coleshill, Buckinghamshire; and in Grimston, North Elmham, Ludham, Reedham, and Pulham St Mary, Norfolk. Many of the other SED instances of /w/ are from reports in which informants have labelled this pronunciation "older", a further indication of course that the merger was disappearing.

(6)   Norfolk seems to have been one of the areas in which this
       merger lasted longest. It is most likely that the merger began
       in London and then spread outwards from there; and that the
       unmerger then followed the same geographical pattern. In a
       paper on vestigial dialect variants (Trudgill 1999), I discussed
       the current high-stereotype level of awareness of this feature
       in the modern county, even though it has totally vanished
       from actual usage. The merger is 'remembered' by the local
       community, decades after its actual disappearance. Most local
       people in the area over a certain age 'know' that *village* used
       to be pronounced *willage* and that *very* used to be pronounced
       wery. The longevity of this folk memory is rather remarkable.
       As a child, I regularly associated with Traditional Dialect
       speakers who were born as early as the 1860s. However, I never
       heard anyone use this feature except as a joke or quotation.
       Discussions with older Norfolk people who actually remember
       hearing it (e.g. my mother, b. 1918) suggest that it was in wide-
       spread normal unselfconscious use only until the 1920s. The
       fact that modern dialect writers still use the feature is there-
       fore highly noteworthy. For example, Michael Brindred in his
       local dialect column in the Norwich-based *Eastern Daily Press*
       of 26th August 1998 wrote *anniversary* as <anniwarsary>. The
       dialect feature has remained a stereotype for generations after
       its disappearance from actual speech.

A merger of /v/ and /w/ is not too surprising. The functional load of
this opposition in English is rather low, and minimal pairs are very
few. However, in modern England the merger has clearly now been
reversed, as we saw above: it is probably safe to say that no native
English speaker anywhere in England now fails to contrast /w/ and
/v/. The principle concerning the irreversibility of mergers therefore
suggests that we should consider very carefully whether the above
reports of a merger can in fact be correct. We have to ask: was there
really a genuine merger, which has been reversed; or was it simply a
near-merger à la Labov?

Finding the answer to this question is not going to be easy. The difference between apparent and genuine mergers is a matter of fine phonetic detail, and it would be useful if we could accurately reconstruct the phonetics of the reported /w/ – /v/ merger. Obviously, however, it is now impossible to reassemble in any detail the phonetics of what happened in southeast England since there are no native speakers of English anywhere in the British Isles who have this feature and, if Norfolk is typical, nor have there been for many decades. Nor is the merger to be found anywhere in the major colonial varieties of English: there is no evidence of it at all in modern American, Canadian, Australian, New Zealand or South African English.

However, an exciting avenue of exploration is opened up to us by the fact that there actually are other varieties of English where the merger is reportedly still extant. There are accounts of the phonologies of a large number of the lesser-known colonial varieties of English spoken, as mentioned above, in small communities in the North Atlantic, South Atlantic, North Pacific and South Pacific, where the merger is said to be alive and well. And it is therefore to these varieties that this discussion now turns.

The fact that these varieties are "lesser known" may in truth not be a coincidence. There is evidence that small, isolated communities may produce slower rates of linguistic change than larger communities (see Trudgill 2001). This has been explained by Milroy and Milroy (1985) and J. Milroy (1992), who distinguish between communities with dense, multiplex social networks and communities with loose networks. From their work, notably in Belfast, they conclude that dense networks lead to strong social ties, which then lead to closer maintenance of community norms, in language as in other forms of behaviour. On the other hand, loose networks lead to weaker social ties and so to a relative lack of maintenance of community norms. The Milroys therefore argue that "linguistic change is slow to the extent that the relevant populations are well established and bound by strong ties whereas it is rapid to the extent that weak ties exist in populations" (1985: 375; see also L. Milroy 2000). Dense social networks are most likely to be found in small, stable communities with few external contacts and a high degree of social cohesion. Loose social networks are more liable to develop in larger, unstable communities which have relatively many external contacts and a relative lack of social cohesion. Linguistic change is therefore liable, other things being equal, to be faster in larger than in smaller communities.

It therefore seems possible that these lesser-known varieties of English may in some respects be more representative of earlier stages of English as spoken in England than modern English English itself. Thus, if we can show that these lesser-known varieties genuinely do have a merger, then we can hypothesise that it is present in these varieties as a result of having been transported to the locations concerned in the phonologies of speakers emigrating from the southeast of England. That is, these varieties have retained an originally south of England feature which has been lost in its initial homeland.

Similarly, if it emerges that these varieties rather have a near-merger, we can hypothesise that this, instead, was what was transported from England.

REPORTS OF MERGERS IN LESSER-KNOWN ENGLISHES

I have been able to find the following reports of the /w/ – /v/ merger in lesser-known varieties of English:

North Atlantic

Bermuda
Ayres (1933: 10) reports a merger of /w/ and /v/ (see below).

Bahamas
Wells (1982: 589) reports for one White Bahamian English speaker "the phonemic merger of standard /v/ and /w/ into a single phoneme with the allophones [w] and [v] in complementary distribution. The [w] allophone occurs in initial position ... but the [v] allophone elsewhere."

Montserrat

Wells (1982: 568) reports *village* as occurring with initial [w], for example.

St Vincent

Wells (1982: 568) writes that "Vincentians are among those for whom the use of [w] for standard [v] has been reported".

Bay Islands

According to Warantz (1983: 84), the phonology of the native English of the Bay Islands off the coast of Honduras has "the merging of /w/ and /v/ in certain environments".

South Atlantic

Tristan da Cunha

Tristan English is reported as having the merger by Zettersten. In his discussion of consonants he writes: "[v] > [w]: [wɛri] 'very'" (1969: 72).

St Helena

Schreier *et al.* (2006) write that "phonologically, the most salient characteristics of basilectal St Helena English include ... the V – W merger".

North Pacific

Bonin Islands

According to Long (1998, 2000), /v/ and /w/ are merged, and [v] and [w] are in complementary distribution.

South Pacific

Pitcairn

Ross and Moverley (1964: 154) claim that in Pitcairnese /v/ is generally [w] in word-initial, word-final and intervocalic position. They say that there is no evidence that the merger took place in preconsonantal position, where /v/ is realised as [v]. Actually, however, since /w/ does not occur in preconsonantal position in English, this would in fact appear to be evidence of a merger, since [w] and [v] are in complementary distribution according to this description.

Norfolk Island

Flint (1964: 196 ff.) reports [w] in *valley* and *invitation*, for example.

Palmerston

Ehrhart-Kneher (1996: 530) shows that Palmerston has both [v] and [w]. For words derived from English /w/, her data show [w] as in *ui* 'we', *uan* 'one' and *uash* 'wash'. For etymonic /v/, there is variation between [w] and [v], apparently in complementary distribution. In medial and final position, all examples show [v], as in *ev* 'have'. In initial position, however, /v/ consistently becomes [w] as in *ueri* 'very'. This seems to suggest a total merger of original /v/ and /w/.

THE SUBSTRATUM PROBLEM

Thus in eleven different varieties of English in widely separated areas of the world, a genuine merger of /v/ and /w/ has been reported. This would seem on the face of it to represent good evidence that this same merger did in fact take place in the southeast of England, where it has now disappeared, but whence it was exported to the colonial overseas varieties.

However, there is an important reason why these reports of the /w/ – /v/ merger cannot, without further examination, be interpreted unambiguously – as colonial remnants of a phenomenon which has disappeared in the mother country – as evidence for the merger in England. This is that there is an alternative explanation which could be advanced: the mergers in the colonial varieties could be due to a substratum effect resulting from the influence of other languages which may have been in contact with them. Let us now consider these in turn.

North Atlantic

Bahamas

The Bahamas consists of an archipelago of about 700 islands to the southeast of Florida, with a population of about 270,000. Serious

English involvement began in 1648 when Bermuda was suffering from religious disputes and Captain William Sayle, a former governor, decided to look for an island where religious dissidents could worship. He sailed to the Bahamas with about seventy settlers, Bermudian dissidents and others who had come directly from England. Their plantation colony was largely unsuccessful, and a number of settlers returned to Bermuda. Other Bermudian migrants continued to arrive, however, and the island of New Providence was settled from Bermuda in 1656. After the American Revolution, from 1782 onwards, many American Loyalists also fled to the Bahamas, which had the effect of doubling the white population. The English of white Bahamians, then, has two main sources: the Bermudian English of the original settlers, and the North American English of the Loyalists. Some of the Loyalists were from the American South, but Abaco and the northern Eleuthera Islands in particular were settled by Americans from New England and New York (Holm and Shilling 1982). There was also some later white immigration from the Miskito coast of Central America when this area was ceded by Britain to Spain in 1786, and Andros Island in particular was settled from there.

There are certainly linguistic differences between the different islands of the Bahamas to this day. It is possible then that the /v/ – /w/ merger, rather than arriving directly from England, came from Bermuda or from Central America, from where there are also reports of the merger. Holm, however, argues for a different explanation. A majority of the modern population of the Bahamas is of African descent. Black Bahamians too have different origins (see Holm 1980), some being descended from slaves who actually arrived in the Bahamas directly, others being originally from the Caribbean or the American South – post-1782 immigration had the effect of trebling the black population since many Loyalists brought their slaves with them. According to Holm and Shilling (1982: vii), Black Bahamian English is probably most like the mainland American creole Gullah. It is certainly "closer to white English than comparable varieties in the Caribbean proper, but much further from white English than the vernacular Black English of the United States". Holm argues strongly that the Bahamian /v/ – /w/ merger is the result of African influence. This is also an origin countenanced for the West Indies as a whole by Wells, who writes, "it is not clear whether this phenomenon ... arose independently in the West Indies through the influence of an African substratum lacking /v/" (1982: 568). This is a possibility we have to consider since Welmers (1973: 52) states that typical West African consonant systems have /w/ but no /v/, a point which is supported by Clements (2000: 125). The Ewe language, on the other hand, has /w/ as well as /β/ and /v/ (Ladefoged 1968: 25), and also /Φ/, according to Clements (2000: 127).

Holm argues further that the presence of the merger in white speech is the result of influence from the majority black population.

Bay Islands

The Bay Islands are a group of eight small islands about 55 kilometres off the northern Honduras coast. They were first sighted by Columbus in 1502 and were settled in 1642 by English buccaneers. Between 1650 and 1850 Spain, Honduras and England disputed ownership of the islands. The islands were officially annexed by Britain in 1852 but were then ceded to Honduras in 1859. White English-speaking Protestants formed the majority of the population until about 1900, when Hispanic Hondurans from the mainland began settling, but indigenous anglophones still form about 85 per cent of the population. There are currently about 20,000 inhabitants, of black, white and mixed-race origin. An African substratum cannot be ruled out here, but seems less likely than in the Bahamas.

Bermuda

Bermuda is a British colony about 900 kilometres east of Cape Hatteras, North Carolina, USA. The first anglophones to arrive were English Puritans who were shipwrecked in 1609. In 1612, sixty English settlers were sent to colonise the islands, and Bermuda became a crown colony in 1684. African slaves were transported to Bermuda as early as 1616, and soon the black population was larger than the white one. Today about 60 per cent of the population are of African origin; whites are mostly of British origin, but descendants of Portuguese labourers from Madeira and the Azores who arrived during the 1800s are also to be found and some Portuguese is still spoken. There are noticeable differences between the speech of blacks and whites, the former being more Caribbean in character, the latter more like the English of coastal South Carolina (see Trudgill 1986). Once again, an African substratum has to be considered.

A further complication is that there were a large number of historical connections between these three different communities. There was considerable to-ing and fro-ing of anglophones between the Bahamas and Bermuda, as well as between the Bay Islands of Honduras, the Caymans and the Bahamas (Parsons 1954). We cannot exclude the possibility, therefore, that in any one of these territories, the merger arrived not from England but from one of the other communities.

South Atlantic

St Helena

There is a clear substratum problem with the English of St Helena as well. This island is situated in the South Atlantic Ocean, 1,930 kilometres west of Angola. Its nearest neighbour is Ascension Island, approximately 1,100 kilometres to the northwest. St Helena's population of approximately 6,000 is of mixed European, African and Asian origin. English is the only language spoken on the island (for the first and only full scientific description of St Helena English, see Schreier 2008). From the time when it was claimed by the British East India Company in 1658, a concerted policy of settlement was implemented, and Company employees (soldiers and servants) and 'planters' were recruited to St Helena, along with slaves supplied on request by East India Company ships. Little is known about the origins of the British settlers, but there is some evidence that most of them came from southern England. Even less is known about the origins of the non-white population, but various records show that slaves were imported from the Guinea Coast, the Indian subcontinent and Madagascar, and to a lesser extent from the Cape area of South Africa, the West Indies, Malaya and the Maldives. St Helenian English, which is perhaps best described as a creoloid (see Chapter 2), is thus the result of contacts between regional dialects of English English and many other languages. An African or other substratum origin for the /v/ – /w/ merger is thus possible.

Tristan da Cunha

This British dependent territory consists of six small islands which are about halfway between southern Africa and South America. The only populated island, Tristan da Cunha, has an area of about 100 square kilometres and a population of about 290. It is said to be the most remote permanently inhabited settlement in the world, the nearest habitation being St Helena, which is about 2,300 kilometres away. The islands were discovered in 1506 by a Portuguese sailor, Tristao da Cunha. A British garrison was stationed on Tristan da Cunha in 1816 as a result of fears that it might be used as a base for an attempt to rescue Napoleon from St Helena, and the islands were formally annexed by Britain. When the garrison was withdrawn the following year, three British soldiers, one of them with his wife and children, obtained permission to stay behind and settle permanently.

In the 1820s shipwrecked sailors and castaways from all parts of the British Isles added to the population, and six women, some of whom seem to have been freed non-white slaves, emigrated from St Helena in 1827, one of them with four daughters. In the 1830s and 1840s several US American whalers arrived, as well as three non-anglophone seamen – a Dutchman and two Danes. The population increased rapidly, and by 1842 the island community consisted of ten families totalling seventy-five people. There were thus three influential groups in the community's early formation period. First, the British group, the colony's founders, consisting of soldiers, castaways and shipwrecked sailors from the British Isles; second, the women who arrived from St Helena in 1827; and third, the US American whalers and European sailors who settled between 1833 and 1849. There was very little trade with passing ships in the second half of the nineteenth century and the influx of settlers declined drastically, the only newcomers being a weaver from Yorkshire in the 1860s, two stranded sailors from Italy who settled in 1892, and two Irish sisters who arrived in 1908.

Despite repeated language contact at various stages of the formation process, the present-day population is entirely anglophone. Sociohistorically, there were three types of contact: dialect contact between the British and American dialects spoken by the anglophone founders; language contact between English and the native tongues of the non-anglophone settlers (i.e. Dutch, Danish and Italian); and contact with the English-based creoloid spoken by the women from St Helena. It is possible that the /v/ – /w/ merger on Tristan could therefore have an origin in southern England; and/or through influence from Dutch and/or Danish and/or Italian; and/or through African influence via the English of St Helena (Schreier 2003).

North Pacific

Bonin Islands

These Japanese-owned islands, known in Japanese as Ogasawara-gunto, are in the central Pacific Ocean, about 800 kilometres southeast of Japan proper. The population is about 2,000. The islands were discovered by the Spanish navigator Ruy López de Villalobos in 1543. They were claimed by the USA in 1823 and by Britain in 1825. They were formally annexed by Japan in 1876, but after World War II they were placed under US military control and returned to Japan in 1968. The originally uninhabited islands were first settled in 1830 by fifteen people: five seamen (two Americans, one Englishman, one Dane and one Italian) and ten Hawaiians (five men and five women). This founding population was later joined by whalers, shipwrecked sailors, and drifters of many different origins.

The origins of the English spoken on the islands are discussed further in Chapter 4. Substratum influence concerning the merger as reported by Long (1998, 2000) is difficult to evaluate. The early settlers of the island were a multi-ethnic band whose native tongues consisted of English, Portuguese, Hawaiian, Chamorro and at least a dozen other European and Pacific Island languages. Native speakers of English were a tiny minority in the community and almost all households consisted of speakers of differing languages. A variety of English was used as the common language in the tiny community, and it is often described as being 'broken'. Within the context of the islands' settlement history, two possibilities present themselves to account for the occurrence of the /w/ – /v/ merger. One is that it results from the English spoken by the large number of Polynesian (and other Oceanic language) speakers living on the islands in the nineteenth century. Hawaiian has no contrast between /v/ and /w/: according to Elbert and Pukui (1979: 12–13), /w/ is [w] on Kaua'i and Ni'ihau, [v] on Hawaii, with [v] and [w] occurring as allophonic variants on the other Hawaiian islands. There is evidence that this leads to confusion between /v/ and /w/ in the English of Hawaiians and other Polynesians, but nothing to indicate the kind of complementary distribution found on the Bonins. The other possibility is, of course, that it arrived in the phonologies of native-English-speaking settlers: two early settlers (both males) who exerted a tremendous degree of influence over the community were native speakers of English whose home regions we can pinpoint. One was from Wallington, Surrey, England, which was in the relevant merger zone (for the other speaker, see Chapter 4).

South Pacific

Pitcairn

Pitcairn is an isolated British colony about 2,200 kilometres southeast of Tahiti in the South Pacific. The main and only inhabited island has an area of about 5 square kilometres, and the population in 1992 was fifty-two. The modern population, as is well known, is descended from the mutineers of the British ship HMS *Bounty* and their Tahitian companions. After a lengthy stay on Tahiti, the crew, led by the first mate, Fletcher Christian, mutinied when their voyage to the West Indies had reached only as far as western Polynesia and set their captain William Bligh and a number of loyal sailors adrift. They headed back to Tahiti, where they collected a number of local women and a few men, and from where, fearing discovery by the Royal Navy, many of them set off again. They reached Pitcairn in 1790, where, in the interests of secrecy, they burnt their ship. The island community survived undiscovered until found by American whalers in 1808. It is therefore possible that the merger in Pitcairn English could be the result of Tahitian influence. There is no contrast between /v/ and /w/ in Tahitian: Tryon (1970: 2) writes that Tahitian /v/ is "phonetically [v], as in *vine*" but that "*v* is sometimes pronounced *w*, as a free variant; it is also realised as [β]". Even if the Pitcairn merger does have an origin in English, moreover, there is no guarantee that this was English English: one of the mutineers, Edward Young, came from St Kitts in the Caribbean, some areas of which are reported to have the merger themselves (see above).

Norfolk Island

Norfolk Island is an Australian dependent territory in the southwestern Pacific, about 1,600 kilometres northeast of Sydney. The island, with an area of 35 square kilometres, has a population of about two thousand. In 1856 the Pitcairn Islanders, descendants of the mutineers on the *Bounty*, were resettled on Norfolk because of overcrowding on Pitcairn. Not all of the islanders were happy, however, and eventually two separate groups returned to Pitcairn. Norfolk Island's current population includes about one-third who can claim to be the descendants of mutineers, the remainder being descendants of later settlers, mostly from Australia and New Zealand. Since Norfolk Island English has its origins on Pitcairn, the same problems in ascribing an origin in England to this phenomenon occur.

Palmerston

Palmerston English is a variety spoken on Palmerston Island, Polynesian *Avarau*, a coral atoll in the Cook Islands about 430 kilometres northwest of Rarotonga, by descendants of speakers of the Polynesian language Tongarevan and English speakers. What we know about the settlement is that William Marsters, a ship's carpenter and cooper from Gloucestershire, England, arrived on the uninhabited Palmerston Atoll in 1862. He had three wives, all from Penrhyn (Tongareva) in the Northern Cook Islands. He forced his wives, seventeen children and numerous grandchildren to use English all the time. Virtually the entire population of the island today descends from this patriarch. Ehrhart-Kneher (1996) considers Palmerston English to be a dialectal variety of English rather than a contact language. She writes that it appears to be a classic case of mixing and vernacularisation of a type which has "produced languages which, while new languages, are varieties of English rather than new languages without genetic affiliation in the usual sense". While her analysis focusses on syntax and we cannot ignore her disclaimer that "the transcription used here makes no phonological claims" (1996: 524), she is nonetheless a trained linguist and has based her transcriptions on the IPA alphabet. Once again, the substratum problem is evident since Penrhyn/Tongarevan has /v/ but no /w/ (Clark 1976: 20, quoting Yasuda 1968).

Summary

It would be possible, then, to argue that these Lesser-Known Englishes provide no evidence at all as to the nature of the /w/ – /v/ merger in England. In every case, it is possible to argue that the merger was not imported from England at all but is the result of direct or indirect interference from languages other than English which had no /w/ – /v/ distinction. After all, only a very few of the world's languages have this distinction. An examination of Maddieson (1984) shows that 76 per cent of his sample languages have /w/, but only 21 per cent have /v/, and a mere 11 per cent of the languages in his sample have both /v/ and /w/.

It is also possible to argue, however, that the presence of this merger in so many different varieties of English in so many different parts of the world – seventeen such varieties have been discovered so far – is too much of a coincidence to be *totally* explicable in terms of a substratum effect in *all* cases. Caution about the role of substrata is advisable, but the evidence from around the world may well still be indicative of an earlier merger in England. Given the considerable evidence from England, too, of there having been a merger of /v/ and /w/ in pre-nineteenth-century English in the southeast, there may be enough of a case here to persevere with the data from the Lesser-Known Englishes. In our attempt to solve the puzzle of the unmerged merger, we cannot ignore the evidence which these varieties may be providing us with.

THE TWO-WAY TRANSFER PATTERN

This claim about the relevance of the lesser-known varieties is strengthened by another important piece of evidence which we have so far not discussed. This evidence concerns what we can call an *apparent two-way transfer pattern* or interchange. That is, a number of the reports from England seem to indicate, not that a merger of /w/ and /v/ occurred as a result of a sound change /v/ > /w/, but rather that two different changes occurred: /w/ > /v/, and /v/ > /w/, leading to /w/ appearing where /v/ would be expected, and vice versa. The evidence is as follows:

(1)   Wyld (1956: 292) writes of the interchange of v- and w-:

> This was formerly a London vulgarism, but is now apparently extinct in the Cockney dialect. Personally, I never heard these pronunciations, so well known to the readers of Dickens, Thackeray, and of the earlier numbers of *Punch*. My time for observing such points begins in the late seventies or early eighties of the last [i.e. nineteenth] century, and I never remember noticing this particular feature in actual genuine speech, though I remember quite well, as a boy, hearing middle-aged people say *weal* for *veal* and *vich* for *which*, jocularly, as though in imitation of some actual type of speech with which they were familiar.

He then goes on to suppose that the pronunciation was extant until the 1840s or 1850s. Crucially, he also reports documentary evidence, some of it as early as the fifteenth century, of a two-way transfer pattern, with examples of the same writer using *v* for *w* and *w* for *v*, and cites instances such as *vyne* 'wine' and *vyves* 'wives', as well as *wyce* 'vice' and *woyce* 'voice', suggesting a complex interchange of the two phonemes. This early date is supported by Wakelin (1972: 96), who writes that "this change goes back to ME [Middle English] and is evidenced in place-name spellings from much of southern England from the second half of the thirteenth century onwards". Wyld also argues (1956: 180) that the merger was "probably not confined to London".

(2)   Wyld (1956: 179) also cites the Scot James Elphinston, born in 1721, as referring to the two-way transfer. And he tells us (p. 182) that the elocutionist John Walker, born in London in 1732, discussed the /v/ – /w/ merger as occurring "among the inhabitants of London, and those not only of the lowest order" and as operating in both directions: *vind* = 'wind' and *weal* = 'veal'. Similarly, Thomas Sheridan (1719–88) discusses *veal/weal* as well as *winter/vinter*.

(3)   The two-way transfer is also reflected, as Wyld mentions, in the stereotypical nineteenth-century Cockney portrayed, famously, in the speech of Dickens' character Sam Weller in *The Pickwick Papers*. Dickens writes, for example, <wery> for *very*, but also <vith> for *with*:

I had a reg'lar new fit o' clothes that mornin', gen'l'men of the jury, said Sam, and that was a *wery* partickler and uncommon circumstance *vith* me in those days ... If they wos a pair o' patent double million magnifyin' gas microscopes of hextra power, p'raps I might be able to see through a flight o' stairs and a deal door; but bein' only eyes, you see, my *wision's* limited
(Charles Dickens, *The Pickwick Papers* (1837), Chapter 34 [my italics])

(4)   W. Matthews, in his book *Cockney past and present*, also cites the /v/ – /w/ interchange as being typical of older Cockney (1972: 180–1).

(5)   The SED gives a few examples of w > v as well as the examples of v > w already cited. Wakelin (1972: 96) cites *watch* from Somerset and *wife* from Kent with initial [v].

(6)   Wells (1982: 568) refers to the "V – W Confusion of eighteenth- and nineteenth-century London Cockney".

(7)   Washabaugh (1983: 178) claims that on the Cayman Islands, a location not previously mentioned here, "/v/ and /w/ are sometimes used in the reverse of their English reflexes, e.g., *vejiz* (wages) and *inwestigeyt* (investigate)". Kohlman (n.d.: 13) agrees: "*v* and *w*, which in many words can scarcely be differentiated, and in other words are interchanged. Hence we find 'vessel' is 'wessel,' 'virgin' is 'wirgin,' and 'wood' is 'vood'".

Now a two-way transfer /v/ > /w/ and /w/ > /v/ would be a very mysterious change indeed from a historical linguistic point of view. It is a phenomenon which most historical phonologists would consider extremely unlikely if not totally impossible: two simultaneous changes /w/ > /v/ and /v/ > /w/ must surely be out of the question.

But this then leaves us with a conundrum: why does Dickens show both *v* for *w* and *w* for *v*? And why do we find so many other reports suggest the same thing?

EXPLANATIONS

There would appear to be three different possible explanations:

(1)   There was a near-merger involving a distinction which Dickens did not hear, and which led the writers cited by Wyld to employ interchangeable spellings. I cite evidence below for why I do not believe this is what happened.

(2)   A single change /v/ > /w/ did genuinely take place. Occasional forms such as *vyves* are the result of spasmodic hypercorrection leading to non-systematic substitutions in the opposite direction, /w/ > /v/, also. This point of view is supported by Wakelin: "it may be assumed from the statements of various writers that early New English spellings of *v* for etymological *w* reveal hypercorrect pronunciations" (1972: 96). However,

forms such as *vyves* in Dickens are *not* occasional. The consistency with which Dickens converts /v/ to <w> and /w/ to <v> suggests something much more regular and widespread than hypercorrection. Wyld, too, gives numerous examples of substitutions in both directions.

(3)   A complete merger did indeed take place but *it was on some articulation intermediate between [w] and [v]*. It is a principle of phonological perception that listeners notice what is different about accents other than their own, not what is the same. Listeners also normally perceive segments which are alien to their own variety in terms of segments which are native to it. This would have led Dickens, who presumably did not have the merger in his own accent, and who was presumably doing his best to report what he *thought* he heard, to illustrate Weller as speaking in this highly improbable manner. Dickens would have heard this intermediate articulation in *very* as 'not [v] and therefore necessarily [w]' and in *with* as 'not [w] and therefore necessarily [v]'.

The question then is: if there was an intermediate articulation, what was it? An obvious candidate for an articulation intermediate between [v] and [w] is [β], which combines the bilabial place of articulation of [w] with the voiced fricative manner of articulation of [v]. This possibility occurred to Wakelin, who speculates that the merger in England "may have taken place via a bilabial stage /β/" (1972: 96).

Let us now return to our Lesser-Known Englishes data and consider this possibility further. The relevant reports of which I am aware are the following:

(1)   Wells (1982: 568) says of the Caribbean that a bilabial fricative "has been reported".

(2)   Ayres (1933: 10) says that in Bermuda there is "an intermediate sound like Middle German 'w' – it is usually a frictional labial sound".

(3)   Kohlman (n.d.) writes for the Cayman Islands of "a soft blurring that is neither 'v' nor 'w'".

(4)   For the Bahamas, Shilling (1980) writes that "all white speakers ... used [β] variably with 'correct' v and w". Wells, however, disputes this finding: "the essence of the admittedly frequent V – W Confusion is not ... the use of [β] indifferently for both /v/ and /w/" (1982: 589).

(5)   Turner (1949: 25) states that the pronunciation corresponding to both English /v/ and /w/ in Gullah – a variety I have hitherto not cited evidence from – is /β/. McDavid and McDavid (1951: 28) also tell us that "many white folk informants in and near Gullah country replace both /v, w/ by one bilabial voiced spirant /β/".

Here again, there are problems of substratum effect as opposed to inheritance from England. The Cayman Islands, for example, are a British colony of three major islands in the Caribbean, about 290 kilometres northwest of Jamaica. The population is about 25,000. About a quarter of the Caymanians are European, mostly of British origin; about one-quarter are descendants of African slaves; the remainder are of mixed ancestry. The islands were not claimed by any nation until they were ceded to England in 1670. Most of the early settlers were British mariners, buccaneers, shipwrecked passengers, plus land grant-holders from Jamaica, and African slaves. An African substratum therefore has to be considered for the /v/ – /w/ merger. The Gullah /β/ pronunciation is also the basis for the claim, mentioned above, made by Holm for an African substratum effect in the Bahamas. He notes (1980: 56) that Turner points out "that /β/ occurs in many West African languages".

At least one West African language, however, as we have already noted, has /w/, /v/ *and* /β/. To complicate matters further, Ladefoged also states that "the I.P.A. does not provide for the symbolisation of the contrast between a labial velar approximant like the English **w**, and a similar sound with closer articulation which may produce audible friction" (1968: 25), which also occurs in some West African languages.

I now argue that there is reason to believe that these speculations and reports about an intermediate pronunciation are on the right lines, and indeed for Gullah at least we have no reason to suppose that the report is anything other than phonetically totally correct. The suggestion is, however, that, while the Dickensian representations and the other reports of a two-way substitution in England can indeed be explained in terms of the merger being on an articulation intermediate between [v] and [w], and while these constitute evidence to suggest that the reports of a total merger in England were indeed entirely correct, the articulation in question in southeastern England may not have been – or may not only have been – [β].

This assertion is based again on data from Lesser-Known Englishes. In this case, however, it is based on work done by myself rather than on second-hand reports. These are phonetic and phonological analyses carried out on six different lesser-known varieties of English, three of which we have already discussed, which all still have a genuine merger of historical /w/ and /v/ on precisely the same articulation. This articulation, however, is not a voiced bilabial fricative but rather a *bilabial approximant*. That is, it is an articulation which bears the same relationship to [β] as [ɹ] does to [z], and [j] to [ʝ], and [ɰ] to [ɣ]. There is no single IPA symbol for this consonant so, just as one has to write [ð̞] if one wants to distinguish the Danish dental approximate from the English [ð], so one has to use here the symbol [β̞] in order to distinguish it from [β]. Laver (1994: 302) writes: "Apart from the symbols specified above, all other central approximants can be transcribed by adding a subscript diacritic [˔] to the corresponding fricative symbol, meaning 'more open stricture'."

The articulation of [β̞] involves no audible friction, no lip-rounding (except before rounded vowels), and there is no approximation of the tongue towards the velum as there is for [w].

The six varieties that have been analysed are:

(1) Pitcairnese English, as investigated by Källgård (1993), who very kindly made his tape-recordings from Pitcairn in 1980 available to me. My analysis implies that the transcriptions of Ross and Moverley are incorrect. Pitcairnese speakers consistently use [β̞].

(2) Tristan da Cunha, as investigated by Schreier (2003), where at least some speakers have this articulation. That is, the analyses and transcriptions of Zettersten are not totally correct (see also Trudgill and Schreier 2006).

(3) St Helena, as reported in Schreier (2008), and based on recordings kindly made available by Karen Lavarello-Schreier.

(4) The English of the white community on Bequia, in the Caribbean Grenadines, as investigated by Williams (1987), who kindly made his recordings available to me. Bequia, the largest and northernmost of the Vincentian Grenadines, is situated in the Windward Antilles approximately 14 kilometres from St Vincent. Bequia has an area of 18 square kilometres and a population of around 7,200. Little has been written about the settlement history of Bequia and virtually nothing has appeared on the history of white settlement (however, see Williams 1987). There are two separate white communities on Bequia: Sugar Hill and Mt Pleasant. Some of the whites in these two communities derive from relocation schemes entered into by the governments of Barbados and St Vincent beginning in the 1850s and lasting up until 1880. Like most other white communities in the Caribbean, white Bequerians have tended to remain in isolation and adhere to rules of colour endogamy.

(5) The English of the white community on Saba, in the Dutch Antilles, as also investigated by Williams (1985, 1987). Saba is the smallest of the Windward Netherlands Antilles, having a total land area of less than 13 square kilometres. The population of Saba is approximately 1,600, although about 400

of these are foreign medical students. Even though Saba has been a colonial possession of the Netherlands intermittently since the mid-seventeenth century, varieties of English have been stable vernaculars of communication among local Sabans throughout the recorded history of the island (see Hartog 1988; Johnson 1989; Williams 1985, 1987, forthcoming). Saba has the highest ratio of whites to blacks of any of the English-speaking West Indies. The earliest white settlement on Saba was at the historic village of Mary's Point that was relocated by the Dutch government in 1933 (see Williams forthcoming). Presently, the largest white populations are to be found in the villages of Upper Hell's Gate, Lower Hell's Gate and Windwardside. All of these communities are descended from early English-speaking settlers who came during the middle of the seventeenth century from St Kitts, many of these Presbyterian Scots; and from Barbados, many of these escaped or freed indentured servants. The whites of Saba have maintained separateness from the blacks on the island, with most blacks taking up residence in the village of The Bottom following emancipation in 1863 (Johnson 1989: 10).

(6)   Particularly valuable has been fieldwork on the basilectal English of the white community on Anguilla carried out by Jeff Williams, with some assistance from me. Anguilla is a British dependency in the northern Leeward Antilles, approximately 235 kilometres east of Puerto Rico. The most recent population census of Anguilla lists nearly 12,000 inhabitants. The majority of the islanders are classified as either black or brown (mixed), with only a handful of 'clear-skinned' (white) people. The white population of Anguilla, at present concentrated in the community of Island Harbour, had two probable historical sources. One was the settlement of English speakers from St Kitts who began arriving on Anguilla around 1650 to collect salt and grow tobacco (Burns 1954: 350). Some of these early settlers founded the historic village of Sandy Hill whose

only remaining feature today is a cemetery. The other source was the shipwreck of the English brigantine *Antelope* that was wrecked off an islet called Scrub Island, only a few kilometres northeast of Island Harbour village, in 1771. The ship was sailing from Grenada to England when it ran onto the reef. A trio of brothers and their wives, the Websters, survived the wreck and made their way to Anguilla, and established the community of Island Harbour. Although the white population of Anguilla has had contact with the black and mixed populations of the island, a pattern of colour endogamy has prevailed up until recently.

Our fieldwork revealed that this same [β] pronunciation is the norm in this Anguillan community too; but there is the added bonus that, since this phonetic detail was now an object of our research, it was possible for us to see with our own eyes, as well as just hear from tapes, that no lip-rounding occurs in the pronunciation of the (identical) consonants of *will* and *village* (except before the two rounded vowels /u:/ and /u/). To cite just one of our informants: Mr Elbert Webster, born 1919, of Island Harbour, Anguilla, employs this articulation throughout in items such as *away, well, Webster, where, visit, vex, voice, everyone, television, love.*

(Our observations are also supported by Wolfram and Thomas (2002) who report on an isolated area of coastal North Carolina – in work we were not aware of until we had completed our research in Anguilla – saying that "one of the noteworthy patterns apparently found in earlier Pamlico Sound English is the merger of /v/ and /w/ . . . The LAMSAS Hyde County interview with the speaker born in 1858 indicates a number of instances where [β] is transcribed for both /v/ and /w/." According to Wolfram (p.c.), this feature is no longer found in the area.)

It is of course vital that we should state unequivocally that we are entirely confident that what we are hearing in these six locations is not a near-merger. We have had to consider this possibility not only because of Labov's persuasive work but also because Kohlman's (n.d.) description of colloquial Caymanian English contains the phrase "the 'v's' in such words as 'invited,' 'several,' 'have,' and the 'w's' in 'worship,' 'work,' and 'wife,' are pronounced the same, *or almost the same*" [my emphasis]. Happily, the consonants involved in the speech of our Anguillian informants are not only audibly but also visibly identical as between the two lexical sets.

An African substratum is less likely as a source for this pronunciation in the speech of white than black Caribbean speakers, though I concede that it is possible. (According to Ladefoged (1968: 25) there are complex relationships between several different labial fricatives and approximants in many West African languages, with some languages lacking /v/ and /w/ but having instead a voiced bilabial or labiodental approximant.) Perhaps we should consider, too, the possibility of a Gaelic substratum, since some seventeenth-century whites transported to the Caribbean were speakers of Irish, which lacks /w/ as such (O Dochartaigh 1984: 298), though Anders Ahlqvist reports (p.c.) that in fact many Irish dialects realise the distinction between /v/ and palatalised /vʲ/ in a manner which resembles the English /w/ – /v/ distinction. It is true that both de Bhaldraithe (1945: 30–1) and Frick (1899: 64–8) report voiced bilabial fricative articulations in the dialects of Irish they describe, but they also both make it clear that voiced labiodental fricative articulations occur too.

In any case, bearing in mind the observations of Tristan, St Helena and Pitcairn English, it is particularly crucial to note that the bilabial approximant articulation is one which is extraordinarily rare in the languages of the world: Maddieson (1984: 96) shows that only 1.9 per cent of his sample languages have this consonant. A contrast between /v/ and /w/ is not common in the world's languages, but the presence of [β] is enormously uncommon. I therefore conclude that these different communities, scattered as they are in different widely separated parts of the world, and sharing an unusual articulation found in only a very small percentage of the world's languages, inherited this articulation from a common source, namely the dialectal English of the southeast of England.

THE ROLE OF DIALECT CONTACT
IN RESTORATION

There is evidence from Lesser-Known Englishes, then, for two different types of merger in southern England. In one, the merger was on [w] and [v] as allophones of a single phoneme, as totally reliably reported by Wells (1982: 589) for White Bahamian, for example. In the other, as experienced by Williams and me on Anguilla, there was a merger of historical /w/ and /v/ on [β] or [β̞] or both. How do we account for this rather puzzling situation?

Given that there is now reason to believe that there was a genuine merger in the south of England, we have to conclude that there was also a genuine reversal of the merger. And we therefore have to turn, as an explanation for the undoing of this merger, to the dialect-contact hypothesis. There is indeed, happily, evidence that dialect contact is exactly the correct explanation of how the /w/ – /v/ confusion was 'repaired', once again from Lesser-Known Englishes. Reports mentioned above, from varieties other than the six just mentioned, show signs of a partial loss of the merger. I interpret this as evidence that the merger did occur in these localities but is currently in the process of being reversed. This process has only just begun in Montserrat, for instance, where Wells (1982: 568) says that the merger "is restricted to the speech of the older uneducated population, and even for them lexically restricted, since *vote* has [v], not [w]". For Norfolk Island, Flint (1964: 196 ff.) reports, as we have seen, [w] in *valley* and *invitation*; he also, however, reports [v] in *devil* (p. 208), implying that the merger – which we can suppose from the evidence of Pitcairnese was formerly total – has been reversed and that the /w/ for /v/ pronunciation has become very lexically restricted. Even more importantly, our younger Anguillian informants lack the merger also: what is happening in Anguilla now, I would argue, is what started happening in the southeast of England 150 years ago.

I therefore suppose the following. There was indeed an early genuine merger in southeastern England of /v/ and /w/ on [β]. This Anguilla-type merger on an articulation intermediate between [v] and [w] led listeners who did not have it to report – and in the case of Dickens, to portray – /v/ for /w/ and vice versa. This merger was carried, perhaps in the seventeenth century, to other parts of the world, mainly to the early colonies such as those of the Caribbean, in some of which it still remains. In southeastern England, on the other hand, it was reversed as a result of contact with middle-class accents and accents from further north and west in England which did not have the merger.

Again there is evidence from Lesser-Known Englishes as to how this reversal took place: what happened in the south of England is probably what – we can infer from Wells' observations – is beginning to happen on Montserrat. There the contact-induced de-merger process has not yet led to a total re-establishment of two separate lexical sets but it has led to the replacement of the low-status form [β] by the acrolectal [w] and [v] articulations, which, however, continue for the moment to be widely used in members of the "wrong" lexical sets. We can suppose that in England, too, the merger was reversed by means of an intermediate Bahamian-type stage in which the mainstream English forms [w] and [v] were used instead of [β] but, for a while, allophonically rather than contrastively. This later, chronologically intermediate system is the one which is illustrated in the SED records and is the subject of the Norfolk "folk memory"; and the one which was also exported, probably in the eighteenth century, to later colonial Englishes, such as that of the Bonin Islands.

Note that I am not arguing here against the near-merger hypothesis as such. The conclusion to the investigation of the particular puzzle of the /w/ – /v/ merger, however, is that it is probable in this case that a near-merger is not what happened. In parts of southern England, the consonants /v/ and /w/ were genuinely merged on [β]. They were then unmerged again, via an intermediate stage in which [w] and [v] were allophones of the same phoneme. This merger does not survive in any of the major varieties of English around the world. But because of isolation from the influence of mainstream varieties as well as small community size and a consequent slow rate of linguistic change, it has survived, in both its original and intermediate stages, in a large number of Lesser-Known Englishes. Evidence from these little-studied varieties suggests rather strongly that "once a merger" is not necessarily "always a merger".

4 The last Yankee in the Pacific

In this chapter we now move the chronological focus forwards to language-contact events associated with the colonial expansion of English which took place in the 1800s; and we once again concentrate on Lesser-Known Englishes, though in this case we deal with only one of the varieties that we met in Chapter 3, the English of the Bonin Islands. Bonin Islands English may well be the least known of all the Lesser-Known Englishes; and it is certainly one of the most fascinating and remarkable varieties of English in the entire world.

It is remarkable in terms of its history, as we shall see. And it is also remarkable in terms of its scholarship: it was totally unknown to the international community of English linguistics scholars until it was discovered in the 1990s – and "discovered" is an entirely appropriate word – by Danny Long. Long is himself also rather remarkable: an American linguist who teaches Japanese dialectology in Japan to Japanese students, in Japanese, he was alerted to the possible presence of an anglophone community on the Bonins (Ogasawara) by a Japanese television documentary. This showed an interview, in fluent native Japanese, with an elderly man on the Bonins who, however, looked to be of European origin, and whose name was the very un-Japanese Abel Savory. This led Long to investigate material on the history of the islands; and then to take the 28-hour boat trip from Tokyo to Chichijima, the main island of Ogasawara, where he met

Danny Long and I are very grateful to Mary Shepardson, who made the original recordings analysed in this chapter; Irene Savory Lambert, who first brought the tapes to our attention and allowed us to borrow and copy them; Dr Beret Strong, grandniece of Mary Shepardson and keeper of her Bonin field materials; and Edith Washington and the Washington clan, whose helpful cooperation with this research project we very much appreciated.

Mr Savory in the street. The rest is linguistics history: more or less everything we know about Bonin Islands English is due to Long and to his pioneering work. We are also very fortunate that the discovery was his, as he was uniquely qualified to understand what it was he had discovered.

As noted in Chapter 3, the Bonin Islands chain lies in the northern Pacific Ocean between mainland Japan, which is about 800 kilometres to the north, and the Micronesian Northern Mariana Islands, which are a rather greater distance to the south. (One of the islands of the chain is Iwo Jima, famous as the site of one of the crucial battles of World War II.) As was mentioned in Chapter 3, the islands were totally uninhabited for the whole of human history until 1830, when a small band of European men arrived together with a number of Pacific Islanders, men and women, and settled on Chichijima. Over the next few years, several dozen additional men and women settled on the island.

The settlers lived beyond the control of any national government for a couple of generations, until the islands were claimed by Japan in the 1870s. Within a few years the original settlers and their children and grandchildren, who never numbered more than about one hundred in total, were outnumbered by Japanese settlers, and they took Japanese citizenship. The "Westerners", as these people of mixed European and Pacific Island descent came to be called, retained a sense of unique identity even throughout World War II and until the present day. Following the war and the defeat of Japan, the islands were administered by the United States navy, who allowed only these islanders of non-Japanese descent to remain. In 1968, however, the islands were returned by the USA to Japanese authority, and the ethnically Japanese settlers of the pre-war era, along with their mainland-born offspring and new mainlanders, were allowed to return to the islands, where they once again became the majority. There are today two main centres of habitation, the principal one on Chichijima, with a much smaller one on the island of Hahajima.

THE LINGUISTIC HISTORY

The language history of the Bonins is complex. We know that Austronesian languages brought to the islands by the Pacific Islanders included Hawaiian, Tahitian, North Marquesan, Rotuman, and the Micronesian languages Carolinian, Kiribati, Ponapean and Chamorro. There were also speakers of language varieties from China, the Philippines and Bougainville as well as Malagasy; and some of the most influential men on the island were native speakers of the European languages English, Portuguese, German, Italian, French (and probably Breton) and Danish.

However, Long's research points to the fact that from the very beginning English was used as the lingua franca in the settlement, and that it subsequently became the first language of children born on the island (Long 1999): it was the only common language for the original settlers. Long argues that it would have been spoken by the non-native speakers in a pidginised form – and by some of them in a considerably pidginised form. This does not mean, however, that he postulates the existence of any kind of actual pidgin: unlike in typical pidgin-formation situations, native speakers of the source language were always present, i.e. a native English target or model was always available, and a continuous native-speaker tradition survived.

Long (1999) and I believe, rather, that contact between English speakers, on the one hand, and speakers of other European and Pacific Island languages, on the other, led to the development of an English-based creoloid (see Chapter 2) which became the basilectal variety in the community. At the same time, mainstream English continued to be spoken natively, and a continuum developed between an acrolectal Mainstream Bonin English and this basilectal Bonin English Creoloid.

After forty years of relative isolation, in the 1870s the anglophone islands were claimed by Japan, with the subsequent arrival of large numbers of Japanese-speaking settlers. This resulted in a language-contact situation of extreme complexity. As far as Japanese was concerned, dialect contact resulting from the influx of people from many different parts of Japan led to the development of a new dialect, a mixed Ogasawara Japanese Koiné. This new dialect then came into contact with the Bonin English Creoloid, a form of language contact which gave rise to language intertwining (Bakker and Mous 1994), and the development of an Ogasawara Mixed Language, as described by Long (2007), which has a Japanese matrix, i.e. it is grammatically more Japanese than English. By about 1900, therefore, there existed a complex linguistic community where young adults spoke some or all of: Mainstream Bonin English, Bonin English Creoloid (with a continuum of varieties between these two), the Ogasawara Japanese–English Mixed Language and the new Ogasawara Japanese Koiné.

We have records of "Westerners" who were monolingual in English as late as the 1950s: George Webb, 1870–1951, is said to have been more or less incapable of speaking Japanese in spite of the fact that he had lived through the late 1930s, when the use of English was the object of increasing suspicion and oppression on the part of the Japanese authorities. But during the course of the twentieth century, Mainstream Bonin English and Bonin English Creoloid both became progressively weaker in terms of proportions of speakers and of speakers' linguistic abilities: English became an endangered language. However, in 1945, when the USA took control of the islands and the Japanese inhabitants were not allowed to return from mainland Japan where they had been evacuated towards the end of the war, Mainstream English received a boost through the presence of American military personnel and English-medium education. The Ogasawara Japanese Koiné survived as a home language in at least some families, but when the islands were handed back to Japan in 1968, this became increasingly influenced by Standard (or at least mainstream) Japanese. It is also worth noting that the Mixed Language acquired a special role between 1945 and 1968, when it was the only variety available to the Westerners which could distinguish them from the American military personnel.

Today, all younger people are fluent in Standard Japanese, while some elderly people still speak the original Japanese Koiné. Westerners over fifty years old are still comfortable speaking the Japanese–English Mixed Language among themselves, and this tends to be truest of the expatriates living in the USA who have not been influenced by recent developments on the island. (Many of these people left at the time of the 1968 reversion to Japanese rule or soon afterwards and have never experienced life in Standard Japanese.)

The Bonin English Creoloid does not survive in general use, but can resurface when speakers of the Mixed Language who have had little exposure to English communicate with monolingual anglophones: on such occasions they show an ability to shift out of the Mixed Language into the English creoloid, filtering out the Japanese components of the mix.

American English survives as a foreign language among school children and young adults who have learnt it in school, but only to the extent that it does in the rest of Japan. It survives as a second language among those Westerners who received their schooling in English between 1945 and 1968, particularly if they have worked (as many of them have) in the USA, Guam or the Northern Marianas.

But of the original Mainstream Bonin English, there is no trace.

It is, however, the original Mainstream Bonin English which is the topic of this investigation. This is because there are two intriguing questions which we would like to answer in this chapter: what was the original pre-World War II Mainstream Bonin English actually like; and, if we can establish what it was like, why was it like that?

UNCLE CHARLIE

Happily, the answer to the first question can be supplied, as a result of the fortunate availability of recordings of a single speaker of this variety. The tape-recordings were made in 1971 by Dr Mary Shepardson (1906–97), an anthropologist best known for her work with the Navajo of North America. She conducted the recorded interviews on the main island of Chichijima during late July and early August 1971 with her colleague Blodwen Hammond. They interviewed many of the "Westerners", but the longest of their interviews by far were those with Charles Washington (1881–1972). He was called Uncle Charlie, "Uncle" being a traditional term of familiar respect in island society. The researchers seem to have developed a particular affinity for Uncle Charlie, and listening to the tapes one can easily understand why: he has a wit that charms the listener immediately. And of course the subsequent total disappearance of the original Mainstream Bonin English makes these recordings of Charles Washington particularly important.

In her field notes from 1971, Dr Shepardson writes of the initial frustration she and her research partner Hammond felt on the island about making contact with the inhabitants, and their joy at meeting Uncle Charlie:

> Strictly personal note: as I type this I am suffused with the emotions that I was experiencing in Chichi at this particular time. Went looking for Uncle Charlie because we needed him – we had to be doing something, getting some information, making each day count! It was completely frustrating to be told that the group could speak English if they wanted to. It made me feel inadequate – made me feel that I should be able to get to them somehow … Actually U. C. was a much better informant than anyone else for several reasons: he has intellectual curiosity, he has some interest in the world outside of Chichi, he has been in the outside world, etc.

Complete transcriptions of the interviews have been published as a research report in Japan (Long 2001). A complete Japanese translation of the interviews has also been published for the benefit of Uncle Charlie's younger descendants (Long 2002). The recordings were made with Mr Washington's permission, and the tapes and some preliminary transcriptions were made available by Dr Beret Strong, Professor Shepardson's great-niece and the executor of her

Bonin research materials. The final transcriptions were made by Yoshiyuki Asahi and Daniel Long.

Charles Washington was born in 1881 "under the rising sun", as he says in the interviews, meaning that the Bonin Islands had by that time become part of Japan. Charlie himself was born a Japanese citizen to parents who had become naturalised just a few years previously, and he never held any other nationality. He was educated in Japanese government schools, which he attended until a young teenager, or as he says, "I went to school for quite a while till I got grown up – well, half a man". The Japanese government schools on Ogasawara at that time were bilingual, not only teaching Japanese and English as subjects, but teaching *in* both languages as well.

At the age of 17, Charlie left Ogasawara on a whaling ship (a "blubber hunter", as he says). During the next forty years he participated in ten or so subsequent voyages, of about a year each, whaling or sealing on routes that typically took him past Hakodate, on Hokkaido, to the Sea of Okhotsk, and then on to the Aleutian Islands, before heading down to Victoria, British Columbia, and on to San Francisco.

At school, Charlie learnt to read and write the Japanese *kana* syllabary, but he forgot the *kanji* ideographs he learnt, lamenting "the big block letters, why it's hard to keep in your coconut". Since Japanese is not ordinarily written without *kanji*, except for books for infants, telegrams and so on, this would have limited his social literacy in Japan. When questioned about his English literacy skills, he replies, "I can just about scribble out what I got to say to a friend a little – that's about all".

Charlie only ever spoke Japanese at home with his children, although he specifically mentions "speaking English" with other islanders, especially around Japanese people, when the use of English as an in-group language might have been convenient.

MAINSTREAM BONIN ENGLISH

We can present the most important characteristics of Uncle Charlie's English, as demonstrated on the tape-recordings, under a number of different headings in order to help to give us a picture of the origins of this variety.

Language-contact features

On the recordings, Charlie is clearly at his most acrolectal when speaking to two American academics. Nevertheless, even at this end of the Creoloid–English continuum, his English shows a number of contact features of a type that are also found in second- or foreign-language Englishes around the world.

Grammatically we find regularisations such as:

the plural forms *mans* and *womans*
the past tense of *beat* as *beated*

Also notable is the usage of sentence-initial *was* as an existential corresponding to General English "there was":

Was four daughters all told.

Phonologically, /θ/ and /ð/ do occur but TH-stopping to [t̪] and [d̪] is also found; and word-final /θ/ is also often [s].

The most notable phonological contact feature, however, is consonant-cluster simplification, which also occurs, for example, in forms of African American Vernacular English (AAVE), and Caribbean English. As in all varieties of English, the final consonant of words such as *cask, mast, lost, friend, told, world* is deleted if the next word begins with a consonant, as in *los' one, eas' coast, smalles' guy, jus' put, mus' say, firs' name, bigges' claim, aroun' there*. Moreover, as in General English but unlike in pidgins, creoles and AAVE, the consonant is always present if the next word starts with a vowel, as in *lost it*. What is distinctive here, then, is that the final consonant is deleted pre-pausally: *it was los'*. It is probably this characteristic which also leads to the occasional absence of third-person singular present-tense *-s*, plural *-s* and past-tense *-ed*, i.e. the absence is probably a phonological rather than grammatical phenomenon.

We can say, then, that even though a continuous native-speaker tradition was maintained on Chichijima, and there was no break in the transmission of native English from one generation to another, the effects of the massive language contact that took place on the island can still be discerned in these creoloid-type features which are present even in acrolectal native local English.

Traditional Dialect features

Otherwise, the English we find on the recordings is of a type one would expect to find in a native anglophone community. Interestingly, however, some of the pronunciations are of a kind that is normally associated with Traditional Dialects, in the sense of Wells (1982). In Wells' usage, *Traditional Dialect* is a term corresponding to German *Mundart* or French *patois* which refers to dialects which have been relatively unaffected by koinéisation, urbanisation or by contact with Standard English. In the English-speaking world, Traditional Dialects are found only in England, northern Ireland, the Lowlands of Scotland and Newfoundland, though some dialectologists would also include the American dialects of the Ozarks and the Appalachians under this heading. Such dialects are linguistically conservative compared to other dialects, and diverge linguistically from one another and the standard variety quite considerably. For example, while *We're not coming* and *We ain't comin'* are both what Wells calls General English, standard and nonstandard respectively, *Us byun't a-comin* is a Traditional Dialect form (from the English upper southwest). The forms that are found in the English of Uncle Charlie which can be described in this way include:

Sit	/sɛt/
Just	/dʒɛst/
Catch	/kɛtʃ/
Further	/fʌðə/

And he pronounces words such as *hoist, join, joint* and *point* with /aɪ/.

Nonstandard features

Apart from the features just mentioned, Uncle Charlie's English is obviously a variety of General English (Wells 1982) as found in most parts of the world. It is, however, General English of a nonstandard type. The following features from the recordings of Uncle Charlie can be found in all or many nonstandard forms of English around the world:

> multiple negation: *she didn't have nothing aboard*
> double modals: *he might couldn't make the harbour*
> distal plural demonstrative *them*: *them days*
> relative pronoun *what*: *I forgot all what I learned*
> nonstandard preterites: *I always drawed my advance before I left*

This is evidence, if any were needed, that English was not brought to the Bonins by middle-class educated speakers, but by groups of sailors and adventurers.

Conservative features

It is also interesting that Uncle Charlie's English is clearly conservative in its phonology. He was born in 1881, but there are a number of features which are surprisingly old-fashioned even for a speaker with this birthdate. (In Chapter 7 we discuss the notion of *colonial lag*, a term which refers to the thesis that colonial varieties of English and other European colonial languages are, or may be, demonstrably more conservative than metropolitan varieties.)

(1) Clear versus dark /l/
In modern RP and many other forms of English English, /l/ is normally 'clear' before a following vowel or /j/, but 'dark' before a consonant, including /w/, or a pause, regardless of word boundaries.

However, the *Survey of English Dialects* materials show that in the Traditional Dialects of the 1950s/60s, dark /l/ was found only south of a line passing between Shropshire and Hereford and proceeding more or less due east to pass between Norfolk and Suffolk. In modern English English dialects, on the other hand, dark /l/ is now found everywhere except in the northeast. No form of Irish English has dark /l/, clear /l/ being usual in all environments, as it is in the Scottish Highlands. In the Lowlands of Scotland, on the other hand, dark /l/ is usual in all phonological environments, as it is also in modern North American English.

Uncle Charlie's /l/ is clear in all positions.

(2) Long Mid Diphthonging

Wells' term (1982) Long Mid Diphthonging refers to the historical change in English of the vowel of FACE from [e:] to [eɪ] and of GOAT from [o:] to [oʊ]. Long Mid Diphthonging is absent from Uncle Charlie's English, i.e. the vowels of FACE and GOAT are pure monophthongs. MacMahon cites references to Long Mid Diphthonging in England for FACE in 1711 (1994: 450) and for GOAT in 1795 (1994: 459).

(3) Diphthong Shift

This term was introduced by Wells (1982: 256) to refer to the most recent ongoing developments in English associated with the Great Vowel Shift in which the diphthongs /iː, uː, ei, oi, ou, ai, au/ show continuing movement of their first elements beyond those reached by British RP. For example, /ai/ is the result of the diphthongisation of Middle English /iː/ in which the first element has gone from [i] through [ɪ] and [ə] and [ɜ] to [ɐ] and [a]. Diphthong Shift for /ai/ now involves more recent and continuing movement of the initial element of the type [a > ʌ > ɑ > ɒ].

For the vowels of PRICE and MOUTH, the modern qualities of the first elements of these diphthongs in RP, i.e. [a] and [ɑ] respectively, are thought to have been achieved by the last quarter of the nineteenth century (MacMahon 1994: 464–6). For FACE and GOAT, MacMahon cites references to [ei] in FACE from 1711 and [ou] in GOAT from 1795 (1994: 450–9). The slightly diphthongal variants of FLEECE and GOOSE typical of modern RP are described by Sweet for 1878 (quoted in MacMahon 1994: 461).

Uncle Charlie has no Diphthong Shift for any of the vowels /i:, u:, ei, oi, ou, ai, au/.

(4) The STRUT *vowel*

The STRUT vowel is a recent arrival in the phonological inventory of English, and many local varieties in northern and central England do not have it. What happened was that in the late 1500s the vowel /ʊ/ began to lose its lip-rounding in certain environments and lexical items in the southeast of England, giving [ɤ]. According to Gimson (1962), this subsequently lowered to [ʌ] in the eighteenth century, and a vowel a little front of [ʌ] seems to have been the RP norm at the beginning of the twentieth century. During the course of the twentieth century it then fronted to [ɐ], which is the pronunciation found in RP today (see Roach 1983: 16). Modern North American English also generally has some kind of central vowel, though often not as open as [ɐ]. In the English of London and other parts of the southeast, however, the fronting has progressed further, giving "an open front vowel very close to Cardinal [a]" (Gimson 1962: 103). This is also true of Australasian English.

Uncle Charlie's STRUT vowel retains the conservative back-vowel quality [ʌ].

ORIGINS

Uncle Charlie's English, then, is a rather conservative type of non-standard English, commensurate with what we imagine to be the social backgrounds of the speakers who first brought the language to Chichijima, plus a small number of contact features. But what can Uncle Charlie's English tell us about the regional origins of his Mainstream Bonin English? Where did it come from? Was it, too, like the Japanese dialect of the Bonins, a koiné resulting from dialect mixture, or can we pinpoint a single point of regional provenance?

In fact, the immediate impression one receives on first hearing the recording is that Uncle Charlie is an American. For example, intervocalic /t/ as in *better* is most often, but not always, a voiced flap [ɾ] rather than the [t] or [ʔ] one would expect from British English. Similarly, he has YOD-dropping after /t, d, n/, i.e. there is no /j/ in *tune*, *during*, *new*. And he does not have the /h/-dropping that one would expect from most regional English English accents. He also uses the conservative American discourse marker *why*:

> *When there's a storm, why, they'd put a bar across.*

But if Uncle Charlie's English originally came from North America, what can we say more precisely about its regional origins? In fact there are a number of clues.

(1) First of all, my analyses of the Shepardson tapes show that words such as *foreign* have the vowel of LOT and not NORTH, so that *horrible* does not rhyme with *deplorable*. The merger of vowels before /r/ in polysyllables – producing typical American rhymes such as *horrible–deplorable*, *hurry–furry*, *marry–berry* is found in most of North America away from the East Coast (Trudgill and Hannah 2008). Its absence from our data here means that we can suppose that Uncle Charlie's phonology is Eastern North American in origin.

(2) His accent is non-rhotic. It thus has:

NEAR   [ɪə]
SQUARE [eə]
CURE   [ʊə]
NURSE [ɜː – ɜ]

This feature also supports the thesis of an East Coast origin, non-rhoticity, as is well known, being found in the United States only in Eastern New England, New York City and the coastal South.

Given that we have had this degree of success in tracking down the regional origins of Mainstream Bonins English, are we now able to refine our geographical analysis even more? It turns out that we are. The following three features provide important and indeed entirely conclusive evidence.

(3) Uncle Charlie's vowel in the lexical set of LOT is a rounded [ɒ]. This quality is typical of most of the English-speaking world outside North America, but given that we have supposed that this variety is North American in origin, it points to Eastern New England, since everywhere else in North America has unrounded [ɑ] (Wells 1982).

(4) The vowel /aː/, which is phonetically very front, occurs not only in the START lexical set but also in PALM, and in a number of BATH words. For example:

> *lance, chance, plant, commander*
> *can't, half*
> *father, Guam*

Interestingly, words such as *after, mast, ask* which involve pre-voiceless fricative environments mostly have /æ/ (see the discussion of variability in Boston in Wells 1982: 523, based on Kurath and McDavid 1961).

(5) The major non-rhotic accents of English around the world – Australian, New Zealand, South African and English English – have merged the lexical sets of THOUGHT and NORTH/FORCE on /ɔː/, such that pairs like *court–caught, tort–taught, sort–sought, torque–talk, lord–laud, lore–law, more–maw, Thor–thaw* are homophonous.

On the other hand, a number of rhotic accents, such as Scottish, Canadian and, increasingly, American, have the LOT–THOUGHT merger, such that pairs like *cot–caught, tot–taught, knotty–naughty, rot–wrought, not–nought, Don–Dawn, hock–hawk, chock–chalk, stock–stalk* are homophonous.

The English of Eastern New England, however, is unique in combining both of these features (Wells 1982: 524–5, based on Kurath and McDavid 1961). It is non-rhotic, with *stork* and *stalk* identical, but it also has the LOT–THOUGHT merger so that *stalk* is homophonous with *stock* as well. This is the only native variety of English

Table 1. *Comparison of Bonin English and other English vowel systems*

	LOT	THOUGHT	NORTH	FORCE
Conservative General American	a	ɔ	ɔr	or
Modern General American	a	ɔ	ɔr	
Canadian	a		or	
Scots	ɔ		ɔr	or
Conservative RP	ɒ	ɔ:		ɔə
Modern RP	ɒ	ɔ:		
Eastern New England	ɒ			ɔə
Nineteenth-Century Bonin English	ɒ			oə
	stock	*stalk*	*stork*	*store*

in the entire world in which the lexical sets of *stork, stock* and *stalk* are identical.

There is a further complication, however: while most non-rhotic accents of English have merged the vowels of NORTH (from ME short /ɔ /+/r/) and FORCE (from ME long /ɔ:/+/r/), as in *horse–hoarse, warn–worn, for–four,* Eastern New England has not, preserving the opposition as /ɒ/ versus /oə/ as shown in Table 1.

It is this remarkably distinctive and indeed unique Eastern New England system which Uncle Charlie has preserved. He has /ɒ/ in *top, lot, caught, saw, north, short,* but /oə/ in *poor, door, four, course, (a)board, (a)shore.*

Interestingly, his phonetics are not identical with modern Eastern New England English: *shore* and *show* are distinguished as /ʃoə/ vs. /ʃo:/ since, as we have seen, the GOAT vowel is a pure monophthong. We can interpret this, as we did above, as a conservative feature, reflecting nineteenth-century as opposed to modern Bostonian English.

There can be absolutely no doubt, then, that we have suc-
ceeded in tracking down the regional origins of Mainstream Bonin
English: it came originally from the area of Boston, Massachusetts,
USA. We do not and cannot know exactly how this happened, but
one of the Americans who settled in the Bonins was Uncle Charlie's
grandfather, who came from the Boston area. The only plausible
explanation for Uncle Charlie's vowel system, and his native, acrolectal variety of English overall, has to be that he inherited it from his
maternal grandfather Nathaniel Savory, of Bradford, Massachusetts,
as it was transmitted down to him through the Mainstream Bonin
English of his mother and other second-generation islanders. We
shall have more to say about this in the Epilogue to this book.

5 An American lack of dynamism

The most important events which I will be describing in this chapter once again occurred during the nineteenth century, but our geographical focus is now on the Atlantic rather than the Pacific Ocean. Linguistically, too, I move from the consideration of an Eastern New England-derived variety of English to an examination of North American English as a whole, in comparison to other English varieties.

In considering differences between the North American Englishes of Canada and the USA, on the one hand, and British Isles English, on the other, it is fairly obviously the case that we should be able to ascribe these differences to one or more of a number of mechanisms (Trudgill 2004):

(1) North American English has adapted to new topographical and biological features unknown in Britain: for example, as is well known, the word *robin* in North America refers to a bird which is different from its referent in Britain; and the word *bluff* has been extended to refer to an inland cliff or headland along a river.

(2) Since the departure of English for America, linguistic changes have occurred in Britain which have not occurred in North America: for example, the glottalling of intervocalic and word-final /t/, as in *better, bet* [bɛʔə, bɛʔ] is typical of British but not of North American English (Wells 1982), and is clearly a nineteenth-century innovation that occurred in Britain.

(3) Since the arrival of English from Britain, linguistic changes have taken place in North America which have not occurred

in Britain: for example, the voicing of intervocalic /t/ and the flapping of intervocalic /t/ and /d/ as in *city* [sɪɾi] are typical of North American and not of British English (Wells 1982).

(4) North American English has experienced forms of language contact with indigenous languages which have, obviously, not been experienced by British English: for example, American English has borrowed lexical items such as *skunk* and *caucus* from Native American languages (Romaine 2001).

(5) North American English has experienced forms of language contact with other European languages in the colonial situation (Romaine 2001) which have not been experienced by British English: for example, American English has borrowed lexical items such as *cookie* 'biscuit' from Dutch and *key* 'islet' from Spanish. We can also suppose that North American grammatical constructions such as *Are you coming with?* and *I like to skate* (as opposed to *I like skating*) are the result of German and/or Yiddish influence (see Trudgill 1986; Mufwene 2001: 162)

(6) North American English has been subject to processes associated with *dialect contact*. Although of course the geographical and social origins of the settlers were different in each location, none of the early anglophone settlements on the east coast of what is now the United States was settled from a single location in England. We can therefore assume that, very early on, contact between different British dialects would have occurred in the American settlements which would have led to the appearance of new, mixed dialects not precisely like any dialect spoken in the homeland.

In this chapter our investigation attempts to sort out which of these six processes has been involved in the evolution of two important differences between North American English and the Englishes of the British Isles (Britain and Ireland). Both of these differences have to do with the main verb *have*.

The first concerns the grammatical behaviour of this verb in the two varieties. North American English (we must except from this some of the varieties of Newfoundland influenced by Irish English) typically employs *do*-support in constructions such as:

(1) Do you have any coffee?

while British Isles English has traditionally not required *do*-support:

(2) Have you any coffee?

The second has to do with the fact that North American English typically does not use *have* in expressions such as:

(3) I took a shower.

whereas British Isles English does:

(4) I had a shower.

Why is this? How did this situation come about? And is there any connection between the two differences?

Given that in both cases South African, Australian and New Zealand English align with British Isles English rather than North American, it would be good to know why North American English is the odd one out.

(There are of course degrees of variability within all these varieties, but the claim in this chapter is that at least in terms of tendencies, the assertions made here about these different varieties, based on handbooks, observations and consultation with informants over many years, are essentially sufficiently correct for conclusions to be drawn.)

STATIVE VERSUS DYNAMIC *HAVE*

As is well known, the verb *to have* in modern English is one of three verbs in the language which have the status of 'primary verb' (Quirk *et al.* 1985). That is, it can function either as an auxiliary verb, like the modals, or as a main verb, like the full verbs.

Auxiliary verbs in English function as 'operators' (Quirk *et al.* 1985) which do not require *do*-support and are employed in negation, interrogation, ellipsis and emphasis. They also have phonologically reduced forms, and can co-occur with other reduced forms such as *'s* and *n't*:

(5a) I will not go.
      Will you go? Yes, I will.
      I WILL go.
      I'll go.
      I won't go.

(5b) *I don't will go.
      *Do you will go? Yes, I do.
      *I DO will go.

Full verbs, on the other hand, require *do*-support in interrogation, negation and emphasis; have no function in ellipsis; have no reduced forms; and cannot co-occur with other reduced forms:

(6a) I do not swim.
      Do you swim? Yes, I do.
      I DO swim.

(6b) *I swim not.
      *Swim you? Yes, I swim.
      *I swimn't

(Stressed *I SWIM* has a contrastive lexical verb, i.e. *I swim rather than dive*, whereas *I DO swim* has contrastive polarity.)
      We might therefore expect to see this pattern occurring also in the case of the two *haves*, with auxiliary *have* behaving like *will* and main verb *have* behaving like *swim*. And indeed we do see precisely this pattern in North American English:

      AUXILIARY *have*
(7a) I have not seen him.
      Have you seen him? Yes, I have.

I HAVE seen him.

I've seen him.

He's seen him.

He hasn't seen him.

(7b) *I do not have seen him.

*Do you have seen him? Yes, I do.

*I DO have seen him.

MAIN VERB *have*

(8a) I don't have a good time there.

Do you have a good time there? No, I don't.

I DON'T have a good time there.

(8b) *I haven't a good time there.

*Have you a good time there? No, I haven't.

*I HAVEN'T a good time there.

*I've a good time there.

*He's a good time there.

It is of considerable interest, however, that, even allowing for variable usage in all varieties, it is possible to claim that, broadly speaking, different regional forms of English around the world, including varieties of Standard English, tend to vary in the extent to which they reproduce this expected, North American English pattern.

English English, for example, demonstrates a split system in which main verb *have* differs in its behaviour from auxiliary *have*, but only in certain cases. Traditionally, English English (see Quirk *et al.* 1985) has distinguished between the grammatical behaviour of main verb *have* in dynamic meanings and its behaviour in stative meanings. *Have* "in dynamic senses such as 'receive', 'take', 'experience' and in idioms with an eventive object (e.g. *have* breakfast = 'eat breakfast')" (Quirk *et al.* 1985: 132) behaves like a full verb, as in North American English:

(9a) Do you have coffee with breakfast? Yes, I do.

I don't have coffee with breakfast.

I DO have coffee with breakfast.

(9b) *I've coffee with breakfast.

Stative *have*, on the other hand, where the meaning indicates an ongoing state involving possession, behaves, unlike in North American English, like auxiliary *have* (which is itself always stative, of course) and does not require *do*-support:

(10) Have you (any) coffee in the cupboard?
      I haven't (any) coffee in the cupboard.
      I HAVE some coffee in the cupboard.
      I've some coffee in the cupboard.

We thus have a contrast, as confirmed by Biber *et al.* (1999: 162, 216), between North American English *Do you have (any) coffee (in the cupboard)?* and traditional English English *Have you (any) coffee (in the cupboard)?* This is the source of Peter Strevens' joke (1972: 48):

(11) *American woman*:   Do you have children?
      English woman: Yes, one a year!

This English English distinction between the grammatical behaviour of stative and dynamic *have* is one which appears to have been extant for around 250 years at least (see below).

In all forms of English, finite forms of stative *have* can also be replaced by *have got*, although this is more common in British than in American English (Biber *et al.* 1999: 162, 216). As Quirk *et al.* (1985: 132) say, we should:

> note the following contrast between stative and dynamic meanings:
> Had she *got* her baby at the clinic? ['Was her baby at the clinic with her?']
> *Did* she *have* her baby at the clinic? ['Did she give birth to her baby at the clinic?']

Especially in American English, the second sentence could have both these meanings.

Chronology

This distinction between dynamic and stative *have* with respect to presence versus absence of *do*-support in English English can be accounted for in diachronic terms. Ellegård (1953) showed that *do*-support in general was introduced into English at different rates depending on whether the construction involved was declarative, negative, interrogative or negative interrogative (see also Denison 1993; Garrett 1998). But the development was actually rather more complicated than that, since the type of verb concerned also seems to have been important: some verbs lagged behind in this process, and Barber (1997: 196) argues that *do*-support spread more rapidly in the case of transitive than intransitive verbs.

Stage 1

The earliest historical stage in the development of *do*-support with *have* is thus one in which *have* is one of those verbs which lagged behind – the stage in which all forms of *have* resisted *do*-support. It is important to notice that this is the system which is still alive and well today in many varieties of British Isles English. In many forms (I stress 'many' as there is of course variability even within these varieties) of Scottish and Irish English, for example, main verb *have* still does not require *do*-support at all, and it can also occur in and with phonologically reduced forms:

(12) Had you a good time? Yes, we had.
Have you coffee with breakfast? Yes, I have.
We'd a good time.
I've coffee with breakfast.
We HAD a good time.
I HAVE coffee with breakfast.
We hadn't a good time.
I haven't coffee with breakfast.

That is, main verb and auxiliary *have* behave alike; and stative *have* also behaves like dynamic *have*.

This means that the claim by Quirk *et al.* (1985: 776) that "the dynamic main verb *have* requires DO as an operator" so that *They haven't an argument every day, We hadn't a party last week, I hadn't a look at your material* are "ungrammatical", while quite true of many varieties of English, is not true of the English (including the Standard English) of Scotland and Ireland, where these sentences are perfectly grammatical. (I acknowledge that there are pragmatic constraints on the extent to which these constructions are likely, or not, to occur in Scottish and Irish English, but these are not relevant to my argument since the fact is that they are genuinely grammatical, as informants confirm.)

Stage 2

The Stage 1 Scottish/Irish-type system was the system which was found in all varieties of English until well into the eighteenth century at least. The next stage in the chronological development consisted of the introduction of *do*-support into constructions with *have*. Ellegård (1953) dates the beginning of this process to the late 1700s. Dietrich (1949: 39–40) concurs, saying that the origins of *do*-support with *have* must go back to the end of the eighteenth century or perhaps earlier in "vulgärer und dialektischer Sprache", although he also dates the full rise to the first quarter of the nineteenth century (1949: 36).

This Stage 2 introduction of *do*-support into constructions with *have* did not happen haphazardly. If we look at *do*-support generally, it seems that it was first introduced into constructions with dynamic verbs or verbs with dynamic meaning, before later being introduced into constructions with stative verbs. Ellegård (1953) shows, for example, that a few high-frequency stative verbs such as *know, say* and *think* resisted the usage of *do*-support, at least in negatives, until as late as the nineteenth century. In addition, Barber (1997: 196) writes:

> There were also differences between individual verbs, some of them resisting the *do* construction more than others. Verbs that

Table 2. Do-*support with negative verb forms*

| Period | Main group | | Know group | |
	total	% +DO	total	% +DO
1500–1570	246	18.7	60	1.7
1570–1640	234	24.8	92	8.7
1640–1710	184	63.0	73	38.4

(*source:* Nurmi 1999: 146)

resisted the use of *do* in negative sentences include *care, come, doubt, know, mistake, speak* and *trow* ... Verbs that resisted the *do* construction in questions include *come, dare, do, have, hear, mean, need, say, think.*

Nurmi's work (1999) supports this. Her research on negative verb forms enables us to compare negation with and without *do*-support systematically. Her '*know* group' coincides largely with the verbs Ellegård mentions, and consists of *know, boot, trow, care, doubt, mistake, fear, skill* and *list,* plus *misdoubt, misknow.* Her 'main group' consists of all other verbs.

When *do*-support did eventually begin to be introduced into constructions with *have,* therefore, it was thus, in line with this general trend, introduced at first only into constructions with dynamic *have.* The earliest examples of *have* taking *do*-support from the Chadwyck-Healey online database 1280–1915 (see below) come from the 1700s and do indeed involve dynamic meanings. Other literary examples are later and can be found, for example, in James Miller: "But don't have an Ague-Fit now when you come to the Proof" (1737, *The Universal Passion,* Act V, Scene 1); and in examples cited by Dietrich (1949), such as Jane Austen: "Do have the goodness to hear me my first act" (1812–14, *Mansfield Park*), and Charles Dickens: "The license was made out, and she did have him" (1837–38, *The Pickwick Papers*), "Do you ever have the nightmare?", "Does she ever have the nightmare?" (1843–44; *Martin Chuzzlewit*).

The system described above as being typical of English English thus represents a second, more recent stage of development than that employed in Scotland and Ireland.

Stage 3

Finally, the North American system, where *do*-support has been introduced also in the case of stative *have*, obviously represents a third, even more recent stage, where the transition of *have* from the status of a verb which did not require *do*-support to one which does has gone to completion. It is also the case that North American English does not permit phonological contractions of the type *I've some coffee.*

Importantly, it is now clear that in modern usage this is beginning to be true of English English as well. We have used the word "traditionally" a number of times above in recognition of the fact that in the English of the south of England among younger speakers today, the situation is currently changing in the direction of the North American system. After a period of stability of about 250 years, dynamic and stative *have* are no longer so consistently treated differently. This change is very recent: Strevens (1972: 48) dates his first hearing of the usage of stative *have* with *do*-support in the (it is true, typically conservative) English English of a BBC news bulletin to February 1972. Quirk *et al.* (1985: 131) exaggerate somewhat when they say that *We don't have any butter* "is also common in British English nowadays" since it is still rare not only in Scotland and Ireland but also in parts of northern England. Similarly, they say that past-tense usages of stative *have* as an operator, as in *Had she any news?* are "now somewhat uncommon" in British English, whereas they are actually still very common indeed with older speakers even in the south of England, and in Scotland and Ireland generally. Scottish and Irish speakers are also much more likely than English English speakers to use this kind of construction in *wh*-questions, as in *What kind of car have they?*, which is labelled as "occasional" for British English by Quirk *et al.* (1985: 818).

Our first clue, then, is that Irish and Scottish English are more conservative in this respect generally than English English, which is in turn more conservative than North American English. This places this phenomenon clearly in mechanism category 3, as outlined at the beginning of this chapter: the difference between British and American English can be explained by saying that since the arrival of English from Britain, a linguistic change has taken place in North America which has not (yet) occurred (fully) in the British Isles.

RESTRICTED COLLOCATIONS

The second difference between British and American English involving the verb *have*, as we saw above, concerns the appearance and non-appearance of dynamic main verb *have* in certain restricted collocations (or "bound collocations", Brinton and Akimoto 1999: 1) in the two varieties (see Trudgill and Hannah 2008). Quirk *et al.* (1985: 751–2) observe that there are "some common collocations of verb and eventive object where the noun heads are derived from verbs", and "it will be noticed that several noun phrases collocate with both *have* and *take*. In such cases, *have* is the typical British verb and *take* is the typical American verb". Similarly, Algeo (1995), who discusses the definitions of expanded predicates and the rhetorical motivations for their use, using the one-million-word Brown (American English) and Lancaster/Oslo-Bergen (British English) corpora, finds that: "The difference is not strong, but it is clear. Even within corpora of the limited size of Brown and LOB, where there is a slant in preference, British lists *have*, American *take*" (p. 211). Comparing the verbs *do*, *give*, *have*, *make* and *take* in the corpora, Algeo concludes (p. 213) that:

> British uses *have* as the verb of an expanded predicate nearly twice as often as American does and in about one and three-quarters as many different constructions. *Have* is the British verb of preference, accounting for 41 per cent of both types and tokens of expanded predicates, whereas in American it

accounts for only 28 per cent of tokens and 26 per cent of types. The British preference for *have* casts a different light on the *have/take* difference noted above. The difference is not that American favours *take* but that British favours *have*.

Stein and Quirk (1991: 197) also find that *have* is much more frequent than *take* in collocations of this type in their British English fiction corpus (see also Wierzbicka 1982: 756).

Thus, British speakers say:

(13) I had a bath.

whereas North American speakers say:

(14) I took a bath.

There are very many such locutions involving the differential usage of *have* and *take*:

have/take a	bite	drink	guess	*holiday/vacation*	
	look	nap	rest	seat	swim
	shower	sleep	walk	wash	etc.

There are, interestingly, also many other expressions where British *have* corresponds or may correspond in North American English to some verb other than *have* (or *take*). In North American English, for example, it is possible in service encounters to say:

(15) Can I get a sandwich?

which is ungrammatical, or at least has been so until very recently,[1] in British English, where one would instead have to say:

(16) Can I have a sandwich?

[1] The original version of this paper was written in 1999: younger speakers in England and New Zealand – at least – can now be heard using this locution very frequently. This seems, however, to be entirely confined to requests in service encounters, and may represent some kind of idiomatic loan from North American English.

Similarly, North Americans can say:

(17) Should we eat lunch?

which again is ungrammatical or at least unusual in British English, where one would have to say:

(18) Shall we have lunch?

North Americans may *smoke a cigarette* whereas in British English one would more normally say *have a cigarette*; and North Americans may *drink coffee* while British speakers tend to *have coffee*.

Of course there are many locutions where the two major types of English agree in their usage of *have* and *take*. But the conclusion I draw from the differences that do exist is that in North American English, *take, get, eat*, etc. are used instead of *have* because *have* in North American English *is not sufficiently dynamic*.

North American *have* obviously does have a certain degree of dynamism, because Americans can in fact *have lunch*, and they can certainly *have coffee* as well as *drink coffee* with breakfast. But I hypothesise that its degree of dynamism is not as high as in British English and that the necessarily more dynamic verbs such as *get* and *take* are therefore preferred in many contexts.

Chronology

If my hypothesis is correct, then why is this so?

One obvious and important historical linguistic question we have to try to answer here is the following. The verb *to have* was originally a stative verb which in Old English indicated possession only. However, it later gradually acquired dynamic meanings in certain contexts through a process of semantic expansion, possibly including metonymic processes of the type POSSESS > COME TO POSSESS > RECEIVE > TAKE > EAT, etc.

Is it therefore the case that North American English *have* never acquired the same degree of dynamism as British English? At a first examination this seems unlikely: by Middle English the process of acquisition of dynamism by *have* was already under way. It is true that Matsumoto (1999: 70) shows that, in Middle English, constructions with *have* tend to be stative, e.g. *haven breth* 'be alive', whereas constructions with *take* tend to be dynamic, e.g. *taken breth* 'catch one's breath'. But the *Middle English Dictionary* shows locutions such as *to have craft* 'to practise a trade'; *to have daunce* 'to dance'; *to have langage (speche)* 'to speak, talk'; *to have wordes* 'to speak words'. The Early Modern English section (1500–1700) of the Helsinki Corpus also contains enough examples of dynamic *have* of the modern type for us to be certain that when English first arrived in North America such meanings were already available. Examples include:

(19) The child must have wine and sugar.
      We shall have a good gammon of bacon.
      He would have their blood.
      to have a little sack posset
      to have punishment
      You have had a quart of ale.
      we had communication with

And it is also obviously true, as we have already noted, that *have* in modern North American English may be dynamic. Dynamic *have* therefore quite clearly left the British Isles and crossed the Atlantic to North America.

However, it is still perfectly possible that North American English *have*, although it did have some dynamism, never acquired *sufficient* dynamism for it to be totally suitable for use in the type of restricted collocation we discussed above. The hypothesis is, therefore, that all varieties of English formerly employed locutions such as *to take a bath*, but that these have gradually been lost in British English because of an increase in the dynamism of *have*, which permitted it to replace *take* etc.; and that this never happened in North American English.

In order to demonstrate that this is in fact the case, it is necessary to show that British English used to employ *take* etc. in these collocations, but, subsequent to the departure of English for North America, gradually abandoned them in favour of *have*.

Some of the evidence we need on this point is supplied in the case of *take* by the *Middle English Dictionary*. This gives the following collocations:

(20) *to take bath*   'to take a bath'
     to take ese   'to take (one's) rest, rest oneself'
     to take nap   'to take a nap'
     to take reste (restinge) 'take (one's) rest, go to bed'
     to take slep (slepinge) 'to sleep, fall asleep'

In addition, Claridge's empirical study of Early Modern English (2000: 122) shows that the most frequent verbs in what she calls 'verbo-nominal constructions' in the Lampeter Corpus (1640–1740) data are *make* (530 tokens), *take* (491 tokens), *give* (336 tokens) and *have* (143 tokens). So at that point in time *take* was more frequent than *have* in a variety of verbo-nominal collocations.

Further evidence comes from the *Oxford English Dictionary*, which lists British English locutions with *take* occurring as late as the eighteenth century (2nd edn. 1989, *take*, v., VIII, 52):

(21) **1766,** Goldsm. *Vic.- W.* xxviii: "My wife, my daughter and herself were taking a walk together."

Forms with *have* in British English are indeed more recent: the OED cites the following (2nd ed. 1989, *have*, v. I, 11.b):

(22) **1868,** W. Collins, *Moonst.* iii: "I went and had a look at the bedroom."
     1891, Mrs. Walford, *Pinch of Exper.* 268: "Rhoda went, had an enchanting walk."

Hiltunen, moreover, writes of *have* that it is "noteworthy that collocations of the most concrete kind, which are so often given as the most typical examples of a verbal phrase, e.g. *to have a look/bath/drink/shave/walk* and the like, are almost completely absent" (1999: 148) in his Early Modern English material.

The Chadwyck-Healey English Drama databases confirm Hiltunen's findings: eventive collocations with *have* are not common before the nineteenth century in British English, as can be seen in Table 3. The figures also reveal a general increase in the use of forms with *have* after 1800 and a corresponding decrease in forms with *take*.

The collocations were searched for in the database in sequences where the verb (in any person or tense) was immediately followed by the noun. The figures are based, first, on the online Chadwyck-Healey English Drama database, which consists of 4,000 plays by 1,200 authors from the late thirteenth to the early twentieth century. All the plays that were first performed between 1500 and 1800 were searched for the pre-1800 figures and those first performed between 1800 and 1915 for the post-1800 figures. Secondly, pre-1800 fiction data come from two Chadwyck-Healey electronic databases: Early English Prose Fiction, drawing on over 200 complete works in fictional prose from the period 1500–1700; and Eighteenth-Century Fiction, comprising ninety-six complete works in English prose from the period 1700–80 by writers from the British Isles, including Sterne's *Tristram Shandy*, Richardson's *Clarissa* and *Pamela*, and of Swift's *Gulliver's Travels*. Thirdly, post-1800 fiction figures were retrieved from the Chadwyck-Healey Nineteenth-Century Fiction database, which consists of 250 novels from the period 1782–1903, including works by all the major Victorian novelists such as Dickens, Thackeray, the Brontës, Eliot and Hardy.

The second clue, then, is that North American English represents an earlier stage of development as far as these idioms are concerned, as compared to British English. That is, *have*-avoidance in these restricted collocations in North America is the result of the fact that North American English *have* never acquired as much dynamism as British English *have*, and therefore never replaced *take*, as it was able to do in Britain.

This places the phenomenon clearly in mechanism category 2, as outlined at the beginning of this chapter: the difference between

Table 3. Have *and* take *in the Chadwyck-Healey databases*

	pre-1800			post-1800		
	take	*have*	% **have**	*take*	*have*	% **have**
a walk	182	2	1	184	28	13
a nap	107	3	3	27	5	16
a ride	11	0	0	25	12	32
a bite	2	0	0	9	8	47
a drink	9	1	10	20	18	47
(a) rest	45	55	53	30	28	48
a glance	0	1	100	6	9	60
a look	7	8	53	47	151	76
a bath	1	4	80	2	11	85
a fall	11	46	81	0	46	100
a tour	8	0	0	0	1	100
a guess	0	2	100	0	10	100
a swig	0	0	0	0	1	100
Total:	383	122	24	350	328	48

British and American English can be explained by saying that since the departure of English for America, a linguistic change has occurred in Britain which has not occurred in North America.

LANGUAGE CONTACT

This still leaves us, however, with a major puzzle: how can we explain this North American conservatism?

It seems that the full range of dynamic meanings that we now see available in British English became fully developed only after the departure of English for North America, where these meanings never developed to the same extent. But why would that have been? I hypothesise that this lag (see further Chapter 6) or halt in the ongoing and centuries-long development in the English language, once it arrived in North America, was the result of large-scale contact between North American English and continental European languages, something which did not occur in the British Isles or in the other major anglophone areas of the world – which is why, as noted above, North American English is the odd variety out.

The suggestion is that the lack of a further development in dynamism in North American English *have* has resulted from the inhibiting influence of other European languages concerning the meanings of *have*; and that this influence was exerted in the multilingual melting pot that came with massive and mainly nineteenth-century European immigration, especially to the USA. That is, the influence of languages other than English blocked the development of the dynamic meanings which was occurring at this time in British English, as illustrated in these restricted collocations.

How this could have happened can be seen by examining verbs for *to have* in a range of European languages. Verbs in many European languages which correspond to English *have*, such as French *avoir*, German *haben*, Dutch *hebben*, Scandinavian *ha*, clearly have less dynamism than their English counterpart. In very many European languages we can therefore find, as in North American English, expressions rendering English dynamic *have* in locutions such as those cited above which employ verbs that are translations of the more obviously dynamic verb *take*: Spanish *tomar el té* 'to take tea'; Italian *prendere un caffé* 'to take coffee'; French *prendre le petit déjeuner* 'to take breakfast'; Polish *wziac kapiel/prysznic* 'take a bath/shower'.

European languages may also use constructions with other more obviously dynamic verbs translating English *make/do*: Greek *kano mia volta* 'to make a walk'; Italian *far colazione* 'to do breakfast'. Or they may, again as in North American English, in service encounters use a verb corresponding to *get*: Norwegian *få et smørbrød* and Polish *dostac bulke* 'to get a sandwich'. Alternatively, as in North American English, European languages may use a more specific dynamic verb semantically connected to the noun object: Spanish *fumar un pitillo* and Greek *kapnizo ena tsigharo* 'to smoke a cigarette'; French *manger un sandwich* 'to eat a sandwich'; Greek *troo proino* 'to eat breakfast'; Polish *jesc obiad* 'to eat dinner' and *pic herbate* 'to drink tea'. They may also use a specific dynamic verb without an object rather than a dynamic verb plus eventive noun: Spanish *comer*, Italian *cenare* and French *dîner* 'to dine'; German *frühstücken* 'to breakfast'. Verbs of this type may also occur in passive form: Greek *ksekourazomai* 'I am rested = I have a rest'; or in a reflexive form: Polish *wykapac sie* 'to bathe oneself'.

These facts therefore also place this phenomenon in mechanism category 5, as outlined at the beginning of this chapter: the difference between British and American English can be explained by saying that North American English has experienced forms of language contact with other European languages in the colonial situation which have not been experienced by British English.

CONNECTIONS

What we have found, then, is that while Scottish and Irish English, and to a lesser extent English English, are conservative as compared to North American English in their use of *do*-support with *have*, they are on the other hand more innovative than North American English in their use of dynamic *have* in restricted collocations.

Is this just a coincidence, or is there any connection between these two phenomena? Can we relate the loss of the distinction in grammatical behaviour between dynamic and stative *have* in North American English to the apparent lack of development of dynamism in the meaning of main verb *have* generally, as illustrated in the use of other dynamic verbs in these restricted collocations?

At first sight, this would appear to be a problematical conjecture. After all, if dynamic *have* is actually not very dynamic in North American English, then one might expect it to behave more like stative *have* in English English. This is, in fact, not what happens. On the contrary, it is stative *have* in North American English which behaves like dynamic *have* in English English:

(23) Do you have (any) coffee in the cupboard?

My interpretation of this is as follows. It is quite simply the case that since dynamic *have* is not very dynamic in North American English, and there is therefore not so much difference in meaning between dynamic and stative *have*, then both forms could more readily, and thus more speedily in terms of chronological development, be handled in the same way grammatically. Basically, since dynamic *have* is not very dynamic, one can afford to treat stative *have* as if it were dynamic also. Because *have* in North American English is lacking in dynamism, it is possible to say *Do they have coffee in the cupboard?* without addressees imagining coffee-drinking taking place in extraordinary places.

It is also possible that language contact might have played a role here too. It is well known that in contact situations speakers often overgeneralise rules and apply analogical extensions. After *have* had split into two items, the main verb and the auxiliary, the difference between the two was – syntactically – that the main verb could occur alone as the only verb in a clause while the auxiliary could not. The dynamic versus stative meaning difference, when it arose, was a less recognisable difference since in both cases *have* was the only verb that could determine the type of constituents that were needed in the clause. That meant, for a non-native learner of English, that while the syntactic distinction is obvious (i.e. if *have* is the only verb in the clause, it is analysed as the main verb and needs *do*-support; if it modifies another verb in the sentences, it is itself the auxiliary and the other verb is the main verb, which does not need *do*-support), the semantic distinction (dynamic/stative) is less recognisable and more difficult to grasp. American English is much more regular in this respect and thus easier for learners to master.

We can hypothesise therefore that the regularisation process was a simplification which was hastened in American English by the presence of large numbers of non-native speakers in the population. This is once again therefore a case of mechanism category 5 – an example of language contact leading, as it is well known to do, to simplification of the type that occurs in its most extreme form in the development of pidgin languages, as we have seen in earlier chapters.

But why exactly has the merger of grammatical behaviours been in this direction? Why has stative *have* become like dynamic *have* and not vice versa? The answer to this question would appear to be that this is part of the broader chronological trend outlined above for English verbs to acquire rather than to lose the characteristic of requiring *do*-support. This long-term development involving *have* can be seen as part of a wider development in which the number of verbs in English which behave like auxiliaries has for a considerable time been undergoing reduction. This development has actually involved a complex series of changes (see Ellegård 1953; Hudson 1997; Ogura 1994), but the legitimacy of this interpretation of events is especially clear in contemporary English in the case of the semi-modals such as *need*, *dare* and *ought to*, which are currently moving or have moved from auxiliary-type to full-verb-type behaviour:

> (24)   I used not to go. > I didn't use to go.
>
> You needn't go. > You don't need to go.

CONCLUSION

Two conflicting trends have been at work in English over the last six hundred years or so. One has been, as just mentioned, for fewer verbs to behave like auxiliaries. The second has been, as we saw above, for the increasing acquisition of dynamic meanings by the verb *to have*. Different varieties of English are at different stages of development with respect to these two interacting trends.

In its treatment of dynamic *have*, North American English is both more innovative and more conservative in comparison with other varieties of English around the world. The innovative behaviour of North American English, as demonstrated in the greater rapidity of its adoption of *do*-support with *have*, is paradoxically due to its conservatism in its failure to gain as much dynamism in the meanings of this verb as British and other varieties of the language. This failure, as illustrated in the usage of verbs other than *have* in restricted collocations in North American English, is likely to be the result of large-scale contact with languages other than English, such as French, German and Yiddish – something which is absent from the histories of British Isles and Southern Hemisphere varieties of English – which brought the ongoing development of a wider range of dynamic meanings of *have* to a halt. It was, then, this failure to gain dynamism, perhaps coupled with the simplification which often accompanies language contact, which brought about or – more likely in view of the long-term chronological trend outlined above – accelerated the change in question. This was the change in which dynamic *have* lost its distinctive grammatical behaviour as a result of stative *have* coming to acquire the same grammatical characteristics.

The answer to the question we posed at the beginning of this chapter is thus a complex one: the two differences we have been discussing are the result of linguistic changes which have occurred in North America but not in Britain; changes which have occurred in Britain but not in North America; *and* contact between North American English and other European languages. This contact is not manifested directly as it is in the case of loanwords or obvious calques, but can be deduced to have resulted in two consequences which can be observed only indirectly: the suppression of a change in progress which has continued in other varieties of the language around the world, as a result of syntactic and semantic transfer in which a kind of negative calquing has led to the maintenance of the grammatical status quo; and a process of regularisation of a type which is also typical of the kind of simplification which occurs in language-contact situations.

6 Colonial lag?

In Chapter 5 we saw that in some respects North American English is more conservative than the English of England; and I ventured to employ the word *lag* in that context. I now go on to explore this term in more detail. Once again in this chapter we will be concentrating on the 1800s, but – reflecting the geographical spread of the English language itself during that period – we now begin to pay attention to the Englishes of the Southern Hemisphere as well.

The particular version of the term 'lag' I intend to discuss here was first introduced into the linguistics literature by the American linguist Albert H. Marckwardt. He wrote, in connection with the history of English in the United States:

> These post-colonial survivals of earlier phases of mother country culture, taken in conjunction with the retention of earlier linguistic features, have made what I should like to call a colonial lag. I mean to suggest by this term nothing more than that in a transplanted civilisation, such as ours undeniably is, certain features which it possesses remain static over a period of time. Transplanting usually results in a time lag before the organism, be it a geranium or a brook trout, becomes adapted to its new environment. There is no reason why the same principle should not apply to a people, their language, and their culture.
>
> (Marckwardt 1958: 80)

The term 'colonial lag' has acquired some considerable currency in the literature, and has been much discussed in works on the history of English (see Görlach 1987; Hickey 2003; Dollinger 2008). The legitimacy of the term has also been disputed with some vigour, as the subtitle of Görlach's paper shows: "The *alleged* conservative character of American English and other 'colonial' varieties" [my italics].

In this chapter, however, I actually support the validity of Marckwardt's notion, to an extent; and I assert that there is at least one sense in which 'colonial lag' is actually a demonstrable linguistic reality. I also strengthen this assertion by producing an explanation for why colonial lag occurs – although this has nothing to do with the "adaptation to a new environment" factor proposed by Marckwardt. And I give actual linguistic examples of the colonial lag phenomenon, focussing on New Zealand and Australia.

The English of New Zealand is the most recently formed major variety of natively spoken English in the world, with only the English of the Falkland Islands postdating it as a colonial native variety of English. The English language, obviously, arrived in New Zealand from the British Isles, and the crucial formation period for the variety was almost certainly between 1840 and 1860 (Trudgill 2004). I argue here that colonial lag in New Zealand and elsewhere occurred because of an unusual set of circumstances which are typical of colonial new-dialect-formation situations. And, because of a unique data set to which I have been fortunate enough to have had access, I am able to demonstrate in this case how these circumstances combined to produce the lag effect. The data set enables us to account for the occurrence of colonial lag, and to provide illustrations of the phenomenon as it applies to New Zealand relative to British English. By implication, we can suppose that the same kind of process occurred in other similar situations, such as in the formation of American English or Canadian French.

The data which are discussed in this chapter are derived from the Origins of New Zealand English (ONZE) project led by Professor Elizabeth Gordon and carried out from Canterbury University, Christchurch (Gordon *et al.* 2004; Trudgill 2004; Trudgill *et al.* 2000). The ONZE research project was based on analyses of recordings collected by the National Broadcasting Corporation of New Zealand between 1946 and 1948. These were made by the Corporation's

Mobile Disc Recording Unit, which travelled around towns in both the North Island and South Island of New Zealand recording oral history for broadcasting purposes. The recordings were of pioneer reminiscences, many obtained from people who were children of the first European settlers in New Zealand. The first ONZE project analyses that I carried out were of the speech of the oldest people recorded, ninety-five speakers who were born between 1850 and 1889, the first generation of New Zealand-born anglophones.

Consider the following data in the light of information from this project.

(A) THE PRONUNCIATION OF /r/

In modern Britain, five different phonetic realisations of /r/ are extant:

(1)   the sharply recessive voiced uvular fricative [ʁ] which is confined to the northeast of England and some areas of Scotland (see the discussion of Mrs McFarlane in Chapter 8; and Wells 1982: 368; Glauser 1994);

(2)   the alveolar flap [ɾ] which is usually associated today with Scotland and parts of the north of England;

(3)   the retroflex approximant [ɻ] which is most typical of south-western England (Wells 1982: 342);

(4)   the postalveolar approximant [ɹ] most usually associated with RP and much of south and central England;

(5)   the labiodental approximant [ʋ] which is currently gaining ground very rapidly amongst younger speakers in England (see Trudgill 1988).

There is no doubt at all that number (5), the labiodental approximant, is a new pronunciation. Of the other three widespread variants, we can assume on phonetic grounds that the flap is the oldest and the postalveolar approximant the newest, with the retroflex variant being chronologically intermediate. We can suppose that even earlier forms of English may have had a roll or trill. Bailey (1996: 99) indicates that "weakening of r from a trilled consonant was first reported in Britain at the end of the sixteenth century" (see also Wells 1982: 370). This gives us a history of lenition in the realisation of /r/ as follows:

$$[r > ɾ > ɻ > ɹ > ʋ]$$

That is, the relative chronology is clear. What is less certain is the absolute chronology. When, for example, did the variant [ɹ] become the most usual and widespread variant?

Here the ONZE recordings are of considerable interest. The normal pronunciation of /r/ in New Zealand and Australia today is also, as in most of England, [ɹ], although on average rather more retroflexed, i.e. more conservative, than in England (Trudgill 2004). However, analysis of the ONZE tapes shows that the pronunciation of /r/ as a flapped [ɾ] is extremely common on these recordings. This, moreover, is not simply true of speakers who have some kind of north of England or Scottish connection. In fact, it is employed, most often variably, by 57 per cent of the informants investigated.

There is thus a strong suggestion that the weakening of the flap to an approximant in the Midlands and south of England is a very recent phenomenon dating from approximately the middle of the nineteenth century, and rather later in New Zealand.

(B) THE LEXICAL SET OF BATH

It is well known that accents of English treat lexical items such as *dance, laugh, path, plant* in two different ways. Accents in the north of England and North America have /æ/ in such words, while RP and accents in the south of England have /a:/. This is sometimes explained by historians of the English language as having resulted from a lengthening of /æ/ (presumably [a]) and later phonologisation to /a:/ in the environment before the front voiceless fricatives /f, θ, s/, as in *laugh, path, grass*; and before certain clusters of nasals followed by obstruents, as in *sample, demand, plant, dance, branch*. It is, of course, recognised that the development must have been more complicated than that: for one thing, there are many exceptions, such as *ample, grand, ant, romance*.

One interesting problem here is that many Australians, as well as speakers with certain Welsh accents (see Trudgill and Hannah 2008; Hughes and Trudgill 1995), are in a kind of intermediate position between English southerners, on the one hand, and Americans and English northerners, on the other: they have /æ/ in words such as *sample* which involve a nasal but /aː/ in words with voiceless fricatives such as *laugh*. Other Australians, however, have the south of England system, which is also, crucially, true of modern New Zealanders. Wells (1982: 233) points out that Leeward Islanders in the Caribbean also have the split system, while other West Indians do not. Wells speculates that the split system that we find in Wales, Australia and the Leeward Islands – all, in a sense, colonial varieties – but not elsewhere, "may well be because in eighteenth-century south-east England these *dance*-type words were still fluctuating between a short and long vowel; or indeed they may still generally have had a short vowel, and have gone over to the long vowel only later".

In my view, it is the latter hypothesis which is correct. I would want to argue that we are dealing here with two separate sound changes. The evidence from the ONZE recordings is again very strong. We obviously have to exclude from our observations speakers who do not have a distinction between the TRAP and START/PALM vowels, /æ/ and /aː/, e.g. they rhyme *lager* and *dagger* – presumably as a result of English West Country and/or Scottish input – as well as those with obvious north of England accents who have /æ/ throughout. Once we have done that, we can observe that very many ONZE speakers consistently have the split system: they have /aː/ in the lexical set of *after, grass, path* but /æ/ in the set of *dance, plant, sample*. In all, 48 per cent have this pattern. This strongly suggests that the change from /æ/ to /aː/ in the south of England (and in RP) was in fact two separate changes: the first involved pre-voiceless fricative environments which, however, as is widely agreed, must postdate the settlement of North America; this took place a good deal earlier than the second change, which involved combinations of nasals and obstruents and which cannot on this evidence have become general in England until the second half of the nineteenth century.

(c) THE CLOTH VOWEL

Paralleling the lengthening of /a/ before the front voiceless fricatives /f, θ, s/ in the set of BATH (see above), there was also a change of short o to /ɔ:/ in the same environments, also in the south rather than the north of England. Wells (1982: 203) refers to both these changes as *pre-fricative lengthening*, and dates the beginnings of the lengthening to the end of the seventeenth century. Intriguingly, the change to /ɔ:/, unlike the change to /a:/, is currently reversing, so that in England it is now mostly conservative RP speakers and speakers of low-status regional accents who retain this feature, other accents having gone back to /ɒ/ in this set. The *Survey of English Dialects* (SED), however, using data collected in the 1950s and 1960s, shows the whole of the south of England as having /ɔ:/. It is therefore interesting to note the extent to which this pronunciation is the norm among the ONZE speakers. We have to exclude from this computation those speakers who have the Scottish merger of the vowels of LOT and THOUGHT (see Chapter 8), as also occurs in many forms of North American English. Of the remainder, 70 per cent pronounce the lexical set of *off, froth, cross* with /ɔ:/ rather than /ɒ/, indicating that in the nineteenth century it was not only speakers of Traditional Dialects who had this feature in southern England. Interestingly, moreover, we can note that /ɔ:/ is still today a good deal more common in New Zealand (and Australia) than it is in England.

(d) T GLOTTALLING

Wells (1982: 261) writes that the realisation of syllable-final /t/ as [ʔ] in Britain "must have spread very fast in the course of the present century" and indeed there is plenty of evidence that this is exactly right. According to Bailey (1996: 76), observers have been commentating on the phenomenon only since 1860, and early references were almost exclusively to Scotland and to London. The SED records show hardly any instances of T Glottalling, as Wells calls it, except in the London area and East Anglia. And there is convincing evidence that it reached western areas such as Cardiff (see Mees 1977) and Liverpool only very recently. In many studies (see for example Trudgill 1988) it has been shown that younger speakers demonstrate more T Glottalling than older speakers. It is hardly surprising, therefore, that there is hardly any glottalling in the speech of our elderly New Zealanders, a confirmation, if one were needed, of the relatively recent development of this phenomenon in England.

(E) PRE-GLOTTALISATION

However, the following is also of considerable interest. When I first started listening to the ONZE tapes, I noticed that there was something about even those speakers who sounded very English that was strange – something which gave their speech a distinctly un-British and/or old-fashioned ring to it, to my ears. I eventually realised what it was: the ONZE speakers also show very little evidence indeed of pre-glottalisation (Wells 1982: 260). That is, they do not employ a glottal stop before /p, t, k, tʃ/ in items such as *hopeless* [hoʊʔplɪs], *match* [mæʔtʃ]. Pre-glottalisation of this type is today very usual indeed in very many – perhaps most – English English accents, including RP. As Wells points out, however, it is something which has attracted very little comment from either amateur or professional observers in Britain (although it may be one of the things which leads Americans to describe British accents as "clipped"). We therefore have no good information which might lead us to any satisfactory indication of its dating. Our New Zealand evidence, however, suggests that pre-glottalisation in Britain, too, is a recent and probably late nineteenth-century phenomenon. New Zealand English, moreover, still lacks pre-glottalisation.

COLONIAL LAG

New Zealand English, then, as spoken by elderly people in the 1940s offers many helpful insights into what English English was like in the mid-nineteenth century. As a result of the predominantly upper-working-class and middle-class background of the migrants, moreover, we have access, through New Zealand English, to information on the forms of English English about which we otherwise know least – the majority but neglected speech forms of those mid-nineteenth-century British people who were not speakers of Standard English or of Traditional Dialects. The fact that these elderly, ordinary speakers were actually recorded en masse at a time when recording techniques were rudimentary, and oral history in its infancy, was an extraordinary stroke of good fortune.

Importantly for this chapter, however, even today New Zealand and Australian English still lag behind English English with respect to the features discussed:

(a) New Zealand and Australian /r/ is still more retroflexed than English English /r/, i.e. these two forms of English are behind in terms of the chronological progression outline above.

(b) Australian *dance* typically has still conservative /æ/ rather than /aː/.

(c) New Zealand and Australian CLOTH words are more likely to have originally innovative but now conservative /ɔː/ than English English.

(d) New Zealand and Australian English lack innovative T Glottalling, or at least have only recently acquired it (Holmes 1997).

(e) New Zealand and Australian English lack innovative pre-glottalisation.

Of course, it is not my intention to suggest that the Southern Hemisphere Englishes are, overall, conservative as such. Naturally, innovations have occurred in these varieties which have not occurred in Britain. Twentieth-century endogenous changes in New Zealand English include:

- the centralisation of the KIT vowel (Trudgill *et al.* 1998; Bell 1997);
- the merger, as a consequence of this, of the KIT vowel with schwa (Wells 1982);
- the ongoing raising of the DRESS and TRAP vowels to articulations closer than [e] and [ɛ] respectively, a change which is linked to the movements involving KIT and probably STRUT in a chain shift;
- the merger of the vowels of the NEAR and SQUARE sets (Maclagan and Gordon 1996: 131).

The claim I am actually making here is rather that the Southern Hemisphere Englishes are conservative with respect to the five features (a)–(e), which were eighteenth- and nineteenth-century innovations that began in England. And the question I'm attempting to answer is why this is – why is colonial lag in this sense a reality?

We can begin this answer by noting that the conventional sociolinguistic wisdom is that young children speak like their peers rather than, for example, like their parents or teachers (see Trudgill 1986: 220). This conventional wisdom is necessarily correct – otherwise, regionally distinct dialects would never have survived in the face of the increased geographical mobility of modern societies. In any case, the evidence for the thesis is overwhelming: in the context of families moving from one dialect area to another, the phenomenon of total childhood accommodation is the object of so much and such widespread observation and comment on the part of non-linguists that it does not really need scientific confirmation. American parents moving to London, England, know very well that before too long their younger children, at least, will sound like Londoners. No one expresses any surprise, though they may express regret, if a Welsh-accented family moving to East Anglia quite quickly comes to consist of adults who still sound Welsh and young children who sound as if they have lived in Suffolk all their lives.

It is true that occasional individuals may be found of whom this is not true, but these are usually socially maladjusted, non-integrated people whose lack of linguistic accommodation to their peers is a sign of social pathology (see Newbrook 1982). Payne (1980) has also suggested that after a certain age children may not master perfectly all the intricate details of phonological conditioning in a new variety they are exposed to, although the children she studied were in an area with an unusually large number of incomers. Chambers (1992), too, has shown that older children do not necessarily accommodate so completely or so successfully as younger children. And Kazazis (1970) has warned that the degree of accommodation normally demonstrated by children in the anglophone world may be at least partly culture specific rather than a universal. There are also a number of situations where children may become bidialectal in a peer-group dialect *and* a family dialect (see Trudgill 1986: 32). But the general trend, at least in most European-style communities, is very clear: up to a certain age, normal children accommodate rapidly and totally, or almost totally, to the speech of any new peer group of which they become long-term members.

The relevance for the puzzle we are trying to solve here, however, is that there are certain situations where this total accommodation to the peer group does not actually occur. Berthele (2000), for example, has investigated the Swiss-German speech of a group of children at a private school in Fribourg, Switzerland, in which, for religious and historical reasons, there has been a tradition of speaking Bernese German rather than the local Fribourg German, and where children come from a very wide range of non-local linguistic backgrounds, arriving at the school speaking many different varieties of German or no German at all. Here, it emerges from Berthele's pioneering study that individual children adopt individual strategies whose eventual linguistic outcome is determined in part by their integration into the social structure of the class.

Now, typically, as already mentioned, children acquire the dialect and accent of their peers. However, in early anglophone New Zealand, just as in the Fribourg school mentioned above, there was no single, established peer-dialect for children to acquire. This, of course, is typical of all situations involving the kind of dialect contact, dialect mixture, koinéisation and new-dialect formation (see Trudgill 1986) that occurs in colonial and other similar situations, such as the development of new towns (see Kerswill 1994). It would also therefore presumably have been a feature, as I indicated above, of many early anglophone North American settlements which gave rise to the colonial lag phenomenon referred to by Marckwardt.

In the New Zealand data, it can be seen that this situation can lead to two different scenarios. First, in some of the New Zealand cases I analysed, it is clear that certain elderly speakers, as children 120 to 160 years ago, acquired, unusually, something very close indeed to the English, Scottish or Irish English dialects of their parents, for the very good reason that there was nothing else for them to acquire. These are people who were raised in very isolated rural communities. One of our informants, for example, grew up in a community which consisted entirely of herself, her many siblings, and her mother and father, and which was forty miles by rowing boat from the next settlement. Thus, some such people who never set foot in Scotland sound totally Scottish because their parents were Scottish. In another case, an informant whose parents were from Kent sounds utterly Irish, apparently because he was brought up by an Irish washerwoman. The speech of these isolated people is therefore to a considerable extent fossilised in the sense that it represents forms of speech typical of a generation older than would normally be the case.

Secondly and more frequently, in other cases the lack of a single peer-group model led, as in Fribourg, to fascinating and varied individual dialect-mixture processes (see Trudgill 1998). This is, it seems, what happens in the case of people brought up in mixed, non-isolated communities where dialect contact took place early on. It emerges that the mixed speech of these non-isolated speakers is also interesting in precisely the same way as that of the isolated speakers because, even though they do employ innovative combinations, these turn out to be combinations of *conservative* features. Their speech features, then, when looked at individually, are equally fossilised. It is also noteworthy that in the case of these speakers, there seems to be generally no very great connection between their speech and that of their parents.

My suggestion is, then, that we therefore have recordings available to us which give important insights into the way in which vernacular English was spoken in the British Isles by people born a generation earlier. The colonial situation, that is, enables us to push back the time depth available to us for historical linguistic studies in the sense that we are able to investigate speech which is, as it were, one generation earlier than would be the case with British-born speakers, and for which we do not have large-scale sound-recorded evidence.

For example, if we ask how the ONZE core-speakers acquired the now archaic flap pronunciation of /r/, the answer is clear: English was brought to New Zealand by their parents' generation, and so these New Zealand-born informants can have acquired it only from the speech of people of that generation – and that generation, of course, consisted of speakers who were born in the British Isles in the period from approximately 1820 onwards. The fact is that speakers born in New Zealand in 1850 used forms typical of their parents' speech, and that in listening to people born in 1850 it is therefore *as if* we were actually listening to recordings of people born in the 1820s – something which normally we are not able to do. For instance, early on in the project, members of the ONZE team argued, on the basis of these recordings and on the supposition of colonial lag in the sense in which I am using the term here, that the English short front vowels /ɪ, ɛ, æ/ of the lexical sets of KIT, DRESS, TRAP, which are often phonetically very close in the ONZE recordings, were probably much closer in nineteenth-century English English than they are today (see Trudgill *et al.* 1998).

So in such colonial settings, total accommodation by children to the speech of their peer group did not happen because it could not. The children of early colonial Australia and New Zealand, and we must assume the United States and Canada and other colonies, were unable to accommodate to a peer-group dialect because there was no common peer-group dialect for them to accommodate to. Rather, they typically, with the exception of the isolated speakers we just mentioned, developed mixtures of features derived from those present in the speech of members of their parents' generation.

'Colonial lag', as this term was first used by Marckwardt, is then a linguistic reality which can indeed be explained in terms of the transplantation of colonial societies. 'Lag' in this linguistic sense has nothing to do with adaptation to a new environment. It is simply a delay in the normal progression and development of linguistic change which lasts for about one generation, and which arises solely as an automatic consequence of the fact that there is no common peer-group dialect for children to acquire in first-generation colonial situations involving dialect mixture, and where therefore the speech of the older generation provides the model. Colonial lag must therefore, I would submit, have been a feature of those early varieties of North American English discussed by Marckwardt which developed in dialect-contact environments, as well as all or most other colonial dialects of whatever language.

7   "The new non-rhotic style"

The final two chapters of this book continue with a focus on Southern Hemisphere Englishes, specifically those of Australia and New Zealand.

Varieties of English, as is well known, fall into two categories with respect to the phonotactics of /r/. Some varieties are 'non-rhotic', i.e. they lack non-prevocalic /r/ and, while they have /r/ in words such as *rack*, *track*, *carry*, they lack /r/ in words such as *cart* or *car* (except where the latter is followed by a vowel). Other varieties are 'rhotic', i.e. they permit the occurrence of /r/ before a consonant or pause in words such as *cart* or *car*. Notice the use of the term 'permit' here: while there is an absolute prohibition in non-rhotic accents on the occurrence of /r/ preconsonantally and pre-pausally, it is not necessarily the case that historical non-prevocalic /r/ will actually occur 100 per cent of the time in rhotic accents, as there are many such accents where rhoticity is variable.

This division between rhotic and non-rhotic accents is a fundamentally important distinction between two radically different types of English segmental phonology. This involves not only word phonotactics but also:

- the structure of vowel systems, with non-rhotic accents having a set of vowels not found in rhotic accents – such as the vowel of the lexical set of SQUARE;
- the sandhi phenomena 'linking' and 'intrusive' /r/ (see below);
- dialect-contact phenomena such as analogical /r/, phonotactic /r/, hyperadaptive /r/ and hyperdialectal /r/ (Trudgill 1986: 72–8).

As far as these two categories of accent are concerned, Irish English and Scottish English are well known to be rhotic. North American English is generally thought of as being rhotic also, although there are a number of US varieties which are or have historically been non-rhotic: eastern New England, New York City and the southeast, as we saw in Chapter 4, plus African American Vernacular English, together with AAVE-speaking diaspora communities, e.g. in Nova Scotia, the Dominican Republic and Liberia (Poplack 2000; Poplack and Tagliamonte 1989; Singler 1997). There are also a small number of Canadian enclave varieties which are or were non-rhotic: Lunenburg county, Nova Scotia (Emeneau 1975); southern and western New Brunswick (Bailey 1982: 143, citing Kurath *et al.* 1939–43), including Grand Manan Island off the coast of Maine (Murray 1996); and Bay Roberts in Newfoundland (Wells 1982: 500; Kirwin 2001: 447), together with a number of other Newfoundland enclaves (Chambers 1991: 102).

English and Welsh English are most often thought of as being non-rhotic, although there are actually a number of areas in England and some in Wales which are not: southwestern England generally; adjacent areas of eastern Wales; southern Pembrokeshire in southwest Wales; and northern Lancashire. The Southern Hemisphere English varieties of Australia, New Zealand, South Africa, the Falkland Islands and Tristan da Cunha are also non-rhotic, with the exception of the Southland region of New Zealand. In the Caribbean, some varieties are rhotic and some not (Wells 1982). Many second-language varieties of English, such as West African, East African, Southern African, South Asian, Malaysian and Singaporean English, are also non-rhotic, while Philippines English is rhotic (Trudgill and Hannah 2008).

SOUTHERN HEMISPHERE NON-RHOTICITY

This division of the world's Englishes into rhotic and non-rhotic types is clearly due to the fact that the former are conservative in not having undergone rhoticity-loss, whereas the latter have. Rhoticity-loss was the outcome of a phonological change where /r/ disappeared before a following consonant or pause: /r/ remained in *rat, trap, carry* but was now absent from *cart, car,* although /r/ did remain in *car* where it was followed immediately by another word beginning with a vowel, as in *car engine.* Accents with variable rhoticity most often represent cases where the loss of rhoticity is partial and still ongoing, i.e. increasing diachronically, as in Southland, New Zealand (Bartlett 2003), and in England, where rhoticity is generally recessive. In the USA, on the other hand, variability can be the result of the re-introduction of rhoticity into formerly non-rhotic areas, as in New York City (Labov 1966).

The alternation in *car*-type words between forms with and without /r/, depending on whether there is a following vowel or not, was originally the outcome of the phonological change in which /r/ was retained only before a vowel, but has now become reinterpreted in most non-rhotic accents as being the result of a low-level and deeply automatic rule of /r/-insertion, so that non-rhotic speakers have an /r/ in *idea of* as well as in *car engine* (for further consequences, see Trudgill 1986: 71–8). The /r/ in *idea of* is often called 'intrusive /r/', and that in *car engine* 'linking /r/', even though synchronically they are one and the same phenomenon.

The beginnings of this loss of rhoticity, i.e. the loss of non-prevocalic /r/ in English, have generally been dated by historians of the language as having begun in southern England in the eighteenth century. Bailey (1996: 100) says of English English that "the shift from consonantal to vocalic *r*, though sporadic earlier, gathered force at the end of the eighteenth century"; and Strang (1970: 112) writes that "in post-vocalic position, finally or pre-consonantally, /r/ was weakened in articulation in the 17c and reduced to a vocalic segment early in the 18c".

It is therefore obvious, and has been widely accepted (e.g. Trudgill 1986), that Irish English, Canadian English and American English are rhotic because the English language was exported to these colonial areas from England before or during the seventeenth century, i.e. *before* the linguistic change of loss of rhoticity in England began; and that the Southern Hemisphere Englishes are non-rhotic because English was exported to these areas in the nineteenth century, i.e. *after* the loss of rhoticity.

This fact is so self-explanatory that no one has ever thought to question it. Wells (1982: 592 [my italics]) writes that:

> The Australian and New Zealand accents of English are very similar to one another. South African, although differing in a number of important respects, also has a general similarity to Australian. These facts are not surprising when we consider that all three territories were settled from Britain at about the same time, the English language becoming established in each around the beginning of the nineteenth century. *All reflect, therefore, the developments which had taken place in the south of England up to that time: they are non-rhotic . . .*

Bailey (1996: 105) also says that the loss of /r/ came *"just in time for the English of Australia, New Zealand, and South Africa to be drawn within the sphere of the change"* [my italics].

And Trask (1994: 26), in describing the distribution of rhotic and non-rhotic accents around the world, writes that at one time all speakers of English were rhotic, so "this type of pronunciation was carried to North America, which was settled in the seventeenth century". He then goes on to say: "in the eighteenth century, however, the new, non-rhotic style of pronunciation appeared in the southeast of England"; and "Australia, New Zealand and South Africa were largely settled in the nineteenth century by immigrants from England, who took with them the new non-rhotic style".

THE PROBLEM

In the 1990s, however, this widely accepted orthodoxy was shown not to be correct. The realisation that this was so came initially from the study of the history of New Zealand English; and more specifically from the Origins of New Zealand English (ONZE) project, as described in Chapter 6.

One of the most remarkable of the features which emerged from my analyses of the speech of the ONZE informants concerned rhoticity: a surprising 98 per cent of the ninety-five speakers whose speech I investigated were rhotic to a greater or lesser degree (Gordon *et al.* 2004), thereby demonstrating unequivocally that it most certainly cannot have been the case that non-rhoticity was exported to New Zealand from England. Other information then came to hand. Bauer (1997: 411–12) cites additional evidence for the presence of rhoticity throughout the South Island of New Zealand in the 1860s; and Branford (1994: 436) writes that there are also indications that nineteenth-century South African English was rhotic too: he discusses early borrowings from English into Xhosa, such as *tichela* 'teacher', where the /l/ corresponds to English /r/, indicating a word-final /r/ and thus a rhotic pronunciation in nineteenth-century South African English.

Subsequently, even more evidence came to light to confound the original orthodoxy – and this happened entirely by chance. Elizabeth Gordon and I were analysing recordings of Australians born during the late nineteenth century, for the purposes of comparing their speech with that of New Zealanders of the same age from our ONZE informants. Our data consisted of recordings of elderly Australians which were made in 1988 as part of the New South Wales bicentennial oral history project.[1] A preliminary step consisted of an examination of one hour of recorded speech for each of the twelve oldest speakers, six male and six female, who were born between 1889 and 1899.

It was once again a surprise to find that, of these speakers, the six men were *all rhotic* to varying degrees. (The six women, on the other hand, were all non-rhotic.) The details of the six male rhotic speakers are as in Table 4.

The tapes were all listened to and checked independently by both of us, and we are entirely agreed about the presence and absence

---

[1] The recordings were very kindly made available to us by the copyright holders, the Mitchell Library in Sydney.

Table 4. *Rhotic Australian speakers*

Speaker	Year/Place born	% Rhoticity (no. tokens)
Mr G. Golby	1889 (Dalgety)	20 (49/240)
Mr Reg Green	1897 (Tingha)	8 (29/357)
Mr Arthur Debenham	1897 (Pampoolah)	8 (34/395)
Mr A. Richardson	1889 (Sydney)	4 (25/580)
Mr Arthur Emblem	1897 (Tamworth)	4 (19/454)
Mr Don Taylor	1891 (Avalon)	1 (8/557)

of /r/s, and about the percentages (any doubtful cases were treated as non-rhotic).

Our surprise did not come from the discovery that Australian English used to be rhotic. In Trudgill *et al.* (2000: 124) we had ventured to claim, on the basis of the new and surprising New Zealand evidence, that "given that New Zealand was settled later than Australia, we are happy to assert that Australian English must ... have been rather rhotic at one stage also". The point was, of course, that if it was rhoticity rather than *non*-rhoticity which had been transported from the homeland to New Zealand, then non-rhoticity can hardly have been taken to the other two Southern Hemisphere colonies either, because English speakers left Britain for these locations *earlier* than they left for New Zealand, at a time when the loss-of-rhoticity innovation was less advanced. (We can say very roughly that large-scale anglophone settlement of Australia dates from *c.* 1800, South Africa 1820 and New Zealand 1840.) We had absolutely no direct evidence for our assertion, of course, and we most certainly did not expect to find any, given the much greater time-depth involved in the development of Australian as opposed to New Zealand English. The surprise came from the fact that we were now able to present evidence that our hypothetical deduction had been entirely correct.

Of course, it might be objected that the levels of Australian rhoticity we have found are so low as to be meaningless. I would dispute this vigorously. A speaker who has only 1 per cent rhoticity is nevertheless most definitely rhotic. Mr Taylor has a phonotactic system which *does* permit the occurrence of /r/ in non-prevocalic position in a way that would not be possible, for example, in my (English English) speech – 'variably rhotic' is still 'rhotic'. And speakers do not suddenly introduce segments into their speech at random, for no reason: Mr Taylor's meagre eight rhotic tokens in an hour of recording are actually powerful evidence of a nineteenth-century form of speech in his community where rhoticity was phonotactically permitted. There can be no doubt, we suggest, that Australian English, while today totally non-rhotic, was indeed formerly rhotic.

It would therefore seem to be incontestably the case that nineteenth-century New Zealand and Australian English were not non-rhotic. And it seems perfectly possible that South African English was not non-rhotic either at that time.

So how did we get it so wrong? It was accepted as obvious that the Southern Hemisphere Englishes were non-rhotic because what the settlers took with them to the new colonies was nineteenth-century non-rhotic English, as opposed to the earlier rhotic English which travelled across the Atlantic. But, obvious as it may have seemed, this is not what actually happened.

So what did happen? There are two questions that have to be tackled to take into account our new findings. First, how did it come about that the English which arrived in the Southern Hemisphere in the 1800s was rhotic? And given that it was, why are the modern Southern Hemisphere varieties non-rhotic?

THE FIRST QUESTION

The first difficulty we have is that, as Bailey and Strang and indeed others are agreed, English in southern England lost non-prevocalic /r/ in the 1700s. But if that is so, how can it be that the English-speaking nineteenth-century Southern Hemisphere settlers, very many of whom came from the south of England, produced colonial varieties of English that were rhotic?

To start with a consideration of the New Zealand data first, how did it happen that most of the New Zealand-born children of the first anglophone settlers, our ONZE informants, were rhotic? I would suggest that the only reasonable response to the ONZE evidence is to conclude that at the time of the anglophone settlement of New Zealand, the mid-nineteenth century, England *cannot* have been mainly non-rhotic. In fact, it must actually have still been very rhotic. There is no other explanation for the very low proportion of non-rhotic speakers among the ONZE informants.

Happily, if we look beyond the standard history of the English language texts, we can see that the orthodox story of /r/-loss in England is very misleading, as has also been argued by Windross (1994). For example, Beal (1999: 7–8) tells us that Walker (1791), in saying that /r/ is "sometimes entirely sunk", is referring "only to the most advanced dialect" of his day, colloquial London English. Hallam, quoted in MacMahon (1983: 28), also shows that rhoticity continued to be a feature of some upper-class speech into the 1870s, citing the accents of Disraeli (b. 1804) and Prince Leopold (b. 1853), the fourth son of Queen Victoria (see also the discussion in Lass 1997: 6.2).

The most important evidence, however, comes from dialectology. An examination of the relevant dialectological works shows that most regional accents in England lagged way behind London English, and that Bailey's (1996: 102) statement that "resistance to the spreading London fashion was, however, not long sustained" is a considerable exaggeration as far as regional accents are concerned. If we work backwards chronologically, the evidence from modern dialectology is rather clear on this point. On the basis of data contained in the major dialectological surveys of England from different periods, I have produced Map 3 which shows areas of England which were rhotic in different ways at different times in local dialects. We can note the following different areas:

(1)   Areas labelled '1' consist of localities that are shown as still fully rhotic in the *Survey of English Dialects* (SED) records from

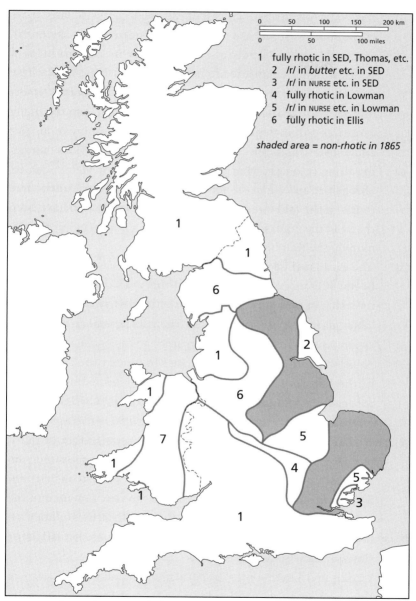

1 fully rhotic in SED, Thomas, etc.
2 /r/ in *butter* etc. in SED
3 /r/ in NURSE etc. in SED
4 fully rhotic in Lowman
5 /r/ in NURSE etc. in Lowman
6 fully rhotic in Ellis

shaded area = non-rhotic in 1865

Map 3 The survival of rhoticity

the 1950s/60s. As can be seen, these areas comprise large parts
of the southwest and the northwest of England, plus the northeast (and Scotland). I have also included in this category areas of
Wales which are indicated to be rhotic by Thomas (1994): these
are "the rural communities of the west and the north" where
it is a feature "carried over" from Welsh (p. 128); and the many
centuries-old anglophone areas of southern Pembroke (p. 131)
and Gower; and the Marches – the areas of Wales bordering directly on the rhotic English counties of Herefordshire,
Shropshire and Gloucestershire.[2] Obviously, if these areas were
rhotic in the mid-twentieth century, they would also have been
rhotic at the point in time crucial for the solution of our puzzle,
namely the first half of the nineteenth century.

(2)   The area labelled '2' on my map consists of eastern Yorkshire.
In the SED records, the dialects in this area are shown to have
retention of non-prevocalic /r/, but only in unstressed final syl-
lables, as in *butter*. This area too, then, had not been non-rhotic
as late as the mid-twentieth century.

(3)   Area '3' incorporates those localities in Essex which are shown
in the SED as still having retained non-prevocalic /r/, but in
this case only in the lexical set of NURSE, e.g. in words such as
worms.

(4)   We can then extend our knowledge about the extent of rhoticity in Britain back in time by consulting the material given
in Kurath and Lowman (1970). This work is based on brilliant
field research carried out by the American Guy Lowman in the
1930s. The area labelled '4' covers those localities which are
not rhotic in the SED materials but which appear as still being
rhotic in Lowman's data.

(5)   Kurath and Lowman (1970: 29) also shows additional areas of
the south and east Midlands, as well as of Essex and Suffolk,

---

[2] I have also assumed, following Thomas (1994), that there was rhoticity in the
second-language English of those areas of Wales which were Welsh-speaking in
the mid-nineteenth century – labelled '7'.

which retained /r/ in the lexical set of NURSE. These appear on the map with '5'.

(6) The oldest dialect materials I have consulted are those of Ellis (1889), which are based on research carried out on the ground in the 1860s. Areas which are described in Ellis as being rhotic are here shown with '6'. The details that can be derived from Ellis concerning the limits of those areas which he gives as rhotic but which had become non-rhotic by the time of the later research work, are as follows:

In Ellis's area 20, "Border Midland", which is equivalent to Lincolnshire, Ellis explicitly states (p. 297) that /r/ is vocalised or omitted. This is confirmed by his transcriptions.

In area 24, "Eastern West Midland", which is essentially south Yorkshire, rhoticity is variable but present, including in Sheffield and Rotherham.

In area 25, "Western Mid Midland", which centres on Cheshire, the transcriptions all show rhoticity.

In area 26, "Eastern Mid Midland", which centres on Derbyshire, transcriptions show total rhoticity except in the far east of that county.

In area 27, "East Midland", which is equivalent to Nottinghamshire, transcriptions show lack of rhoticity, except in East Retford in the north bordering the Eastern West Midland.

In area 29, "Eastern South Midland", all the transcriptions show rhoticity except for those for Lichfield, Staffordshire, and Atherstone and Enderby, Leicestershire.

Transcriptions for area 30, "East Northern", generally do not show rhoticity (except in the east where it shows up, as expected – see (2) above – in items such as *butter*).

The whole of area 31, "West Northern", has transcriptions showing rhoticity.

Naturally, all the other areas given as rhotic under (1)–(5) above are also rhotic in Ellis.

Map 3 therefore shows, crucially, those areas of England and Wales for which we have *no* evidence of rhoticity in the mid-nineteenth century. They cover only a relatively small area of Britain and lie in two separate corridors. The first runs south from the North Riding of Yorkshire through the Vale of York into north and central Lincolnshire, taking in nearly all of Nottinghamshire and adjacent areas of Derbyshire, Leicestershire and Staffordshire. The second includes all of Norfolk, western Suffolk and Essex, eastern Cambridgeshire and Hertfordshire, Middlesex, and northern Surrey and Kent.

We can therefore conclude that it is not even slightly surprising that rhoticity was exported to New Zealand in the nineteenth century since, in addition to the fact that Scotland and Ireland were obviously rhotic as they still are today, the greater part of England and English-speaking Wales was still rhotic at that time also. The areas of the British Isles where rhoticity was unattested in the 1860s were very few indeed. Impressions to the contrary are the result of the undue attention paid by some historians of the English language to upper-class and metropolitan speech.

And since the Southern Hemisphere colonies were actually settled by English speakers some decades before Ellis carried out his research, we can assume that rhoticity was even more widespread in the motherland at the time of the departure of these founding speakers from Britain.

THE SECOND QUESTION

As far as the second question is concerned – why are modern Southern Hemisphere varieties non-rhotic – there would appear to be three possibilities.

First, the existence of a number of current non-rhotic varieties can be accounted for in terms of *migration*. For example, Chambers (1991: 94) ascribes non-rhoticity in Lunenburg, Nova Scotia to "influence from New England", and Trudgill (2001), following a suggestion by Chambers, makes it clearer that this influence took the form of actual emigration from New England (see Chapter 4). For a similar explanation to work for the Southern Hemisphere, we would have to be able to show that the migration of non-rhotic speakers from England, subsequent to the initial settlements of South Africa, Australia and New Zealand, was sufficiently influential for the original rhoticity to be displaced by the newcomers. I am rather sceptical about this possibility, as no other England-based innovations, such as T Glottalling, have arrived in this way, and we can therefore be reasonably confident that later arrivals were not numerous enough for the "founder effect" (Mufwene 1991) to be over-ridden – newcomers (or at least their children) clearly accommodated to Southern Hemisphere English, as one would expect.

Secondly, the existence of some current non-rhotic varieties can be accounted for in terms of *diffusion*. North America was settled by English speakers long before the loss of rhoticity. The fact that some American varieties are currently non-rhotic therefore requires an explanation. The demographic facts rule out migration from England as a factor, and diffusion is the most satisfactory explanation. It is surely not a coincidence that non-rhoticity developed in North America along the East Coast. In particular, the major non-rhotic areas are all focussed on port cities which had close contacts with seventeenth- and eighteenth-century London: eastern New England, focussed on Boston, Massachusetts; New York City; and the American "South", i.e. the southeast, focussed on Richmond, Virginia, Charleston, South Carolina, and Savannah, Georgia. In no case did it spread very far inland, except in the case of speakers of African American Vernacular English, who migrated from the southeast to the rest of the country many decades later, taking their non-rhoticity with them. According to Wells (1982: 220), "the non-rhotic accents are found around the major Atlantic seaports", suggesting that the innovation was acquired in these areas as a result of more face-to-face interaction with, and more long-term accommodation to (Trudgill 1986), non-rhotic English English speakers than would have been the case further inland. Trask (1994: 26), too, says that "non-rhotic speech was also carried across the Atlantic to the coastal cities of the United States, which were in fairly close contact with the mother country".

There is, as far as we know, no similar indicative geographical patterning in Australia, and indeed the Australian rhoticity we have uncovered is sited in the neighbourhood of Sydney, the Australian port which, in terms of contact with London, played a role most like that of Boston. However, the possibility that some form of diffusion was a factor cannot be entirely excluded.

Thirdly, *independent development* is always a possibility, and has indeed been advanced as an explanation for recent r-loss among working-class young people in Edinburgh, Scotland. Romaine (1978: 156) suggests that "r-lessness is a separate competing development in Scots and is *not* being adopted in conscious imitation of a Southern English prestige model". The Newfoundland r-less enclaves may also be susceptible of this type of explanation. And it is also in fact the explanation I favour for loss of rhoticity in Australia, except that, as I shall explain, I do not regard it as being truly independent.

The rhoticity which we see in older Australian speech is best interpreted as the vestigial rhoticity which is typical of the end-stages of rhoticity-loss. The variable rhoticity has a low level of occurrence; the non-prevocalic /r/s tend to be phonetically weaker than in pre-vocalic position (and than in most fully rhotic accents), i.e. they are less fully retroflexed; and /r/ occurs much more frequently in some phonological contexts than others: the preceding vowels which most commonly produce rhoticity are those of NORTH/FORCE and LETTER, unlike in New Zealand English (see Bartlett 2003) and other ves-tigially rhotic varieties, e.g. those of various parts of England, where rhoticity is most common after NURSE (see Trudgill 2004: 70). So this variable and low-level rhoticity must represent the last surviv-ing traces of earlier, fuller rhoticity. There is no other explanation for why six speakers, all unknown to one another, and living in six different places, should display this kind of linguistic behaviour. It is clear that Australian English, just like New Zealand English, used to be rhotic; and that the nearer to the beginning of the nineteenth century, the higher the levels of rhoticity must have been. It is also quite possible that at least some of our six rhotic speakers might have had higher levels of rhoticity when they were younger.

We have been fortunate enough to find, by chance, some of the very last rhotic Australian English speakers, whose phonologies represent the final stages of a sound change which had been going on for very many decades. The evidence is that, far from non-rhoticity being brought to Australia, it was actually rhoticity that arrived; and that the sound change involving loss of rhoticity did not go to total linguistic and society-wide completion until about 1900, in terms of birthdates of speakers.

Whether or not we are also seeing the last stages of a lexical diffusion process (Wang 1969) is not entirely clear. The lexical items in which rhotic tokens occurred in the Australian recordings are as follows, classified according to the preceding vowel:

NEAR: *year, years, shearers*
SQUARE: *chair, there, where*
NURSE: *firm, first, her, were*
START: *apart, bark, car, Carter, McCartney, parsnips, parts, start, started, sweethearts*
NORTH/FORCE: *border, course, door, for, Forster, Forsterton, Fort, fort, four, headquarters, horse, horseback, horsemen, horses, imported, more, morning, quarters, quartz, or, reinforcement, sort, sport, sports*
LETTER: *after, behaviour, blazers, brothers, buyer, Carter, cultured, December, driver, ever, father, father's, Grocer's, jumper, jumpers, mother, or, paper, papers, particular, poster, properly, property, remember, rivers, shearers, sister, sisters, teacher, teachers, timber, understood, Victor, worker's*

In Gordon *et al.* (2004: 182) we note that rhoticity in early New Zealand English was most common in words associated with "old-time activities", notably farming and mining: e.g. *turnip, tractor, rooster, quartz, miner, ore*. It is therefore perhaps suggestive of an association of rhoticity with an older, rural way of life that rhotic tokens of the word *quartz* also appear in our New South Wales data, and that the word which is most commonly pronounced in a rhotic manner by the Australian speakers is *horse* and its derivatives.

We can conclude from our data that, though non-prevocalic /r/ was very widespread in nineteenth-century England, it was also clearly involved in linguistic change: in many areas rhoticity was present but was gradually disappearing. This is what is reflected in our ONZE recordings. The majority of our speakers are rhotic, as we have seen, but most of them are only variably rhotic and many of them are, like our Australian speakers, only vestigially so. In fact, in the data as a whole, rhotic tokens are less numerous than non-rhotic tokens (Gordon *et al.* 2004: 240).

What happened was, I suggest, that New Zealand English did not inherit non-rhoticity from English English as such, but rather inherited an *ongoing process involving loss of rhoticity*. And because of the new data, we are now able to apply the same argument to Australia, although for this variety we do not have any older data comparable to the ONZE corpus. My suggestion is that what was taken to the Southern Hemisphere was a *linguistic change in progress*, such that rhoticity was lost in parallel in England, Australia, New Zealand and South Africa, through processes which we can label, using Sapir's (1921) term, *drift* (Trudgill 2004: 131–44). The seeds of the parallel developments lay in the variability in rhoticity, and gradual loss of rhoticity, which was shared – it has now become clear – between these four varieties of English in the nineteenth century. In the Southland of New Zealand, indeed, the process is still ongoing today, as it is in the still rhotic areas of northern and western England.

8 What became of all the Scots?

In Chapters 6 and 7 we discussed the work of the Origins of New Zealand English project. This research showed that this newest of all of the major native-speaker varieties of English was the result in part of drift, but crucially also of dialect contact and new-dialect formation. Clearly, the dialects which were involved in the initial colonial dialect-contact situation were varieties of English which had been brought to New Zealand from England, Scotland, Wales and Ireland.

These different parts of the British Isles, however, were not evenly represented. In terms of population figures, the Englishes that came into contact in New Zealand (and on the boat during the long trip out) arrived from England, Scotland and Ireland in roughly the proportion 5:2:2. The north of England was underrepresented, and the Welsh contribution was very low (McKinnon 1997). These proportions tally rather well with Bauer's lexical study (Bauer 2000), which shows that there are focal points for the dialectal origins of New Zealand lexis "in Scotland, in Ireland, and in a band stretching from Lincolnshire ... through Nottinghamshire, Warwickshire and Somerset to Devon and Cornwall" (Bauer 2000: 52).

In considering the relative importance of the different forms of British Isles English involved in the dialect mixture which gave rise to modern New Zealand English, no one will doubt the significance of the input from England, on linguistic grounds alone. From a phonological point of view, it is clear that New Zealand English is very closely related typologically to the Englishes of the southeast of England. For instance, both southeastern English English and New Zealand English have the FOOT/STRUT split – unlike accents from the north of England, which have the vowel of FOOT also in the lexical set of STRUT. Both forms of English distinguish between the vowels of TRAP, PALM, LOT and THOUGHT, unlike many forms of American English, and unlike Scottish and Canadian English, which have no LOT/THOUGHT distinction. Both varieties are non-rhotic, as we discussed in the previous chapter, unlike Scottish English. Both southeast of England and New Zealand varieties employ the vowel of PALM and START in the lexical set of BATH, unlike North American English. And, again unlike Scottish English, both varieties also have wide diphthongs (Wells' *Diphthong Shift*) involving a greater amount of tongue movement in the sets of FACE, GOAT, PRICE and MOUTH (New Zealand English, for example, has [aɪ] for FACE where Scottish English has [e˙]).

There would therefore appear to be no room for any role at all for Scottish English in the development of New Zealand English phonology: very few pairs of English accents have phonologies so very unlike one another as those of Scotland and New Zealand. This is even more true of the Traditional Dialect (or indeed language) of Lowland Scotland, Scots, which would have been spoken by many, and perhaps most, of the Scottish immigrants to New Zealand. Bauer (1997) agrees: after attempting to trace the Scottish input to New Zealand phonology, he concluded that Scottish influence cannot be presumed.

There is, however, one New Zealand English phonological feature which has long been thought to be the result of Scottish influence. One of the most striking characteristics of modern New Zealand English is the very centralised KIT vowel. It is particularly salient in Australasia, where it contrasts with the raised and fronted KIT of Australian English. It was earlier hypothesised, for example in Trudgill (1986), that input from the Scottish [ə]-type pronunciation of KIT words was the explanation for the distinctive modern New Zealand central pronunciation of this same vowel. McClure (1994: 65) describes the vowel in Scottish English as being "somewhat lower than the corresponding vowel in English"; and Wells (1982: 404) also says that "in more popular accents it may be considerably opener and/or more retracted" [than in RP].

However, we can now see that this hypothesis is totally wrong. The feature is actually completely absent from the speech of the ONZE core informants, and even those of our core-speakers who are most obviously and consistently Scottish in their phonetics and phonology do not have it. It must therefore in fact be a New Zealand innovation, something which arose in the early years of the twentieth century after the development of New Zealand English as a separate variety. The earlier hypothesis of direct Scottish descent for centralised New Zealand English KIT is an example of the type of error that can occur when one attempts to work backwards from an existing variety without recourse to actual linguistic data.

This apparent total absence of Scottish phonological influence is on the face of it a rather puzzling phenomenon. New Zealand English is full of lexical features of Scottish origin (Bauer 2000) such as the frequent usage of *wee* 'small'. And, at the non-linguistic level, New Zealand is full of Scottish influences of other sorts: people with Scottish surnames, many of whom visit Scotland during their popular "Overseas Experience" trips to the Northern Hemisphere; the Presbyterian church, which was second only to the Anglican church in size until late in the twentieth century (Davidson 1991; McKinnon 1997); Scottish Pipe bands, Caledonian Societies, Masonic Lodges, and elite Scottish heritage schools throughout the country; the University of Otago, the country's oldest university, founded by the strongly pro-education Scottish settlers; and the well-supported Otago rugby football team – "The Highlanders" – whose colours are the blue and gold of the Scottish flag. Indeed, this degree of general Scottish influence is what we would expect in view of the fact, as we saw above, that Scotland supplied more than 20 per cent of the early immigrants to New Zealand (McKinnon 1997). This figure, moreover, does not include Ulster Scots immigrants, whose port of origin would have been recorded as somewhere in Ireland but whose speech would have further added to the Scottish influence on New Zealand English.

So why, then, are we presented with this rather puzzling absence from modern New Zealand phonology of features from a part of the English-speaking world which supplied so many of the immigrants? The basis of this chapter, which now attempts to answer this question, is once again the ONZE research project, as described earlier.

A SCOTTISH-BORN SPEAKER

In addition to the core ONZE informants as described in Chapters 6 and 7, I have also been able to analyse the English of older "pre-core" speakers. These were people who were born outside New Zealand, and who came to New Zealand later in their lives, and who therefore were not included in the project's main study. In spite of this exclusion from the central part of our research, their speech can give us an indication of the nature of the English that was used during the very first, contact stage of the new-dialect-formation process; and it does indeed very often show features from British Isles dialects that have already disappeared from the speech of the first generation of New Zealanders who were the core informants in the ONZE project.

There are a number of pre-core speakers who are of special importance for this chapter because they were born in Scotland. One such speaker, Mrs Susan McFarlane, is of particular interest. She was born about 1845, and, as far as we can tell from the content of her recording, she grew up in Friockheim, in Angus, Scotland. She came to New Zealand in 1878 when she was in her thirties. She was recorded in Dunedin, aged 102. We know that Mrs McFarlane did not go to school; that her father was a gamekeeper; that she worked in service; and that her husband was a prison warder in Perth, Scotland, before emigrating to New Zealand. (We also know that she met Queen Victoria – "a dear little woman".) Her speech, in other words, provides us with a remarkable record of mid-nineteenth-century Scottish English.

It is true of course that Mrs McFarlane shares many phonological features with those of the ONZE core speakers who have Scottish elements in their speech. For example, she is one of a number of speakers on the ONZE tapes who demonstrate Aitken's Law (see below). Mrs McFarlane also preserves as distinct the KIT vowel in *first*, the STRUT vowel in *fur*, and the DRESS vowel in *fern*, as some of the core informants do. She also has a vowel system which resembles the basic Scottish English system in which the vowels of FOOT and GOOSE, TRAP and PALM, and LOT and THOUGHT are not distinct, which is also found in the speech of a number of core informants.

But in addition she has, albeit spasmodically and unsystematically, a number of other Scottish features which differ very dramatically from those found in the speech of any of the New Zealand-born core informants. In analysing these linguistic characteristics, we have to make a distinction between Scottish English, on the one hand, and the Traditional Dialect Scots, on the other. Although Mrs McFarlane has a vowel system which is not unlike that of the other "Scottish" New Zealand speakers, her distribution of lexical items over these Scottish English vowels is sometimes very typical of Scots as opposed to English: she not infrequently uses forms such as *oot, doon, hoose, aboot*, etc.; *airm* 'arm'; *canna* 'can't'; *nae* 'no'; *craw* 'crow'; *mither* 'mother'. She also often has the TRAP vowel in items such as *watch, wash, what, warder, all*. And many of her LOT words actually have the vowel of GOAT, a typical Midland Scottish dialect feature (see Grant and Dixon 1921: 50; Aitken 1984: 100). Her KIT vowel is sometimes also very central, unlike all the other ONZE informants with Scottish-type vowel systems, as was just mentioned.

Mrs McFarlane also has /x/, not just in place names, surnames or the exclamation *och!*, like some of the ONZE core informants, but in items such as /roxt/ 'wrought = worked' (Aitken 1984: 101) too. And she has occasional instances of initial /f/ in items such as *when* (Aitken 1984: 102). Her /r/ is most frequently an alveolar flap, but she also employs a trilled [r] and not infrequently a uvular [ʁ] (see Aitken

1984: 102). And in her pronominal system she uses *hit* 'it' and *wur* 'our' (see Grant and Dixon 1921: 95–8).

The point is, then, that Mrs McFarlane has many dialectal Scots features in her speech that do not occur in the speech of any of the ONZE core informants. Such features would surely have been present also in the speech of many other emigrants from Scotland to New Zealand. And a legitimate question therefore is: why have none of them survived?

NEW ZEALAND-BORN SPEAKERS

This question becomes rather more pressing when we turn to the speech of the actual core informants. Among these speakers, there are also many instances, as we have just seen, of Scottish forms. As far as phonology is concerned, the Scottish Vowel Length Rule, also known as "Aitken's Law" (see Aitken 1984: 94), occurs in the speech of a minority of the informants. According to this rule, which developed from the late sixteenth century onwards and spread out from the West Central Lowlands of Scotland (Johnston 1997a: 67), while all Scottish vowels are basically short and there is no phonemic length distinction in the system as such, all vowels apart from KIT and STRUT are longer before /r/, a voiced fricative or a morpheme boundary than elsewhere. Because of the effect of the morpheme boundary, there is the well-known consequence (see Wells 1982: 400) that *greed* and *agreed* do not rhyme, and that *need* is not homophonous with *kneed*. Aitken's Law also gives rise to very different allophones of /ai/ such that the first element of the PRICE vowel in *tight, tide* [təɪd] is much closer than the first element in *tie, tied* [taed].

Other Scottish phonological features include the fact that a number of core informants also preserve as distinct the KIT vowel in *first*, the STRUT vowel in *fur* and the DRESS vowel in *fern*, like Mrs McFarlane. Others merely have *fern* as distinct from the other two, which are merged. This reflects a similar situation in Scotland itself (Wells 1982). A proportion of speakers do not distinguish between the vowels of FOOT and GOOSE. Some of the speakers, in the Scottish manner, also have TRAP and PALM as not distinct, i.e.

there is no distinction between /æ/ and /a:/, with a vowel often of the type /a/ occurring in both lexical sets. Some speakers have [æ] in TRAP and PALM and [a] in START, but this is an allophonic distinction, with [a] occurring only before /r/. And for a number of speakers, LOT and THOUGHT are not distinct. A number of core informants also employ the voiceless velar fricative /x/ in place names and surnames such as *Cochrane*, and in the exclamation *och!* And a number of speakers demonstrate an assimilation of /r/ and /s/ into retroflex [ʂ] in items such as *first, worse.* (This feature is often associated with the Gaelic- or formerly Gaelic-speaking areas of the Highlands and Islands, but can also be found in Scots-speaking areas – see Johnston 1997b: 511.) We also observe typical Scottish stress patterns, such as *recognise* with stress on the final syllable (Aitken 1984).

In addition, the recordings contain a number of grammatical forms which are clearly of Scottish origin, such as the plural of *sheaf* as *sheafs.* And in the syntax, we find some speakers who use, even in colloquial speech, nominal rather than verbal negation and who say, for example,

> They had no ploughs.
> They would get no food.

rather than *They didn't have any ploughs* and *They wouldn't get any food*, something I also take to be Scottish rather than English English in origin (see Aitken 1984). The use of *for* as a conjunction, as in

> For he liked it very much.

is also likely to be Scottish in origin.

Another particularly interesting regional feature concerns what some writers have referred to as the Northern Subject Rule, as also discussed in Chapters 1 and 2. In the corpus there are speakers who say, for example,

> The roads was bad.

but

> *They were really bad.*

We can suppose an origin here from outside England, i.e. from Scotland, in view of the rarity of other north of England forms.

None of these certainly or possibly Scottish forms have survived into modern New Zealand English either. The puzzle is: why is this?

THE "SCOTTISH" SPEAKERS

In actual fact, the truth is that a number of these Scottish features did survive in New Zealand for quite a long time. This can be demonstrated by means of data provided by a subset of the core informants.

All of the ONZE speakers under analysis were labelled for "Overall Impression": I categorised as many as sixteen of them (about 19 per cent) impressionistically as "Scottish". That is, on a first hearing, the initial reaction on the part of this (English English-speaking) analyst was that these people sounded as if they were Scots.

We can also compare these sixteen informants with Mr E. Bissett, a post-core informant who was born in 1894, later than the other speakers, and the child of New Zealand-born parents. He was recorded at the age of 100 in 1994, as part of a follow-up study of relatives of ONZE informants. He too, rather astonishingly for a native-born New Zealander at the end of the twentieth century, sounded Scottish.

Of the sixteen core speakers, one, Mr Knight of Waitahuna, had parents from England; Mr P. Mason of Balclutha had a mother from Liverpool, England; and the father of Mr Cannon of Milton was from northern Ireland. All the other parents were from Scotland. At least some of Mr Bissett's grandparents were from Scotland, and his mother is one of the sixteen Scottish core informants.

In Table 5, I present a selection of Scottish-sounding features which can be heard in the speech of the "Scottish" subset of the

Table 5. *Scottish features*

Speaker / birth year	TRAP/PALM	GOAT	FACE	NURSE	PRICE	MOUTH	LOT/THOUGHT	FOOT/GOOSE	FLEECE/GOOSE
Mrs H. Cross 1851	S	S	S	S	S	S	S	S	S
Mrs C. Bisset 1875	S	S	S	S	S	S	S	S	S
Mr J. McLew 1875	S	S	S	S	S	S	S	S	S
Mr G. Ross 1878	S	S	S	S	S	S	S	S	S
Mr J. Stewart 1876	x	S	S	*	S	S	S	S	S
Mr D. Falconer 1869	x	*	S	S	S	S	x	S	S
Mr D. Algie 1867	x	S	S	*	*	S	S	S	S
Mr F. Knight 1856	x	S	S	x	S	*	*	S	S
Mr P. Mason 1873	x	*	*	S	S	S	x	S	S
Mr W. Morrison 1873	*	*	*	*	*	*	*	x	S
Mr A. Tweed 1865	x	x	x	S	S	S	S	S	S
Mrs J. Drinnan 1868	x	x	x	x	S	S	S	S	S
Mr E. Bisset 1894	x	x	*	x	x	S	S	S	S
Mrs C. King 1868	x	x	x	x	x	S	S	S	S
Mr R. Welsh 1880	x	*	*	S	x	x	*	*	S
Mr T. Cannon 1876	x	x	x	x	S	S	x	x	S
Miss M. Mason 1875	x	x	x	x	*	S	x	x	x

S = Scottish; x = not Scottish; * = variable

core informants and Mr Bissett. The table is arranged to highlight the implicational scaling that is present in the data. An 'S' in the TRAP/PALM, LOT/THOUGHT and FOOT/GOOSE columns indicates that the speakers do not make a distinction between the phonemes in the relevant lexical sets.

GOAT, FACE, PRICE and MOUTH represent phonemes that are particularly important in the formation of New Zealand English, being some of the first sounds to be noted as having distinctively New Zealand pronunciations (see Gordon 1983, 1998). The table indicates the extent to which speakers retained a distinctively Scottish pronunciation for these vowels, i.e. monophthongal [e] and [o] for FACE and GOAT, and diphthongs with central onsets for PRICE and MOUTH in the appropriate Aitken's Law environments (see above).

An 'S' in the NURSE column indicates that the speaker retained some of the distinctions already mentioned between *first*, *fur* and *fern*. And finally the FLEECE/GOOSE column indicates whether speakers used Scottish monophthongal pronunciations rather than the somewhat diphthongal pronunciations of modern New Zealand English.

From Table 5, we can see that some Scottish features were more persistent than others. Although this is not shown in the table, but as one would expect from Chapter 7, all of these speakers are rhotic to a degree, some of them consistently so. Sixteen out of the seventeen speakers retain monophthongal pronunciations of both GOOSE and FLEECE; and fourteen of them (including one who is variable) do not distinguish between the vowels of GOOSE and FOOT. The latter is perhaps not surprising in view of Wells' assertion (1982: 402) that "in the speech of anglicised Scots this is the one characteristic above all which seems virtually impervious to alteration", and because it is harder to acquire a phoneme distinction than to lose one.

The LOT/THOUGHT merger is not quite as successful, being maintained by thirteen of the Scottish subset (three of whom are variable). Eleven of the speakers variably maintain a distinction between the vowels of *fern* and *fur*, and sometimes of *first* also.

The least "successful" feature is the non-distinction between the vowels of TRAP and PALM. At first sight, this is surprising because it is usually difficult to unmerge a pair of phonemes. Wells points out (1982: 403), however, that many Scots actually do have this distinction, and many of the original Scottish settlers may therefore have brought the distinction with them. The diphthongs of MOUTH and PRICE (in the appropriate Aitken's Law environments) preserve their Scottish-type central onsets for a majority of the speakers but, interestingly, this seems to have lasted longer in the New Zealand context in MOUTH (with thirteen speakers, plus three whose use is variable) than in PRICE (which has only eleven, plus three whose use is variable). Similarly, nine of these speakers have (variably) diphthongal realisations of FACE, and ten have (variably) diphthongal realisations of GOAT.

Once again we may ask: if these features survived for so long in the speech of a good number of nineteenth-century-born New Zealanders who lived until the 1940s, why did they not survive into modern New Zealand English as such?

NEW-DIALECT FORMATION: DETERMINISM

In Trudgill (2004) I claim that the new-dialect formation which resulted from the mixture of dialects brought from the British Isles to New Zealand was not a haphazard process but, on the contrary, deterministic in nature. That is, the newly formed dialect, New Zealand English, which is largely a third-generation outcome of dialect contact and dialect mixture, is characterised at the phonological level by the presence of those features which were in a majority in the first-generation input, except in cases where linguistically unmarked or more simple features are in a large minority and win out over majority features on the grounds of their unmarkedness and/or lack of complexity (unmarking).

The way in which this happened, however, is complex. Notwithstanding the obvious influence of their own parents' dialect(s), for the core informants in our ONZE corpus – the earliest generation of New Zealand-born anglophones, who represent the second stage of new-dialect formation – there was in most early communities no homogeneous local accent for them to acquire as children, as we noted in Chapter 6, but instead a kind of supermarket of vocalic and consonantal variants that were available for inclusion in their developing idiolects. This is of course why colonial and other new dialects consist to a considerable extent of new combinations of old features.

There are, crucially, many inter-individual differences in the way in which these new combinations of old features were formed. It is clear that this implies a degree of randomness concerning which speakers chose which variants, such that different people in the same community may arrive at different combinations even in the case of speakers who have lived in close proximity to one another all their lives and whose parents even had similar origins. But I explain the survival of particular variants at the third-generation stage in terms of their majority status in the speech of the second-stage ONZE informants. And I explain this majority status in terms of the presumed majority status of these variants in the speech of their parents' generation, i.e. in the dialects brought to New Zealand at the first stage by immigrants from different parts of the British Isles. The differential proportions of variants in the ONZE corpus (and thus their later survival or disappearance) are, in other words, not random (see Trudgill *et al.* 2000).

We therefore have to assume the following. The proportions of variants present in the phonologies of groups of second-stage speakers, taken as a whole, derive in a probabilistic manner from, and will therefore reflect at least approximately, the proportions of the same variants present in the different varieties spoken by their parents' generation taken as a whole. The most common variants at the first stage were the ones which were most often selected at the second stage, even though second-generation speakers demonstrated considerable inter-individual variability, stemming from the lack of constraints that a more homogeneous speech community could have imposed; and these most common variants were therefore the ones to survive into the third generation – the new dialect we call New Zealand English.

For example, Modern New Zealand English has both /h/-retention and /ʍ/-retention (though the /w~ʍ/ distinction has now disappeared from the twenty-first-century speech of many younger New Zealanders). This is predictable from the fact that 75 per cent of the Stage 2 ONZE-corpus informants were /h/-retainers and 60 per cent were /ʍ/-retainers, which is, I suggest, because these were also approximately the proportions of such speakers, taken overall, at the earlier immigrant stage, the pre-ONZE corpus Stage 1. What was *not* present at the first stage is, for example, the bizarre combination of /h/-dropping with retention of /ʍ/ demonstrated at the second stage by one of our informants, Mr Ritchie from Arrowtown, in the South Island.

There is, however, an important rider to the thesis that the proportion of variants in the input mixture is represented in the final outcome. The data show that we have to assume there was a frequency threshold for variants represented in the first-stage input. From our knowledge of the origins of the early immigrants to New Zealand, we can be certain that some features must have been present at the first stage which nevertheless did not survive – or barely survived – into the second stage. Such dialect forms, I propose, were at too low a level to be perceived and/or acquired by children at that second stage. I do not profess to know exactly what the appropriate threshold level is, but I am not the first to employ this concept. Lightfoot (1999: 155–6), in his Universal Grammar approach to grammatical change, suggests a dialect-contact context for the change away from verb-second structures in northern mediaeval English:

> Children in Lincolnshire and Yorkshire, as they mingled with southerners, would have heard sentences whose initial elements were non-subjects followed by a finite verb less frequently than the required threshold ... the evidence suggests that 17%

of initial non-subjects does not suffice to trigger a verb-second grammar, but 30% is enough.

We have to suppose, then, that the absence of dialectal features such as those we find in the speech of Mrs McFarlane from the English of the core ONZE informants is the result of a rudimentary levelling process in the early dialect-contact situation, which led to the gradual diminution in use of most Traditional Dialect features at the first stage and their consequent absence from the speech of our second-stage core-speakers. We can suppose that this was because such forms, *looked at individually*, would have been very much in a minority. That is, large numbers of speakers of Traditional Dialects emigrated to New Zealand, but since many individual Traditional Dialect features were found only in rather small geographical areas – hence the observation that such dialects change every few miles or so – there would have been a tendency for such features, perhaps like Mrs McFarlane's /f/ in *when*, to be found in the speech of only very few immigrants.

Similarly, we can suppose that the Scottish forms which appear in the speech of some core and post-core informants, but which did not survive into New Zealand English, fell at the second stage of the new-dialect-formation process. Scottish speakers, while very numerous, were just not numerous enough to influence the eventual phonology of New Zealand English, even if there were enough of them to have a powerful influence on other aspects of New Zealand English, and New Zealand life generally. Even pan-Scottish features could have been present in the speech of no more than 22 per cent of the speakers (remembering the 5:2:2 ratio of immigrants) who came to New Zealand; and minority forms do not survive – 22 per cent was simply not enough.

However, it turns out that this is not the whole story. Further consideration of the details of the new-dialect-formation process is now required. During new-dialect formation, variants from the different dialects involved in a mixture are reduced in number until, usually, only one remains for each variable. Crucially, however, this reduction does not take place in a haphazard manner, as we have just noted. As mentioned above, I have used the term *determinism* to describe this process (Trudgill 2004). I argue that New Zealand English is a variety which, from a phonological point of view, is basically a southeast-of-England sort typologically, *not* because most of the immigrants from Britain to New Zealand came from the English southeast, but because, as it happens, *individual linguistic forms* found in the southeast of England were also, coincidentally (taking all the dialects which contributed to the mixture as a whole), very often majority forms in the original dialect mixture.

In fact, it is very clear that where southeast-of-England forms were not in a majority, they did not survive: a number of non-southeastern forms are extant in New Zealand English, in addition to obvious lexical features of the type discussed by Bauer (2000) such as Scottish *wee* 'small'. For example, /h/-dropping – the pronunciation of *hammer, hill, house*, etc. without initial /h/ – does not survive in New Zealand English in spite of the fact that it was the norm in vernacular varieties in London and everywhere else in the southeast of England. The ONZE data explains why this should have happened. Although /h/-dropping is not uncommon on our recordings (see Maclagan 1998), and although it was mentioned by early commentators on New Zealand English (see Gordon 1983, 1998), only 25 per cent of our speakers use this feature. The Scottish, Irish, Northumbrian and East Anglian /h/-pronouncing variants were in the majority in the mixture and have won out in modern New Zealand English.

The immigration figures cited earlier also help to confirm this thesis. Even if all the immigrants from England combined were /h/-droppers, they constituted only 55 per cent of the arrivals and were almost matched numerically by incomers from Scotland and Ireland, areas where /h/-dropping was and is still unknown. However, not all the immigrants from England were /h/-droppers, because some of them came from peripheral areas of England, such as East Anglia (including Essex), where /h/-dropping was not at that time to be found (see Trudgill 1974).

This suggests very strongly that during the crucial first-stage formation period, New Zealand was an area where /h/-droppers were in a minority. And this means that Scottish speakers played an indirect but vital role in producing the absence of /h/-dropping in modern New Zealand English. We are beginning to see, then, that in fact, contrary to one's first impressions, some Scottish English features did indeed survive into New Zealand English, but only if, coincidentally, they happened to be features of other dialects also, to an extent which would make them dominant in the dialect mixture.

Another southeast-of-England feature which did not survive into New Zealand English was the merger of /w/ and /ʍ/, as in *which–witch; where–ware; while–wile*. Here again, we can advance the same explanation. Although the Englishes of nineteenth-century southeastern England had largely merged the initial consonants of *whales* and *Wales*, it was the form used by Scottish, Irish and the remaining non-merging southern English speakers which survived the levelling process for demographic reasons.

One other intriguing example is provided by the word *with*. I am not so inclined to argue deterministically in the case of single lexical items, but the final consonant of this word is interesting. In the English of modern England, *with* is pronounced with /ð/. In Scotland and Ireland, on the other hand, it is pronounced with final /θ/. The voiceless consonant is the one which is most common on the ONZE recordings, and which has survived into most forms of modern New Zealand English, a fact which Bauer (1997: 261) suggests could be evidence of Scottish influence.

NEW-DIALECT FORMATION: INTERDIALECT PHENOMENA

There is a further respect in which Scottish English/Scots was influential. Accommodation between speakers during new-dialect formation has been shown to lead to the development of interdialect forms (Trudgill 1986). These can be defined as forms which were not actually present in any of the dialects contributing to the mixture but which arise out of interaction between them. Such forms are of three types: intermediate forms, which result from partial accommodation; simpler or more regular forms; and hyperadaptive forms – the latter two resulting from misanalysis or reanalysis during accommodation.

For example, a common interdialectal feature on the ONZE tapes is hyperadaptive – in fact hypercorrect – initial /h/ in, for example, *and*, *I*, *apple*. About 10 per cent of the informants have some instances of this feature. One of the ONZE informants, Mrs McKeany, who was born in 1866 in Cambridge, North Island, and whose father came from Ireland, is extraordinary in this respect and demonstrates behaviour I have not come across before from any other English speaker: nearly all stressed vowel-initial words in her speech begin with /h/; even more unusually, nearly all words which begin with /w/ actually begin with /ʍ/ in her idiolect. Other speakers make such hyperadaptations only variably. This phenomenon is not totally unknown in England, of course, but my suggestion is that the very high level of occurrence of this phenomenon in the speech of these ONZE speakers indicates that they inherited such hyperadaptations from the speech of people of their parents' generation, among whom it was unusually widespread as a result of misanalyses during the course of accommodation.

I also consider that Scottish speakers contributed to the final form of New Zealand English through the creation of interdialect forms. Their contribution may have been particularly important in helping to influence the final form of the raised New Zealand English front vowels. The vowels of KIT, DRESS, TRAP have a very wide range of realisations on our ONZE recordings (though, as we have seen, centralised KIT is absent). However, the closer variants [i, e, ɛ] are much more common on the recordings than the more open variants associated with the north of England, Scotland and Ireland – 60 per cent of our speakers have DRESS and TRAP vowels which are consistently closer than [ɛ] and [æ] respectively (see Trudgill, Gordon and Lewis 1998) – and it is therefore no surprise that these qualities were the ones associated with the third stage of early New Zealand English (modern New Zealand English has qualities which are even closer – see Trudgill, Gordon and Lewis 1998; Maclagan, Gordon and Lewis 1999).

Nevertheless I also see a role for Scottish English in this development. A number of the core ONZE informants combine unmistakably Scottish accents with an /æ/ which is, very surprisingly, realised as [ɛ]. I say "surprisingly" because "most Scots … have [a – ɑ]" (Wells 1982: 403). This reminds us, however, of the fact that anglicised (or, in the words of the late David Abercrombie, "anglophile") Scottish accents of the type known in Edinburgh as "Morningside" and in Glasgow as "Kelvinside", after the upper-middle-class suburbs with which they are associated, also have [ɛ] in the lexical set of TRAP (Wells 1982: 403). Wells even suggests that in these accents /ɛ/ and /æ/ may be merged before or after velar consonants so that, for example, *kettle* and *cattle* are homophonous.

What is the explanation for this dramatically different vowel quality in these upper-middle-class accents? Grant (1913: 51–2) provides one. He writes of [æ] that "its use by some [Scottish] speakers instead of [a] … is probably an importation from Southern English. It is heard most frequently about Edinburgh and Glasgow. Most Scottish speakers who attempt to pronounce [mæn] say [mɛn] which is the Cockney pronunciation and to be avoided."

The new-dialect-formation scenario implies that informants who have this feature inherited it from speakers of their parents' generation. I do not believe, however, that this feature was imported directly to New Zealand from Kelvinside or Morningside, in view of the lower-middle-class/upper-working-class composition of the majority of groups of migrants to New Zealand. I suggest, rather, that the same mechanism was at work in the New Zealand context as in Glasgow and Edinburgh, and that it gave rise to the same result.

The clue to exactly how this mechanism might have worked comes from the speech of our pre-core speaker Mrs McFarlane. Her behaviour as a Scottish adult accommodating to the speech of non-Scottish others in the New Zealand context gives us an indication of the sorts of processes that may have occurred in the speech of our informants' parents in and on the way to New Zealand as they accommodated to each other, processes which are of course otherwise totally lost to us. That is, I believe that it is reasonable to suggest that what Mrs McFarlane does may be precisely what large numbers of people of Scottish origins also did at the earlier Stage 1 generation for whom we have no evidence.

To explain why Mrs McFarlane's treatment of the TRAP vowel may be significant, it is helpful if we firstly look at what happens to her FACE vowel. (Wells' system of key words representing lexical sets does not really work for Scots, since these dialects are radically different in their vowel systems and distribution of vowels over lexical items from all other varieties of English – Johnston (1997a, 1997b) uses a different set of key words for Scots – but I shall continue in what follows to use Wells' system where this does not cause confusion.) Mrs McFarlane's normal vowel in the lexical set of FACE is, as was and is usual in Scotland, monophthongal [eˑ]. There are also, however, some surprisingly extreme diphthongal tokens of FACE on her recordings. What appears to have happened to bring about this development is very interesting and can be interpreted according to the phonetic clues as follows.

Many Scots dialects (as opposed to Scottish English) have two vowels corresponding to the single PRICE vowel of other varieties. The first of these vowels can be written /ae/ and occurs in Aitken's Law (see above) long environments, as in *fire*, *size*, *live*, *tied*, *pie*. Johnston (1997a, 1997b) refers to this lexical set in Scots as the TRY class. The other can be written /ʌɪ/ and occurs in Aitken's Law short environments, as in *night*, *time*, *tide*. Johnston refers to this lexical set as the BITE class. Although allophonic in Scottish English, these two vowels have to be considered contrastive in many dialects of Scots because of their pronunciation of items such as *pay*. Many varieties of Scots (see Mather and Speitel 1975) – including even, for example, lower-class Edinburgh speech – employ a vowel in the lexical set of *pay, way, stay* – a subset of words that are descended from Older Scots /ai/ rather than /a:/ – which is distinct from the /e/ of FACE etc. and which is a diphthong of the type [ʌi ~ ʌi] (see Grant and Dixon 1921: 57; Aitken 1984: 95). This is identical in many dialects with the BITE vowel and, crucially, distinct from the TRY vowel, such that *pay* and *pie* are not homophonous. Johnston (1997b: 463) writes of words such as *pay*: "The words with final Older Scots /ai/ that do not monophthongise transfer to BITE or TRY; these can be considered a PAY subclass (*ay, may, pay, gey, hay, clay, stay; change, chain; baillie, tailor, gaol*)."

One reasonable conjecture here is that Mrs McFarlane, under the influence of speakers of New Zealand and/or English English, has from time to time accommodated, as it were, phonologically rather than phonetically, by extending this vowel (which is already present in her phonemic inventory; she pronounces *gaol* with /ae/ for instance) to a whole group of words from the FACE set in which she originally did not – and still most often does not – have it. This accommodation strategy resembles the merger strategy labelled "merger by transfer" as outlined in Trudgill and Foxcroft (1978) and Labov (1994), in which two vowels are merged phonologically rather than phonetically by the gradual transfer of lexical items from one vowel to another until all such items have been transferred and the vowel in question therefore disappears. This is thus a feature of *interdialect* (see above).

If this is so, we can employ the same interdialect interpretation in examining Mrs McFarlane's vowel in the lexical set of TRAP. This is variably though not infrequently a dramatically close [ɛ]. (I do not include here her pronunciations of words such as *grass, after, marriage* which are pronounced with the DRESS vowel in very many Scottish dialects – see Grant and Dixon 1921: 44.) This is rather remarkable since, as we saw above, in nearly all forms of Scots and Scottish

English the vowel in this set is a low vowel of the type [a ~ ʌ ~ ɑ], and she herself also often uses a vowel of this quality. A reasonable conjecture, once again, therefore, is that Mrs McFarlane has adopted a similar strategy in this case also. That is, under the influence of people with southeast-of-England-type accents who have a vowel in this lexical set with the phonetic quality [æ], which is radically different from her own, she has replaced this with the vowel from her own phonemic inventory which is closest to theirs, namely her DRESS vowel.

This strategy may have been further encouraged by the fact that there is a small area of Mrs McFarlane's native county of Angus whose Scots Traditional Dialects have a remarkable feature that may be relevant. Friockheim was not one of the fieldwork points for *The linguistic atlas of Scotland* (Mather and Speitel 1975) but is very close to a number of them. It is twelve miles by road southwest of Ferryden; nine miles east of Forfar; eight miles south of Brechin; and eight miles northwest of the coastal town of Arbroath. The Atlas informant from Arbroath, while he is shown as having [a] in *back, bank, strap*, has [ɛ] in certain members of the TRAP set, namely *bad, had, mad, drab, bag, bang*. Johnston (1997b: 486) also writes of the vowel of the lexical set which he labels the CAT class that "the Dundee suburbs up to Arbroath have a distinctive fronting to BET [i.e. DRESS] before /b, g/, so that *bag = beg*".

I suggest that Mrs McFarlane is using an accommodation strategy of a type the results of which appear to be totally absent from the speech of our core informants who, as children, would have been more successful at mastering phonetic detail and at analysing the structure of phonological systems than someone who, like her, arrived as an adult. Crucially, this sort of phonological as opposed to phonetic accommodation, on the part of a number of Scots in the first generation for whom we have no direct evidence, may have played a role in reinforcing the development of the close realisation of TRAP in New Zealand English, not by leading the way in the gradual phonetic raising of TRAP over time but in the total phonological replacement of the TRAP vowel by the DRESS vowel.

CONCLUSION

The ONZE research project has revealed the presence of Scottish features in late nineteenth-century English in New Zealand in quantities that would never be suspected from an inspection of the modern version of this form of the language. Scots dialect features of the type displayed by Mrs McFarlane made it to New Zealand but did not make it into the second stage of the new-dialect-formation process because they were not sufficiently strong demographically to survive the threshold effect or to compete with other features present in the linguistic environment. On the other hand, the ONZE core informants show us that many features of Scottish English did make it to the second stage of new-dialect formation but were not sufficiently strong to make it from there into modern New Zealand English. Scottish English and Scots dialects nevertheless did play a role in the formation of this new variety by reinforcing the influence of other dialects in the survival of certain variants, such as /h/; and in supporting through interdialect forms the developing close variants of the TRAP vowel /æ/ and diphthong-shifted variants of the PRICE vowel /ai/.

It is my contention, then, that the influence of varieties of English from Scotland was indirect but important. The theory of new-dialect formation, with its emphasis on determinism and the threshold effect, as well as its insights concerning interdialect, permits us to see rather clearly the indirect role that these large amounts of Scottish English played in the formation of New Zealand English, in a way that would not be possible on the basis of analysis of the modern language alone.

Epilogue: The critical threshold and interactional synchrony

In the eight chapters which have preceded this Epilogue, I have tried to find solutions to puzzles about why certain language varieties are like they are. In every case, to a greater or lesser extent, those solutions have been couched at least partly in terms of contact between language varieties.

In some cases it was mostly *language* contact that the investigation focussed on. Contact between the West Germanic Old English and the Brythonic Celtic Late British, as discussed in Chapter 1, was clearly language contact. I argued that it was contact between the Old English of the newcomers and the Late British of the indigenous inhabitants that led, originally in the English spoken by adult Brythonic speakers, to the simplification that took place in English during the first centuries of its existence in Britain. The discussion of the surprising but highly probable effects of the Spanish Inquisition on the nature of East Anglian dialects of English in Chapter 2 also saw the importance of contact that was clearly of the language-contact type. It appears to be rather important, too, that the contact involved three languages rather than two: (Walloon) French, (Flemish) Dutch and (Norwich) English. And in Chapter 5, in the discussion of differences in dynamism as between American and British Isles English *to have*, I also discussed contact between English in the United States and other languages such as Dutch, French, Spanish, Yiddish and German. I argued that this contact had had a decelerating effect on the process of linguistic change which had been affecting the verb *to have* for many centuries.

A number of other chapters in the book dealt, on the other hand, with *dialect* contact. Chapters 6, 7 and 8, which were concerned with the origins and development of colonial varieties of

English and especially New Zealand English, investigated different aspects and consequences of the fact that dialect contact leads to dialect mixture. This occurred in the colonies when speakers of different regional forms of British Isles English came into contact and interacted with one another in the new colonial setting in a way that would not have occurred in the homeland.

In yet other chapters in the book, however, it was not really entirely clear if we were dealing with language contact, dialect contact, or both. Obviously, the distinction between dialect contact and language contact is not unproblematical. In Trudgill (1986) I distinguished between the two by employing the rather obvious criterion of mutual intelligibility. This might appear to be an unsatisfactory criterion. It is well known that mutual intelligibility can increase with exposure; it can depend on the willingness of the parties involved to attempt to comprehend each other and to make themselves understood; it may not be equal in both directions; and so on. Crucially, however, mutual intelligibility is not an either/or phenomenon – it admits of many degrees of more-or-less. I suggest, however, that this is actually not a problem. As long as it is understood that there is a continuum of mutual intelligibility, ranging from total, through degrees of partial, to non-existent, then we can suppose that there is also a continuum of contact types, ranging from clear cases of dialect contact, through a whole range of intermediate cases where it is not obvious which term we should use, to clear cases of language contact. The term *semi-communication*, then, which is so often used in the Norwegian–Swedish–Danish context (Haugen 1966; Braunmüller 1997), is not sufficiently precise: we do not have simply "communication", "semi-communication" and "non-communication". What we actually have is a continuum of degrees of communication.

This is illustrated by some of the cases that we have dealt with in this book. The Old English–Old Norse contact I discussed in Chapter 1 probably lay somewhere in the potentially problematical middle of the continuum. As we saw, the degree of mutual intelligibility that existed between Old English and Old Norse remains controversial. Old Norse and Old English were related Germanic languages; and the contact occurred only a few centuries – perhaps as few as six – after the split of Northwest Germanic into North Germanic and West Germanic. It has been widely considered that there would therefore have been enough similarity, or at least lexical similarity, between the two languages at the time in question for communication to have been readily possible in those areas of eastern and northern England where extensive contact took place.

But what "readily" might mean in this context is, of course, a rather open question – the issue has been extensively and helpfully discussed in Townend (2002). In any case, six centuries may have been quite enough for all intelligibility to be lost: Jackson argues that nearly all the sound changes which converted Brythonic into Welsh, Cornish and Breton took place between the middle of the fifth and the end of the sixth century, and that evolution was so rapid that "we can be fairly sure that Vortigern around 450 could not have understood Aneirin around 600" (Jackson 1953: 690).

Another intriguing dialect- versus language-continuum possibility concerns the sixteenth-century presence of Flemish speakers in Norwich. English and Dutch are both West Germanic languages and are obviously closely related. Is it conceivable that some mutual intelligibility was still possible in the 1500s, in a way that it is not today, four and a half centuries later? East Anglian fishermen famously had a rhyme which, in living memory, went:

> *Bread, butter and green cheese*
> *Is good English and good Friese.*

The Frisians, too, still have a version of the same rhyme:

> *Bûter, brea en griene tsiis*
> *Is goed Ingelsk en goed Fries.*

But of course West Frisian is known to be more closely related to English than Dutch is, and in any case such rhymes may well not actually be evidence of a genuinely high level of intelligibility. The best guess is that mutual comprehension was not readily possible in sixteenth-century Norwich, but that it might have been achievable without too much difficulty, given enough exposure. Here, then, "language contact" is probably the more appropriate label for what happened in Norwich in the second half of the sixteenth century.

Chapter 3, where we discussed the merger and subsequent unmerger of /w/ and /v/ in English, dealt with an issue that was problematical in a slightly different way. Here I attempted to use the phenomenon of colonial lag to produce synchronic evidence from lesser-known varieties of English as a way of interpreting the diachrony of the (by now lost) merger in England. The problem was that, although there were many varieties to gather evidence from, in each case I had to consider the possibility that language contact might have been involved and that the evidence I was seeking might be misleading for that reason.

MECHANISMS

Of the two different types of contact, the linguistic consequences of language contact are considerably less mysterious than those stemming from dialect contact. In Chapter 1, we saw that the most far-reaching linguistic effects of language contact are due, as Dahl (2004) elegantly put it, to the disadvantage human adults seem to suffer from in language learning compared to child members of their own species. It is this which, I argued, produced simplification of the type which occurred in Old English, as regularisation and other aspects of simplification make for greater ease of adult learnability by removing linguistic features which are "L2 difficult". The major mechanism that is involved in producing the linguistic consequences associated with language contact has to do with some form of the *critical period* hypothesis.

Intriguingly, some linguists are cautious about accepting this common-sense position that adults are less gifted than children in language acquisition: Anderson and Lightfoot are simply willing to say (2002: 209) that "whatever we learn after the period of normal first-language acquisition, we learn in a different way". But, beginning in the 1970s, there were also, surprisingly, more strongly dissenting voices, both from second-language acquisition studies and formal linguistics. A recent example is Hale (2007: 44), who says: "I do not believe in what is sometimes called the Critical Age Hypothesis".

Swan (2007) has argued that this kind of reluctance on the part of some scholars to accept the obvious is explicable in terms of the linguistic-ideological position taken by some linguists who are "concerned to show, in accordance with the new orthodoxy of the time, that all language development [is] driven by unconscious mechanisms whose operation [is] similar, if not identical, for both L1 and L2", and that any position not compatible with this view "needed to be discredited".

For those who are not so ideologically driven, however, it is clear why adult language contact has the consequences it does. What is not so clear, however, is why exactly dialect contact should have the consequences it does, and in particular why it results in dialect mixture.

Again intriguingly, some linguists have rejected the scenario which sees the one as necessarily leading to the other. Wall (1938), for example, claimed that New Zealand English was not the result of a mixture of British Isles dialects but simply transplanted Cockney. This rejection of the idea that contact leads to mixing is not too surprising – because, after all, why should it? Why should speakers adopt features from dialects other than their own – something which obviously has to happen if mixture is to occur? If we define dialect contact as contact between language varieties that are mutually intelligible, then why would speakers modify their behaviour at all in the presence of speakers of other dialects who, however, are able to understand them perfectly well even if they do not modify their language? Sometimes, of course, if dialects are very different, then a degree of modification may genuinely help with comprehension; but most of the cases of new-dialect formation that are dealt with in the literature do not seem to be explicable solely in those terms.

In fact, however, there are explanations which are available for this phenomenon. The hypothesis which I advanced in Trudgill (1986), which seems to have received some acceptance (e.g. Tuten 2003), is that the fundamental mechanism leading to dialect mixture is accommodation in face-to-face interaction, a concept developed by Howard Giles (1973) and further refined in other publications such as Giles, Coupland and Coupland (1991). Tuten, in his brilliant book, says: "given that most contributing varieties in a prekoine linguistic pool are mutually intelligible ... many of the alterations in speech that take place are not strictly speaking necessary to fulfil communicative needs". He then continues: "Trudgill's emphasis on accommodation reveals rather novel assumptions about why dialect contact leads to change" (Tuten 2003: 29). And it emerges that he agrees with my "novel assumptions".

But actually, of course, an acceptance of the role of dialect mixture, and thus of accommodation, simply leads to yet another question: why is it in fact that speakers do accommodate to each other in face-to-face interaction? Tuten has an answer: "Speakers accommodate to the speech of their interlocutors *in order to promote a sense of common identity*" (Tuten 2003: 29 [my italics]).

Here I part company with Tuten. Although there clearly are sociolinguistic situations where identity plays a role, I see no role for identity factors in colonial new-dialect formation, and I have particular trouble with Tuten's use of the phrase "in order to". But I have to acknowledge that this sort of view about the motivation for accommodation and thus for the development of new colonial dialects is rather widely held.

For example, the Australian lexicographer Bruce Moore (1999) has said, of the development of colonial Englishes, that: "With language one of the most significant markers of national identity, it's not surprising that post-colonial societies like Australia, the United States, Canada, New Zealand, should want to distinguish their language from that of the mother tongue". Schneider, in his article on new varieties of English (2003: 238), also says of the development of these varieties by colonial "settlers in a foreign land" that "the stages and strands of this process are ultimately caused by ... reconstructions of group identities". And Macaulay (2002: 239) states: "I fully expect new dialects to develop in places where a sense of local identity becomes strong enough to create deep-seated loyalty".

Hickey (2003: 215), too, has written in a critique of Trudgill, Gordon, Lewis and Maclagan (2000) that New Zealand English is to "be seen as a product of unconscious choices made across a broad front in a new society to create a distinct linguistic identity". He then goes on to argue that the selection of certain variants available in a dialect mixture "can be interpreted as motivated by speakers' gradual awareness of an embryonic variety of the immigrants' language, something which correlates with the distinctive profile of the new society which is speaking this variety".

In my view, we would do well to be a bit more sceptical than this about explanations for the formation of new colonial varieties couched in terms of identity. I share the kind of view expressed by Mufwene when he writes (2001: 212) of the development of creoles that they were not "created" by their speakers but that they emerged "by accident". I share, too, the scepticism expressed by William Labov on the importance of identity factors in leading to linguistic change. Labov's famous Martha's Vineyard study (1963) is often cited as a typical and very telling example of the important function of identity in producing language change. Strikingly, however, Labov himself does not agree. He writes (2001: 191):

> The Martha's Vineyard study is frequently cited as a demonstration of the importance of the concept of local identity in the motivation of linguistic change. However, we do not often find correlations between degrees of local identification and the progress of sound change.

My claim is that new mixed colonial varieties can and do come into being without identity factors having any involvement at all. We do not need this as an explanatory factor. Of course, since the hey-day of European colonialism, new identities most certainly have developed in most of the colonies. French Canadians are no longer French; Australians are certainly not British; and Afrikaners are very definitely not Dutch; and these new identities do have a strong linguistic component, as Schneider indicates. But my suggestion is that if a common identity is promoted through language, then this happens as a *consequence* of accommodation; it is not its driving force. Identity is not a powerful enough driving force to account for the emergence of new, mixed dialects by accommodation. It is parasitic upon accommodation and is chronologically subsequent to it. Identity factors cannot lead to the development of new linguistic features, and it would be ludicrous to suggest that New Zealand English speakers deliberately developed, say, wide diphthongs in order to symbolise some kind of local or national New Zealand identity. This is of course not necessarily the same thing as saying that once new linguistic features have developed they cannot *become* emblematic, although it is as well to be sceptical about the extent to which this sort of phenomenon does actually occur also.

Labov's view is that, before one jumps to conclusions based on notions of identity, patterns of interaction should always be consulted for possible explanations. Labov's main preoccupation in his writings on this topic has been with the diffusion of linguistic forms; but new-dialect formation, which depends just as much as diffusion on how individual speakers behave linguistically in face-to-face interaction, can be regarded in precisely the same way. Labov argues that "as always, it is good practice to consider first the simpler and more mechanical view that social structure affects linguistic output through changes in frequency of interaction" (Labov 2001: 506). He bases his argument on Bloomfield's assertion (1933: 476) that:

> every speaker is constantly adapting his speech-habits to those of his interlocutors ... The inhabitants of a settlement ... talk much more to each other than to persons who live elsewhere. When any innovation in the way of speaking spreads over a

district, the limit of this spread is sure to be along some lines of weakness in the network of oral communication.

Labov argues that it follows from this that "a large part of the problem of explaining the diffusion of linguistic change is reduced to a simple calculation" (2001: 19). It is purely a matter of who interacts most often with who – a matter of density of communication. Labov then develops the *principle of density*:

> The principle of density implicitly asserts that we do not have to search for a motivating force behind the diffusion of linguistic change. The effect is mechanical and inevitable; the implicit assumption is that social evaluation and attitudes play a minor role.
>
> (Labov 2001: 20)

But why, we can ask, is it "mechanical and inevitable"? What exactly is inevitable about it?

The answer is that it is inevitable because accommodation is not only a subconscious but also a deeply automatic process. It is, as I have argued in Trudgill (2004), the result of the fact that all human beings operate linguistically according to a powerful and very general maxim. Keller (1994: 100) renders this maxim as 'talk like the others talk'.

Keller's maxim, in turn, is the linguistic aspect of a much more general and seemingly universal (and therefore presumably innate) human tendency to 'behavioural coordination', 'behavioural congruence', 'mutual adaptation' or 'interactional synchrony', as it is variously called in the literature. This is an apparently biologically given drive to behave as one's peers do.

There is a copious literature on this topic – see for example Cappella (1981, 1996, 1997); Bernieri and Rosenthal (1991); Burgoon, Stern and Dillman (1995) – which suggests that linguistic accommodation is not driven by social factors such as identity at all but is an automatic consequence of human interaction. Pelech (2002: 9), for example, says that "the innate biological basis of interactional synchrony has been established". He then goes on to say that "the ability to establish interactional synchrony represents an innate human capacity and one of the earliest forms of human communication". This capacity served, and serves, "the basic survival needs of bonding ... safety, and comfort". Cappella (1981) explores further the evolutionary and biological bases for the existence of adaptation processes in the human species. And in Cappella (1997: 65) he says that "mutual adaptation is pervasive" and that it is "arguably the essential characteristic of every interpersonal interaction". Linguistic diffusion and new-dialect formation are "mechanical and inevitable" because linguistic accommodation is automatic; as Cappella (1997: 69) states, it is an aspect of "the relatively automatic behaviors manifested during social interaction".

We should note, however, that Cappella does say that the behaviour involved in accommodation is only "relatively" automatic, the perhaps comforting implication being that it can be overridden in the case of individuals.

This reminds us that we have to consider the evidence provided here by the English of the Bonin Islands, which we discussed in Chapter 4, and where it seems that relatively little accommodation took place. The islands clearly had a considerable history of language contact; and we saw that Uncle Charlie's speech had a number of features which are typical of non-native English, such as the plural forms *mans* and *womans*, and the replacement of original /θ/ by /s/. But there is no evidence of dialect contact at all. We know that the early settlers on the island included native English speakers from England as well as the United States; but Uncle Charlie's English, as we were able to demonstrate, quite clearly descends from a single variety of American English, that of Eastern New England; it is presumably not a coincidence that Charlie's maternal grandfather, Nathaniel Savory, one of the small number of native anglophone original settlers, came from Bradford, Massachusetts. The correct conclusion here would seem to be that there are some highly unusual situations where the normal sequence of dialect contact leading to dialect mixture does not apply.

There are a number of known cases (see Trudgill 2004) of anglophone colonisation where mixing did not occur. These are cases where settlements were derived from single locations in the British Isles, and no mixing could therefore occur. For example, rural dialects of Newfoundland English (i.e. not the dialect of the capital, St John's) are derived more or less directly either from the English southwest or the Irish southeast (Paddock 1982; Kirwin 2001). Rural Falkland Islands English (i.e. not the dialect of the capital, Port Stanley) also differs from settlement to settlement depending on the origins of each community in a single British location (Sudbury 2000; Trudgill 1986), particularly on West Falkland. And the one linguistic colony of the USA that has been studied, the Brazilian settlement of Americana mentioned in Chapter 3, has an English which is entirely derived from the American southeast.

The early situation of English on the Bonin Islands, then, seems to have been one which resembled the situation on West Falkland. We have to conclude that, in spite of the presence of English speakers from other areas, it was as if the English of Eastern New England was the only variety involved – it was certainly the only one which had any impact. We cannot know exactly what happened, but we have to suppose that the key factor was that, unlike the tens of thousands of colonists who arrived in, for example, New Zealand, there were very few people indeed involved in the settlement of the Bonins – including fewer than ten native English speakers. In such a situation, it is not surprising that the influence of a single individual could become paramount.

However, Cappella makes it clear that behavioural congruence is the default; and we can therefore be sure that prolonged large-scale dialect contact involving communities larger than that of the Bonins will always inevitably lead to dialect mixture, as speakers accommodate to one another. And this accommodation in turn leads to new-dialect formation, as there is no single peer-group dialect for children to accommodate to in the new colonial situation. Rather, children are surrounded by an enormously variable set of models. This absence of a single model dialect leads to a situation where children acquire dialects that are very variable, that differ from one another, and that consist for the most part of forms derived, for English, from British dialects but in original combinations not found anywhere in the British Isles. Finally, new-dialect formation occurs when the variants are reduced, in most cases, to one, with the new dialect itself consisting of those variants which were in the majority in the mixture.

My suggestion is therefore that it is this innate tendency to behavioural coordination, not identity, that is the very powerful drive that makes dialect mixture an almost inevitable consequence of dialect contact, to an extent that factors connected with identity would not and could not. The actual linguistic characteristics of any new mixed dialect result from the relatively deterministic principles outlined in Trudgill (2004) and briefly discussed in Chapter 8; and it is the new mixed dialect to which the founder principle – i.e. that the speech of the founding population of a colony determines what its dialect will be like (Mufwene 2001: 28) – then applies. In fact, all the evidence is that large-scale and prolonged dialect contact *always* leads to dialect mixture, and therefore in a sense requires no explanation, and certainly not one in terms of identity.

Perhaps, then, in conclusion, we can say that these investigations in sociohistorical linguistics have been concerned with the way in which the historical-linguistic consequences of the social phenomena of human colonisation and contact are impacted on by two biological phenomena. These are phenomena which appear to be an inherent part of the human condition: the innate language-learning abilities of human children, which are not totally shared by adolescent and adult members of the same species; and the innate biological basis of human interactional synchrony, which is shared by all of us.

Bibliography

Ahlqvist, Anders. 2010. Early Celtic and English. *Australian Celtic Journal* 9: 41–71.

Aitken, Adam J. 1984. Scottish accents and dialects. In P. Trudgill (ed.), *Language in the British Isles*, 94–114. Cambridge University Press.

Algeo, J. 1995. Having a look at the expanded predicate. In B. Aarts and C. F. Meyer (eds.), *The verb in contemporary English*, 203–17. Cambridge University Press.

Anderson, Stephen R. and David Lightfoot. 2002. *The language organ: linguistics as cognitive psychology*. Cambridge University Press.

Andersson, Lars-Gunnar. 2005. What makes a language hard? In C. Kiselman (ed.), *Symposium on communication across cultural boundaries*, 40–8. Prague: Kava-Pech.

Anttila, Raimo. 1989. *Historical and comparative linguistics*. Amsterdam: Benjamins.

Auwera, Johan van der and Inge Genee. 2002. English do: on the convergence of languages and linguists. *English Language and Linguistics* 6: 283–307.

Ayres, H. M. 1933. Bermudian English. *American Speech* 8.1: 6–10.

Bailey, Beryl. 1965. Toward a new perspective in Negro English dialectology. *American Speech* 40: 171–7.

Bailey, Charles J. and Karl Maroldt. 1977. The French lineage of English. In J. Meisel (ed.), *Langues en contact – pidgins – creoles*, 21–53. Tübingen: Narr.

Bailey, Guy, Natalie Maynor and Patricia Cukor-Avila. 1989. Variation in subject-verb concord in Early Modern English. *Language Variation and Change* 1: 285–300.

Bailey, Richard W. 1982. The English language in Canada. In R. W. Bailey and M. Görlach (eds.), *English as a world language*. Ann Arbor: University of Michigan Press.

Bailey, Richard W. 1996. *Nineteenth century English*. Ann Arbor: University of Michigan Press.

Bakker, Peter. 2003. Pidgin inflectional morphology and its implications for creole morphology. In I. Plag (ed.), *Yearbook of morphology 2002*, 3–33. Dordrecht: Kluwer.

Bakker, Peter and Maarten Mous (eds.). 1994. *Mixed languages. 15 case studies in language intertwining*. Amsterdam/Dordrecht: IFOTT/Foris.

Barber, C. 1997. *Early modern English*. Edinburgh University Press.

Bartlett, Christopher. 2003. The Southland variety of English. Ph.D thesis, Otago University.

Battistella, Edwin. 1990. *Markedness: the evaluative superstructure of language*. Albany: SUNY Press.

Bauer, Laurie. 1997. Attempting to trace Scottish influence on New Zealand English. In W. W. Schneider (ed.), *Englishes around the world: studies in honour of Manfred Görlach*, 257–72. Amsterdam/Philadelphia: John Benjamins.

Bauer, Laurie. 2000. The dialectal origins of New Zealand English. In A. Bell and K. Kuiper (eds.), *New Zealand English*, 40–52. Wellington: Victoria University Press.

Baugh, Albert C. and Thomas Cable. 1993. *A history of the English language*. London: Routledge.

Beal, Joan. 1999. *English pronunciation in the eighteenth century: Thomas Spence's 'Grand repository of the English language'*. Oxford: Clarendon Press.

Bell, Allan. 1997. The phonetics of fish and chips in New Zealand: marking national and ethnic identities. *English World-Wide* 18: 243–70.

Benham, Charles. 1960 [1895]. *Essex ballads*. Colchester: Benham Newspapers.

Bernieri, Frank and Robert Rosenthal. 1991. Interpersonal coordination: behavior matching and interactional synchrony. In R. Feldman and B. Rime (eds.), *Fundamentals of nonverbal behavior: studies in emotion and social interaction*, 401–32. New York: Cambridge University Press.

Berthele, Raphael. 2000. *Sprache in der Klasse: eine dialektologisch–soziolinguistische Untersuchung von Primarschulkindern in multilingualem Umfeld*. Tübingen: Niemeyer.

Bhaldraithe, Tomas de. 1945. *The Irish of Cois Fhairrge, Co. Galway: a phonetic study*. Dublin: Institute for Advanced Studies.

Biber, D., S. Johansson, G. Leech, S. Conrad and E. Finegan. 1999. *Longman grammar of spoken and written English*. Harlow: Pearson.

Bloomfield, Leonard. 1933. *Language*. New York: Holt, Rinehart and Winston.

Bradley, H. 1904. *The making of English*. London: Macmillan.

Branford, William. 1994. English in South Africa. In Robert Burchfield (ed.), *The Cambridge history of the English language vol. 5: English in Britain and overseas – origins and development*, 182–429. Cambridge University Press.

Braunmüller, Kurt. 1997. Communication strategies in the area of the Hanseatic league: the approach by semi-communication. *Multilingua* 16: 365–74.

Breeze, Andrew. 2002. Seven types of Celtic loanword. In M. Filppula, J. Klemola and H. Pitkänen (eds.), *The Celtic roots of English*, 175–81. Joensuu University Press.

Brinton, Laurel and Minoji Akimoto (eds.). 1999. *Collocational and idiomatic aspects of composite predicates in the history of English*. Amsterdam: Benjamins.

Britain, David. 1991. Dialect and space: a geolinguistic study of speech variables in the Fens. Ph.D thesis, University of Essex.

Brook, G. L. 1958. *A history of the English language*. London: Deutsch.

Burgoon, Judee, Lesa Stern and Leesa Dillman. 1995. *Interpersonal adaptation: dyadic interaction patterns*. New York: Cambridge University Press.

Burling, Robbins. 1973. *English in black and white*. New York: Holt, Rinehart and Winston.

Burns, Sir A. 1954. *History of the British West Indies*. London: George Allen and Unwin.

Campbell, Lyle. 1997. Amerindian personal pronouns: a second opinion. *Language* 73: 339–51.

Cappella, Joseph. 1981. Mutual influence in expressive behavior: adult–adult and infant–adult dyadic interaction. *Psychological Bulletin* 89: 101–32.

Cappella, Joseph. 1996. Dynamic coordination of vocal and kinesic behavior in dyadic interaction: methods, problems, and interpersonal outcomes. In J. Watt and C. VanLear (eds.), *Dynamic patterns in communication processes*, 353–86. Thousand Oaks: Sage.

Cappella, Joseph. 1997. The development of theory about automated patterns of face-to-face human interaction. In G. Philipsen and T. Albrecht (eds.), *Developing communication theories, SUNY series in human communication processes*, 57–83. Albany: State University of New York Press.

Carpenter, David. 2004. *The struggle for mastery: the Penguin history of Britain 1066–1284*. London: Penguin.

Chambers, J. K. 1991. Canada. In Jenny Cheshire (ed.), *English Around the World: Sociolinguistic Perspectives*, 89–107. Cambridge University Press.

Chambers, J. K. 1992. Dialect acquisition. *Language* 68, 673–705.

Christaller, Walter. 1950. *Das Grundgerüst der räumlichen Ordnung in Europa: die Systeme der europäischen zentralen Orte*. Frankfurt: Kramer.

Clackson, James and Geoffrey Horrocks. 2007. *The Blackwell history of the Latin language*. Oxford: Blackwell.

Clahsen, Harald and P. Muysken. 1996. How adult second language learning differs from child first language development. *Behavioural and Brain Sciences* 19: 721–3.

Claridge, Claudia. 2000. *Multi-word verbs in Early Modern English: a corpus-based study*. Amsterdam: Rodopi.

Clark, Ross. 1976. *Aspects of Polynesian syntax*. Auckland: Linguistic Society of New Zealand.

Clements, G. N. 2000. Phonology. In B. Heine and D. Nurse (eds.), *African languages: an introduction*, 123–60. Cambridge University Press.

Coates, Richard. 2007. Invisible Britons: the view from linguistics. In N. Higham (ed.), *The Britons in Anglo-Saxon England*, 172–91. Woodbridge: Boydell.

Coates, Richard and Nikolas Coupland. 1991. *Contexts of accommodation: developments in applied sociolinguistics*. Cambridge University Press.

Dahl, Östen. 2004. *The growth and maintenance of linguistic complexity*. Amsterdam: Benjamins.

Davidson, Allan. 1991. *Christianity in Aotearoa: a history of church and society in New Zealand*. Wellington: Education for Ministry.

Davis, Norman, Richard Beadle and Colin Richmond (eds.). 2004–5. *Paston letters and papers of the fifteenth century*, 3 vols. (Early English Text Society, supplementary series 20–22). Oxford University Press.

Denison, D. 1993. *English historical syntax*. London: Longman.

Dietrich, G. 1949. *Die Syntax der 'Do'-Umschreibung bei 'have', 'be', 'ought' und 'used (to)', auf sprachgeschichtlicher Grundlage dargestellt*. Brunswick: Georg Westermann Verlag.

Dillard, Joey. 1970. Principles in the history of American English: paradox, virginity and cafeteria. *Florida Reporter* 8.1–2: 32–3.

Dixon, R. M. W. 1997. *The rise and fall of languages*. Cambridge University Press.

Dollinger, Stefan. 2008. *New-dialect formation in Canada: evidence from the English modal auxiliaries*. Amsterdam: John Benjamins.

Edwards, V. K. 1979. *The West Indian language issue in British schools*. London: Routledge.

Ehrhart-Kneher, Sabine. 1996. Palmerston English. In S. A. Wurm, P. Mühlhäusler and D. T. Tryon (eds.), *Atlas of languages of intercultural communication in the Pacific, Asia, and the Americas*, 523–31. Berlin: Mouton de Gruyter.

Ekwall, Eilert. 1960. *The concise Oxford dictionary of place-names*, 4th edn. Oxford University Press.

Elbert, Samuel H. and Mary Kawena Pukui. 1979. *Hawaiian Grammar*. Honolulu: University of Hawai`i Press.

Ellegård, A. 1953. *The auxiliary DO: the establishment and regulation of its use in English*. Stockholm: Almqvist and Wiksell.

Ellis, Alexander. 1889. *On Early English pronunciation*, vol. V. London: Trübner.

Emeneau, M. B. 1975. The dialect of Lunenburg, Nova Scotia. In J. K. Chambers (ed.), *Canadian English: origins and structures*, 34–9. Toronto: Methuen.

Eubank, Lynn. 1996. Negation in early German–English interlanguage: more valueless features in the L2 initial state. *Second Language Research* 12: 73–106.

Evans, D. Simon. 1964. *A Grammar of Middle Welsh*. Dublin: Dublin Institute for Advanced Studies.

Fasold, Ralph. 1972. *Tense marking in Black English: a linguistic and social analysis*. Washington, DC: Center for Applied Linguistics.

Ferguson, Charles A. 1959. Diglossia. *Word* 15: 325–40.

Ferguson, Charles A. 1971. Absence of copula and the notion of simplicity: a study of normal speech, baby talk, foreigner talk, and pidgins. In D. Hymes (ed.), *Pidginisation and creolisation of languages*, 141–50. Cambridge University Press.

Filppula, Markku. 2003. More on the English progressive and the Celtic connection. In H. Tristram (ed.), *The Celtic Englishes III*, 150–68. Heidelberg: Winter.

Fisiak, Jacek. 1968. *A short grammar of Middle English*. Warsaw: Panstwowe Wydawnictwo Naukowe.

Flint, E. H. 1964. The language of Norfolk Island. In A. Ross and A. Moverley (eds.), *The Pitcairnese Language*. London: Andre Deutsch.

Forby, Robert. 1830. *The vocabulary of East Anglia*. London: Nichols.

Fox, Cyril. 1932. *The personality of Britain: its influence on inhabitant and invader in prehistoric and early historic times*. Cardiff: National Museum of Wales.

Frick, Franz N. 1899. *Die Araner Mundart: ein Beitrag zur Erforschung des Westirischen*. Marburg: Elwert.

Garrett, A. 1998. On the origin of auxiliary *do*. *English Language and Linguistics* 2.2: 283–99.

Gelling, Margaret. 1993. *Place-names in the landscape: the geographical roots of Britain's place-names*. London: Dent.

Giles, Howard. 1973. Accent mobility: a model and some data. *Anthropological Linguistics* 15: 87–105.

Giles, Howard, Justine Coupland and Nikolas Coupland. 1991. *Contexts of accommodation: developments in applied sociolinguistics*. Cambridge University Press.

Gimson, A. C. 1962. *An introduction to the pronunciation of English*. London: Edward Arnold.

Glauser, Beat. 1994. Dialect maps: depicting, constructing or distorting linguistic reality. In G. Melchers and N.-L. Johannesson (eds.), *Nonstandard varieties of language*, 35–52. Stockholm: Almqvist and Wiksell.

Gordon, Elizabeth. 1983. New Zealand English pronunciation: an investigation into some early written records. *Te Reo* 26: 29–42.

Gordon, Elizabeth. 1998. The origins of New Zealand Speech: the limits of recovering historical information from written records. *English World-Wide* 19: 61–85.

Gordon, Elizabeth, Lyle Campbell, Jennifer Hay, Margaret Maclagan, Andrea Sudbury and Peter Trudgill. 2004. *The origins of New Zealand English*. Cambridge University Press.

Görlach, Manfred. 1986. Middle English – a creole? In D. Kastovsky and A. Szwedek (eds.), *Linguistics across historical and geographical boundaries*, 329–44. Berlin: de Gruyter.

Görlach, Manfred. 1987. Colonial lag? The alleged conservative character of American English and other 'colonial' varieties. *English World-Wide* 8: 41–60.

Grant, William. 1913. *The pronunciation of English in Scotland*. Cambridge University Press.

Grant, William and James M. Dixon. 1921. *Manual of Modern Scots*. Cambridge University Press.

Green, Barbara and Rachel Young. 1964. *Norwich: the growth of a city*. Norwich: Museums Committee.

Hale, Mark. 2007. *Historical linguistics: theory and method*. Oxford: Blackwell.

Härke, Heinrich. 2002. Kings and warriors: population and landscape from post-Roman to Norman Britain. In P. Slack and R. Ward (eds.), *The peopling of Britain: the shaping of a human landscape*, 145–75. Oxford University Press.

Hartog, J. 1988. *History of Saba*. Saba: O.K.S.N.A.

Haugen, Einar. 1966. Semicommunication: the language gap in Scandinavia. *Sociological Inquiry* 36: 280–97.

Hawkins, John A. 2004. *Efficiency and complexity in grammars*. Oxford University Press.

Heine, Bernd and Tania Kuteva. 2005. *Language contact and grammatical change*. Cambridge University Press.

Henson, Don. 2006. *The origins of the Anglo-Saxons*. Hockwold: Anglo-Saxon Books.

Hickey, Raymond. 2003. How do dialects get the features they have? In *Motives for language change*, 213–39. Cambridge University Press.

Hiltunen, R. 1999. Verbal phrases and phrasal verbs in Early Modern English. In L. J. Brinton and M. Akimoto (eds.), *Collocational and idiomatic aspects of composite predicates in the history of English*, 33–165. Amsterdam: Benjamins.

Hogg, Richard. 1993. *A grammar of Old English I: Phonology*. Oxford: Blackwell.

Hogg, Richard and David Denison. 2006. *A history of the English language*. Cambridge University Press.

Holm, John. 1980. African features in White Bahamian English. *English World-Wide* 1: 45–66.

Holm, John and Alison Shilling. 1982. *Dictionary of Bahamian English*. Cold Spring NY: Lexik House.

Holman, Katherine. 2007. *The northern conquest: Vikings in Britain and Ireland*. Oxford: Signal Books.

Holmes, Janet. 1997. Setting new standards: sound changes and gender in New Zealand English. *English World-Wide* 18.1: 107–42.

Holmqvist, Erik. 1922. *On the history of English present inflections*. Heidelberg: Winter.

Hudson, R. 1997. The rise of auxiliary DO: verb-non-raising or category-strengthening? *Transactions of the Philological Society* 95: 41–72.

Hughes, Arthur and Peter Trudgill. 1995. *English accents and dialects*, 3rd edn. London: Edward Arnold.

Hughey, Ruth (ed.). 1941. *The correspondence of Lady Katherine Paston, 1603–1627*. Norwich: Norfolk Record Society.

Hyltenstam, Kenneth. 1992. Non-native features of near-native speakers: on the ultimate attainment of childhood L2 learners. In R. J. Harris (ed.), *Cognitive processing in bilinguals*, 351–68. Amsterdam: Elsevier.

Jackson, Kenneth H. 1953. *Language and history in early Britain*. Edinburgh University Press.

Johnson, Jacqueline and Elissa Newport. 1989. Critical period effects in second language learning: the influence of maturational state on the acquisition of English as a second language. *Cognitive Psychology* 21: 60–99.

Johnson, W. 1989. *Saban lore: tales from my grandmother's pipe*, 3rd edn. Saba: Lynne Johnson.

Johnston, Paul. 1997a. Old Scots phonology and its regional variation. In C. Jones (ed.), *The Edinburgh history of the Scots language*, 46–111. Edinburgh University Press.

Johnston, Paul. 1997b. Regional variation. In C. Jones (ed.), *The Edinburgh history of the Scots language*, 433–513. Edinburgh University Press.

Källgård, Anders. 1993. Present-day Pitcairnese. *English World-Wide* 14: 71–114.

Kastovsky, Dieter. 1999. Inflectional classes, morphological restructuring, and the dissolution of Old English grammatical gender. In Barbara Unterbeck and Matti Rissanen (eds.), *Gender in grammar and cognition.* Vol. II, 709–27. Berlin: Mouton de Gruyter.

Kazazis, Kostas. 1970. The relative importance of parents and peers in first-language acquisition: the case of some Constantinopolitan families in Athens. *General Linguistics* 10: 111–20.

Keller, Rudi. 1994. *On language change: the invisible hand in language.* London: Routledge.

Kerswill, Paul. 1994. Babel in Buckinghamshire? Pre-school children acquiring accent features in the new town of Milton Keynes. In G. Melchers and N.-L. Johannesson (eds.), *Nonstandard varieties of language,* 64–83. Stockholm: Almqvist and Wiksell.

Kett, John. no date. *Tha's a rum'un, bor!* Woodbridge: Baron.

Ketton-Cremer, R. W. 1957. *Norfolk Assembly.* London: Faber.

Kirwin, William. 2001. Newfoundland English. In J. Algeo (ed.), *The Cambridge history of the English language vol. 6: English in North America,* 441–5. Cambridge University Press.

Klemola, Juhani. 2000. The origins of the Northern Subject Rule: a case of early contact? In Hildegard L. C. Tristram (ed.), *Celtic Englishes II,* 329–46. Heidelberg: Universitätsverlag C. Winter.

Kohlman, Aarona Booker. no date. *Wotcha say: an introduction to colloquial Caymanian.* Grand Cayman: Cayman ARTventures.

Kökeritz, Helge. 1953. *Shakespeare's pronunciation.* New Haven: Yale University Press.

Kroch, A., A. Taylor and D. Ringe. 2000. The Middle English verb-second constraint: a case study in language contact and language change. In Susan Herring, Pieter van Reenen and Lene Schoesler (eds.), *Textual parameters in older language,* 353–91. Amsterdam: Benjamins.

Kurath, Hans. 1928. *American pronunciation.* Oxford: Clarendon.

Kurath, Hans and Guy Lowman. 1970. *The dialect structure of southern England: phonological evidence.* Tuscaloosa: University of Alabama Press.

Kurath, Hans and Raven I. McDavid. 1961. *The pronunciation of English in the Atlantic States.* Ann Arbor: University of Michigan Press.

Kurath, Hans, Marcus L. Hansen, Julia Bloch and Bernard Bloch. 1939–43. *Handbook of the linguistic geography of New England.* Providence: Brown University.

Kusters, Wouter. 2003. *Linguistic complexity: the influence of social change on verbal inflection.* Leiden University Press.

Kytö, Merja. 1993. Third-person singular inflection in early British and American English. *Language Variation and Change* 5: 113–40.

Labov, William. 1963. The social motivation of a sound change. *Word* 19: 273–309.

Labov, William. 1966. *The social stratification of English in New York City.* Washington: Center for Applied Linguistics.

Labov, William. 1972. *Sociolinguistic patterns.* Philadelphia: University of Pennsylvania Press.

Labov, William. 1994. *Principles of linguistic change, vol. 1: internal factors.* Oxford: Blackwell.

Labov, William. 2001. *Principles of linguistic change, vol. 2: social factors.* Oxford: Blackwell.

Labov, William. 2007. Transmission and diffusion. *Language* 81, 344–87.

Ladefoged, Peter. 1968. *A phonetic study of West African languages.* Cambridge University Press.

Laing, Lloyd and Jennifer Laing. 1979. *Anglo-Saxon England.* London: Routledge and Kegan Paul.

Laker, Stephen. 2002. An explanation for the changes *kw-, hw-, xw-* in the English dialects. In M. Filppula, J. Klemola and H. Pitkänen (eds.), *The Celtic roots of English*, 183–98. Joensuu University Press.

Laker, Stephen. 2008. Changing views about Anglo-Saxons and Britons. In H. Aertsen and B. Veldhoen (eds.), *Six papers from the 28th Symposium on Medieval Studies*, 1–38. Leiden University Press.

Laker, Stephen. 2009. Motivations for early phonological change in English: the Brittonic contribution. Ph.D thesis, University of Leiden.

LaPolla, Randy. 2005. Typology and complexity. In J. W. Minett and W. S.-Y. Wang (eds.), *Language acquisition, change and emergence: essays in evolutionary linguistics*, 465–93. Hong Kong: City University Press.

Lass, Roger. 1992. Phonology and morphology. In N. Blake (ed.), *The Cambridge history of the English language vol. II: 1066–1476*, 23–155. Cambridge University Press.

Lass, Roger. 1997. *Historical linguistics and language change.* Cambridge University Press.

Laver, John. 1994. *Principles of phonetics.* Cambridge University Press.

Law, Danny. 2009. Pronominal borrowing among the Maya. *Diachronica*, 26.2: 214–52.

Lenneberg, Eric. 1967. *Biological foundations of language.* New York: Wiley.

Le Page, Robert B. and Andree Tabouret-Keller. 1985. *Acts of identity: creole-based approaches to language and ethnicity*. Cambridge University Press.

Lightfoot, David. 1999. *The development of language: acquisition, change, and evolution*. Oxford: Blackwell.

Long, Daniel (ed.). 1998. *The linguistic culture of the Ogasawara Islands* (Japanese Language Centre Research Reports 6). Osaka: Shoin Women's College.

Long, Daniel (ed.). 1999. Evidence of an English contact language in the 19th century Bonin (Ogasawara) Islands. *English World-Wide* 20.2: 251–86.

Long, Daniel (ed.). 2000. Examining the Bonin (Ogasawara) Islands within the contexts of Pacific language contact. In S. Fischer and W. B. Sperlich (eds.), *Leo Pasifika: proceedings of the fourth international conference on Oceanic Linguistics*, 200–17. Auckland: Institute of Polynesian Languages and Literatures.

Long, Daniel (ed.). 2001. Insights into the vanishing language and culture of the Bonin (Ogasawara) Islands: Mr. Charles Washington's 1971 interviews. In S. Sanada (ed.), *Endangered languages of Japan*, 4685. Kyoto: Endangered Languages of the Pacific Rim Publications Series A4–001.

Long, Daniel (ed.). 2002. *The disappearing English language and culture of the "Westerners" of the Bonin (Ogasawara) Islands*. Kyoto: Endangered Languages of the Pacific Rim Publications Series A4–015.

Long, Daniel (ed.). 2007. *English on the Bonin Islands*. Durham, NC: Duke University Press.

Lutz, Angelika. 2009. Why is West-Saxon English different from Old Saxon? In H. Sauer and J. Story (eds.), *Anglo-Saxon and the Continent*. Tempe, AZ: Arizona Center for Medieval and Renaissance Studies.

Macaulay, Ronald. 2002. I'm off to Philadelphia in the morning. *American Speech* 77: 227–41.

Maclagan, David. 1998. /h/-dropping in early New Zealand English. *New Zealand English Journal* 12: 34–42.

Maclagan, Margaret A. and Elizabeth Gordon. 1996. Out of the AIR and into the EAR: another view of the New Zealand diphthong merger. *Language Variation and Change* 8: 125–47.

Maclagan, Margaret A., Elizabeth Gordon and Gillian Lewis. 1999. Women and sound change: conservative and innovative behaviour by the same speakers. *Language Variation and Change* 11: 19–41.

MacMahon, Michael. 1983. Thomas Hallam and the study of dialect and educated speech. *Transactions of the Yorkshire Dialect Society* 83: 119–31.

MacMahon, Michael. 1994. Phonology. In Suzanne Romaine (ed.), *The Cambridge history of the English language vol. 4: 1776–1997*, 373–535. Cambridge University Press.

Maddieson, Ian. 1984. *Patterns of sounds*. Cambridge University Press.

Marckwardt, Albert. 1958. *American English*. New York: Oxford University Press.

Mather, J. Y. and H. H. Speitel (eds.). 1975. *The linguistic atlas of Scotland*. London: Croom Helm.

Matsumoto, M. 1999. Composite predicates in Middle English. In L. J. Brinton and M. Akimoto (eds.), *Collocational and idiomatic aspects of composite predicates in the history of English*, 59–96. Amsterdam: Benjamins.

Matthews, W. 1972. *Cockney past and present*. London: Routledge and Kegan Paul.

McClure, J. Derrick. 1994. English in Scotland. In Robert Burchfield (ed.), *The Cambridge history of the English Language vol. 5: English in Britain and overseas: origins and development*, 23–93. Cambridge University Press.

McDavid, Raven I. and Virginia McDavid. 1951. The relationship of the speech of American Negroes to the speech of whites. *American Speech* 26: 3–17.

McElhinny, Bonnie. 1993. Copula and auxiliary contraction in the speech of White Americans. *American Speech* 68: 371–99.

McKinnon, Malcolm (ed.). 1997. *New Zealand historical atlas*. Auckland: Bateman.

McWhorter, John. 2007. *Language interrupted*. Oxford University Press.

Mees, Inger. 1977. Language and social class in Cardiff. Ph.D thesis, University of Leiden.

Meisel, Jürgen. 1997. The acquisition of the syntax of negation in French and German: contrasting first and second language development. *Second Language Research* 13: 227–63.

Milroy, James. 1992. Middle English dialectology. In N. Blake (ed.), *The Cambridge history of the English language vol. 2: 1066–1476*. Cambridge University Press, 156–206.

Milroy, James and Lesley Milroy. 1985. Linguistic change, social network and speaker innovation. *Journal of Linguistics* 21: 339–84

Milroy, Lesley. 2000. Social network analysis and the history of English. *European Journal of English Studies* 4.3: 211–16.

Mithun, Marianne. 1999. *The languages of Native North America*. Cambridge University Press.

Mithun, Marianne. 2007. Grammar, contact and time. *Journal of Language Contact – Thema 1*: 133–55. www.jlc-journal.org.

Mittendorf, Ingo and Erich Poppe. 2000. Celtic contacts of the English progressive? In Hildegard Tristram (ed.), *Celtic Englishes II*, 117–45. Heidelberg: Winter.

Moens, William. 1888. *The Walloons and their church at Norwich 1565–1832*. London: Huguenot Society.

Montgomery, Michael, Janet Fuller and Sharon DeMarse. 1993. 'The black men has wives and Sweet harts [and third-person plural -s] Jest like the white men': evidence for verbal -s from written documents on 19th-century African American speech. *Language Variation and Change* 5: 335–57.

Moore, Bruce. 1999. Australian English: Australian identity. *Lingua Franca*. www.abc.net.au/rn/arts/ling/stories/s68786.htm.

Morgan, Kenneth O. 2001. *The Oxford history of Britain*. Oxford University Press.

Mufwene, Salikoko. 1991. Pidgins, creoles, typology, and markedness. In F. Byrne and T. Huebner (eds.), *Development and structures of creole languages: essays in honour of Derek Bickerton*, 123–43. Amsterdam: Benjamins.

Mufwene, Salikoko. 2001. *The ecology of language evolution*. Cambridge University Press.

Mühlhäusler, Peter. 1977. *Pidginisation and simplification of language*. Canberra: Pacific Linguistics.

Murray, R. W. 1996. Historical linguistics. In W. O'Grady, M. Dobrovolsky and F. Katamba (eds.), *Contemporary linguistics: an introduction*, chapter 8. London: Longman.

Newbrook, Mark. 1982. Scot or Scouser? An anomalous informant in outer Merseyside. *English World-Wide* 3: 77–86.

Nichols, Johanna. 1992. *Linguistic diversity in space and time*. Chicago University Press.

Nichols, Johanna. 2007. Review of Ö. Dahl (2004) *The growth and maintenance of linguistic complexity*. *Diachronica* 24, 171–8.

Nichols, Johanna and David A. Peterson. 1996. The Amerind personal pronouns. *Language* 72.2: 336–71.

Nickel, Gerhard. 1966. *Die Expanded Form in Altenglischen*. Neumünster: Wachholtz.

Nielsen, Hans Frede. 1998. *The continental backgrounds of English and its insular development until 1154*. Odense University Press.

Nurmi, A. 1999. *A social history of periphrastic DO*. (Mémoires de la Société Néophilologique de Helsinki 56.) Helsinki: Société Néophilologique.

O Dochartaigh, Cathair. 1984. Irish. In P. Trudgill (ed.), *Language in the British Isles*, 289–305. Cambridge University Press.

Ogura, M. 1994. The development of periphrastic DO in English. *Diachronica* 10.1: 51–85.

Paddock, Harold. 1982. Newfoundland dialects of English. In H. Paddock (ed.), *Languages in Newfoundland and Labrador*, 71–89. St John's: Memorial University.

Parsons, James. 1954. English-speaking settlement of the Western Caribbean. *Yearbook of the Association of Pacific Coast Geographers* 16: 2–16.

Payne, Arvilla. 1980. Factors controlling the acquisition of the Philadelphia dialect by out-of-state children. In W. Labov (ed.), *Locating language in time and space*. New York: Academic Press.

Pelech, William. 2002. Charting the interpersonal underworld: the application of cluster analysis to the study of interpersonal coordination in small groups. *Currents: New Scholarship in the Human Services* 1.1: 1–12.

Pelteret, David. 1995. *Slavery in Early Mediaeval England*. Woodbridge: Boydell Press.

Pettersson, Sofia. 1994. A study of Dutch and Low German elements in the East Midland and East Anglian dialects. Unpublished paper, Stockholm University.

Pinker, Steven. 1994. *The language instinct*. London: Penguin Books.

Poplack, Shana (ed.). 2000. *The English history of African American English*. Oxford: Blackwell.

Poplack, Shana and Sali Tagliamonte. 1989. There's no tense like the present: verbal -s inflection in early Black English. *Language Variation and Change* 1: 47–84.

Poussa, Patricia. 1982. The evolution of Early Standard English: the creolisation hypothesis. *Studia Anglica Posnaniensia* 14: 69–85.

Quirk, Randolph, Sydney Greenbaum, Geoffrey Leech and Jan Svartvik. 1985. *A comprehensive grammar of the English language*. London: Longman.

Rickwood, Douglas. 1984. The Norwich Strangers, 1565–1643: a problem of control. *Proceedings of the Huguenot Society* 24: 119–28.

Roach, Peter. 1983. *English phonetics and phonology*. Cambridge University Press.

Romaine, Suzanne. 1978. Postvocalic /r/ in Scottish English: sound change in progress? In P. Trudgill (ed.), *Sociolinguistic patterns in British English*. London: Edward Arnold.

Romaine, Suzanne. 2001. Contact with other languages. In John Algeo (ed.), *The Cambridge history of the English language vol. 6: English in North America*, 154–83. Cambridge University Press.

Ross, Alan S. C. and A. Moverley. 1964. *The Pitcairnese language*. London: Deutsch.

Sapir, Edward. 1921. *Language*. New York: Harcourt Brace.

Schneider, Edgar. 1983. The origin of verbal – s in Black English. *American Speech* 58: 99–113.

Schneider, Edgar. 2003. The dynamics of New Englishes: from identity construction to dialect birth. *Language* 79.2: 233–81.

Schreier, Daniel. 2003. *Isolation and language change: contemporary and sociohistorical evidence from Tristan da Cunha English*. Basingstoke: Palgrave Macmillan.

Schreier, Daniel. 2008. *St Helenian English: origins, evolution and variation*. Amsterdam/Philadelphia: Benjamins.

Schreier, Daniel, Andrea Sudbury and Sheila Wilson. 2006. English in the South Atlantic. In U. Ammon, N. Dittmar, K. Mattheier and P. Trudgill (eds.), *Sociolinguistics/Soziolinguistik*, 2131–7. Berlin: de Gruyter.

Schreier, Daniel, Peter Trudgill, Edgar Schneider and Jeffrey P. Williams (eds.). 2010. *Lesser-known Englishes*. Cambridge University Press.

Schrijver, Peter. 1999. The Celtic contribution to the development of the early North Sea Germanic vowel system, with special reference to coastal Dutch. *NOWELE* 35: 3–47.

Schrijver, Peter. 2002. The rise and fall of British Latin: evidence from English and Brittonic. In M. Filppula, J. Klemola and H. Pitkänen (eds.), *The Celtic roots of English*, 87–110. Joensuu University Press.

Schrijver, Peter. 2006. What Britons spoke around 400 AD. In N. J. Higham (ed.), *Britons in Anglo-Saxon England*, 165–71. Woodbridge: Boydell.

Schrijver, Peter. 2009. Celtic influence on Old English: phonological and phonetic evidence. In J. Klemola and M. Filppula (eds.), *English Language and Linguistics* 13.2: 193–211.

Shilling, Alison. 1980. Bahamian English – a non-continuum? In R. Day (ed.), *Issues in English creoles*, 133–46. Heidelberg: Groos.

Singler, J. 1997. The configuration of Liberia's Englishes. *World Englishes* 16: 205–31.

Stein, Gabriella and Randolph Quirk. 1991. On having a look in a corpus. In K. Aijmer and B. Altenberg (eds.), *English corpus linguistics*, 197–203. London: Longman.

Strang, Barbara. 1970. *A history of English*. London: Methuen.

Strevens, Peter. 1972. *British and American English*. London: Macmillan.

Sudbury, Andrea. 2000. Dialect contact and koinéisation in the Falkland Islands: development of a new southern hemisphere English? Ph.D thesis, University of Essex.

Swan, Michael. 2007. History is not what happened: the case of contrastive analysis. *International Journal of Applied Linguistics* 17.3: 414–19.

Thomas, Alan. 1994. English in Wales. In R. Burchfield (ed.), *The Cambridge history of the English language vol. 5: English in Britain and overseas – origins and development*, 94–147. Cambridge University Press.

Thomas, Mark G., Michael P. H. Stumpf and Heinrich Härke. 2008. Integration versus apartheid in post-Roman Britain. *Proceedings of the Royal Society B.* 275: 2419–21.

Thomason, Sarah G. 2001. *Language contact: an introduction.* Edinburgh University Press.

Thomason, Sarah G. and Daniel L. Everett. 2005. Pronoun borrowing. *Proceedings of the Berkeley Linguistics Society* 27: 301–15.

Thomason, Sarah G. and Terrence Kaufman. 1988. *Language contact: creolization, and genetic linguistics.* Berkeley: University of California Press.

Townend, Matthew. 2002. *Language and history in Viking Age England: linguistic relations between speakers of Old Norse and Old English.* Turnhout: Brepols.

Trask, R. L. 1994. *Language change.* London: Routledge.

Trask, R. L. 1999. *Key concepts in language and linguistics.* London: Routledge.

Tristram, Hildegard (ed.). 2000. *The Celtic Englishes II.* Heidelberg: Winter.

Tristram, Hildegard (ed.). 2002. Attrition of inflections in English and Welsh. In M. Filppula, J. Klemola and H. Pitkänen (eds.), *The Celtic roots of English*, 111–49. Joensuu University Press.

Tristram, Hildegard (ed.). 2004. Diglossia in Anglo-Saxon England, or what was spoken Old English like? *Studia Anglica Posnaniensia* 40: 87–110.

Tristram, Hildegard (ed.). 2006. Why don't the English speak Welsh? In N. J. Higham (ed.), *Britons in Anglo-Saxon England*, 192–214. Woodbridge: Boydell.

Trudgill, Peter. 1974. *The social differentiation of English in Norwich.* Cambridge University Press.

Trudgill, Peter. 1978. Creolisation in reverse: reduction and simplification in the Albanian dialects of Greece. *Transactions of the Philological Society 1976–77*: 32–50.

Trudgill, Peter. 1983. Language contact and language change: on the rise of the creoloid. In P. Trudgill, *On dialect: social and geographical perspectives*, 102–7. Oxford: Blackwell.

Trudgill, Peter. 1986. *Dialects in contact.* Oxford: Blackwell.

Trudgill, Peter. 1988. Norwich revisited: recent linguistic changes in an English urban dialect. *English World-Wide* 9: 33–49.

Trudgill, Peter. 1990. *The dialects of England.* Oxford: Blackwell.

Trudgill, Peter. 1996a. Dual-source pidgins and reverse creoloids: northern perspectives on language contact. In E. H. Jahr and I. Broch (eds.), *Language contact in the Arctic: northern pidgins and contact languages,* 5–14. Berlin: Mouton de Gruyter.

Trudgill, Peter. 1996b. Language contact and inherent variability: the absence of hypercorrection in East Anglian present-tense verb forms. In J. Klemola, M. Kytö and M. Rissanen (eds.), *Speech past and present: studies in English dialectology in memory of Ossi Ihalainen,* 412–25. Frankfurt: Peter Lang.

Trudgill, Peter. 1998. Third-person singular zero: African American vernacular English, East Anglian dialects and Spanish persecution in the Low Countries. *Folia Linguistica Historica* 18.1–2: 139–48.

Trudgill, Peter. 1999. New-dialect formation and dedialectalisation: embryonic and vestigial variants. *Journal of English Linguistics* 27.4: 319–27.

Trudgill, Peter. 2000. *Sociolinguistics: an introduction to language and society.* London: Penguin.

Trudgill, Peter. 2001. Modern East Anglia as a dialect area. In J. Fisiak and P. Trudgill (eds.), *East Anglian English,* 1–12. Cambridge: Brewer.

Trudgill, Peter. 2003. *A glossary of sociolinguistics.* Edinburgh University Press.

Trudgill, Peter. 2004. *New-dialect formation: the inevitability of colonial Englishes.* Edinburgh University Press.

Trudgill, Peter. 2008. Colonial dialect contact in the history of European languages: on the irrelevance of identity to new-dialect formation. *Language in Society* 37.2: 241–54.

Trudgill, Peter. 2009. Sociolinguistic typology and complexification. In G. Sampson, D. Gil and P. Trudgill (eds.), *Language complexity as an evolving variable,* 97–108. Oxford University Press.

Trudgill, Peter. in preparation. *Language in contact and isolation: on the social determinants of linguistic structure.*

Trudgill, Peter and Tina Foxcroft. 1978. On the sociolinguistics of vocalic mergers: transfer and approximation in East Anglia. In P. Trudgill (ed.), *Sociolinguistic patterns in British English,* 69–79. London: Edward Arnold.

Trudgill, Peter, Elizabeth Gordon and Gillian Lewis. 1998. New-dialect formation and southern hemisphere English: the New Zealand short front vowels. *Journal of Sociolinguistics* 2: 35–51.

Trudgill, Peter, Elizabeth Gordon, Gillian Lewis and Margaret A. Maclagan. 2000. Determinism in new-dialect formation and the genesis of New Zealand English. *Journal of Linguistics* 36: 299–318.

Trudgill, Peter and Jean Hannah. 2008. *International English: a guide to varieties of Standard English*, 5th edn. London: Edward Arnold.

Trudgill, Peter and Daniel Schreier. 2006. The segmental phonology of 19th century Tristan da Cunha English: convergence and local innovation. *English Language and Linguistics* 10.1: 119–41.

Trudgill, Peter, Daniel Schreier, Daniel Long and Jeffrey P. Williams. 2003. On the reversibility of mergers: /w/, /v/ and evidence from Lesser-Known Englishes. *Folia Linguistica Historica* 24/2: 23–46.

Tryon, D. T. 1970. *Conversational Tahitian: an introduction to the Tahitian language of French Polynesia*. Berkeley: University of California Press.

Turner, Lorenzo. 1949. *Africanisms in the Gullah dialect*. University of Chicago Press.

Tuten, Donald. 2003. *Koineization in medieval Spanish*. Berlin: de Gruyter.

Vane, Christine. 1984. The Walloon community in Norwich: the first hundred years. *Proceedings of the Huguenot Society* 24: 129–40.

Vennemann, Theo. 2000. English as a 'Celtic' language: Atlantic influences from above and below. In H. Tristram (ed.), *The Celtic Englishes II*, 399–406. Heidelberg: Winter.

Vennemann, Theo. 2002. On the rise of 'Celtic' syntax in Middle English. In P. J. Lucas and A. M. Lucas (eds.), *Middle English from tongue to text*. Bern: Peter Lang.

Wakelin, Martyn. 1972. *English dialects: an introduction*. London: Athlone.

Wakelin, Martyn. 1984. Rural dialects in England. In P. Trudgill (ed.), *Language in the British Isles*, 70–93. Cambridge University Press.

Wall, Arnold. 1938. *New Zealand English: how it should be spoken*. Auckland: Whitcombe and Tombs.

Wang, William. 1969. Competing changes as a cause of residue. *Language* 45: 9–25.

Warantz, Elissa. 1983. The Bay Islands English of Honduras. In J. Holm (ed.), *Central American English*, 71–94. Amsterdam: Benjamins.

Washabaugh, William. 1983. Creoles of the off-shore islands. In J. Holm (ed.), *Central American English*, 157–80. Amsterdam: Benjamins.

Wells, J. C. 1982. *Accents of English*, 3 vols. Cambridge University Press.

Welmers, William E. 1973. *African language structures*. Berkeley: University of California Press.

Whinnom, Keith. 1971. Linguistic hybridisation and the 'special' case of pidgins and creoles. In Dell Hymes (ed.), *Pidginisation and creolisation of languages*. London: Cambridge University Press.

White, David. 2002. Explaining the innovations of Middle English: what, where, and why? In M. Filppula, J. Klemola and H. Pitkänen (eds.), *The Celtic roots of English*, 153–74. Joensuu University Press.

White, David. 2003. Brittonic influence in the reductions of Middle English nominal morphology. In H. Tristram (ed.), *The Celtic Englishes II*, 29–45. Heidelberg: Winter.

Whitelock, Dorothy. 1952. *The beginnings of English society*. Harmondsworth: Penguin.

Wierzbicka, Anna. 1982. Why can you *have a drink* when you can't **have an eat?* *Language* 58: 753–99.

Williams, Jeffrey P. 1985. Preliminaries to the study of the dialects of white West Indian English. *Nieuwe West-Indische Gids (New West Indian Guide)* 59: 27–44.

Williams, Jeffrey P. 1987. Anglo-Caribbean English: a study of its sociolinguistic history and the development of its aspectual markers. Ph.D thesis, University of Texas at Austin.

Williams, Jeffrey P. forthcoming. White Saban English: a social history. In M. Aceto and J. Williams (eds.), *Eastern Caribbean Englishes*. Amsterdam: John Benjamins.

Windross, Michael. 1994. Loss of postvocalic "r": were the orthoepists really tone-deaf? In D. Kastovsky (ed.), *Studies in Early Modern English*, 429–48. Berlin: Mouton de Gruyter.

Winford, Donald. 1992. Back to the past: the BEV/creole connection revisited. *Language Variation and Change* 4: 311–58.

Wolfram, Walt and Donna Christian. 1976. *Appalachian speech*. Arlington: Center for Applied Linguistics.

Wolfram, Walt and Erik Thomas. 2002. *The development of African American English*. Oxford: Blackwell.

Woolf, Alex. 2007. Apartheid and economics in Anglo-Saxon England. In N. Higham (ed.), *The Britons in Anglo-Saxon England*, 113–29. Woodbridge: Boydell.

Wray, Alison and George Grace. 2006. The consequences of talking to strangers: evolutionary corollaries of socio-cultural influences on linguistic form. *Lingua* 117: 543–78.

Wright, Joseph. 1905. *The English dialect grammar*. Oxford: Froude.

Wright, Laura. 2001. Some morphological features of the Norfolk guild certificates of 1388/9: an exercise in variation. In J. Fisiak and P. Trudgill (eds.), *East Anglian English*, 79–162. Cambridge: Brewer.

Wyld, H. C. 1956. *A History of Modern Colloquial English*, 3rd edn. Oxford: Basil Blackwell.

Yasuda, A. 1968. The structure of the Penrhyn phrase. MA thesis, University of Hawaii.

Zettersten, Arne. 1969. *The English of Tristan da Cunha. (Lund Studies in English* 37.) Lund: Gleerup.

Index

Note: entries in all capital letters are lexical sets; entries with 'm' are maps and 't' are tables.